Goran Žganec was born (1989) and raised in Croatia.

At the age of 23, seeking life adventures, he went to work on a cruise ship where he had difficult but also most valuable experiences. Due to the persuade of his soccer dream, he left the cruiser in 2016 and moved to Germany.

All those adventures inspired him to write this book and motivate people in achieving their goals and dreams. He continues to travel the world and hunt for every opportunity and experience that enriches him even more.

*How the Ship Changed My Life* is his first book.

This book is dedicated to the three groups of people;
To my parents:
"For every advice that you gave me, and all your support."

To all my ex-colleagues from the ship life but also to all of them who were working, work still, and will work on a cruise ship in general.

To all people who travel around the world but also the ones who persuade to achieve their dreams. "Don't ever give up because life can be wonderful."

Goran Žganec

# HOW THE SHIP CHANGED MY LIFE

Your Choice, Your Adventure

AUSTIN MACAULEY PUBLISHERS™

LONDON • CAMBRIDGE • NEW YORK • SHARJAH

A CIP catalogue record for this title is available from the British Library.

ISBN 9781398452114 (Paperback)
ISBN 9781398452121 (ePub e-book)

www.austinmacauley.com

First Published 2023
Austin Macauley Publishers Ltd®
1 Canada Square
Canary Wharf
London
E14 5AA

"Thank you from the bottom of my heart for all adventures we shared together. You were and remained another family which will not be forgotten. For those other unknown 'ship families' I wish you a peaceful sea and safe sailing."

# Foreword

What circumstances can lead a person like me to expose to the general public this kind of reading of this special topic, which I believe many have already heard some versions, but again, nothing like this one. My story is unique without any imaginary and overly inflated experiences but just the brutal reality and natural beauties that this life can offer us. There are two reasons why I wrote this book. One is that too many people questioned me about the ship and that way of life there, and it became annoying for me to repeat the same thing to each individual about such a huge topic while the other reason just came out from me to the surface.

I felt God's voice that this is something I have to do and throughout my writing, I had no idea actually how much I could enjoy expressing myself in words that signify each of my rich experiences and feelings. The ship is my hardest and best experience ever, and I strongly stick to it. I look at this content of the book not only as guidelines full of useful tips but as a small college—a school—where people can learn great things no matter what the life situation is, whether a business career, family, sharing experiences with people of different cultures and nationalities or some life goal.

I hope you enjoy the book.

**If you want to read the extended version, I suggest you leave the short version for last because it can reveal quite a bit of detail to you before you start reading this original large version.**

**Whoever goes to work on the ship, the ship will become part of him for the rest of his life. I can promise you that.**

# 1. Life on a Ship

## 1.1 All you need to know about the preparation and work on a ship: A short version

Preparation and introduction

To work on a ship, you need to have a strong desire, not some superficial kind of desire with the thought 'I'm going to make a lot of money, see the world, meet new people and everything else will be great'. There are many more important things behind this, so it's not smart to just run blind. It is necessary to be aware of what is there because otherwise, people who have a superficial opinion similar to this about working on a cruise ship are disappointed and are usually the first to give up because that reality is way too far from their expectations.

In other words, right at the beginning, before stepping on a vessel, they have an amateurish naive mindset. To work on a cruise ship you need to have nerves of steel, a lot of patience and the ability to create good productive habits. Life on a cruise ship is not easy at all. The work is done for 10–14 hours daily, and they sleep for only a couple of hours. Room/cabin you always share with someone and with how many of them, it depends on the ship. It can be a minimum of 1 and a maximum of 5. As for how old it is best to go to work on a cruise ship, it depends on the person but my personal recommendation is the younger (adult) the better.

1. *What do I need to start with, how and where to apply, what kind of documentation do I need?*

For application, I used one Croatian agency so I suggest the same approach. Regardless of where you are from, search for the nearest work cruise ship agencies and contact them for further info. Count on the fact that as soon as you contact them and express your strong desire and decision to work on a cruise ship, they will immediately begin the procedure of all possible paperwork with you. By that, I don't mean that if you apply today, you're going on a ship next week.

From paperwork, you will need anything and everything—from medical papers, certificates of impunity, IDs, passports, visas to a seaman's book (depends where you are from). If all that paperwork takes some time, don't lose patience already at the beginning and save your nerves for later because definitely, you will need it. Of course, if all documentation is not done within a month or two, then it is necessary to press the others a little bit.

Along with documentation, one of the most important things that are inevitable is the knowledge of the English language. It is not necessary to be a doctor of English grammar but again neither a person who can barely speak five English words. The level of English must be known, should be comprehensible. The simplest and most precise—to understand what you have been told and to know how to respond or communicate.

2. *How much money is enough for all the necessary documentation?*

Since I had so many things in my head from those days until now, it is impossible to remember the exact number today, but I would say more—less around 660 €. It actually depends on what you already have from the documentation. Personally, I think I can say for myself that I did not pay all the documentation more than this figure, but keep in mind that I do not count the money I spent on fuel or bus every time I had to come to the city where the agency is. What occupation and job you are applying for on the ship depends on your previous experience and are in agreement with the agency.

3. *What happens when I have all the documentation attached?*

First comes the English exam that you take on a laptop in an agency where you have to pass 70%, at least back then it was that much, I don't know if they changed anything about it. If I remember correctly, I paid 20€ for that exam. I also remember that they charged others even more. Why? I don't know, I'm just mentioning that you need to be very careful and pay attention to how much you are paying to the agency. For any service you pay them, ask for receipts because they also sometimes play 'their' game.

How does the English exam look like? It's not as complicated as it sounds. The exam keeps different variations of questions. For the best idea, you can check the 'Marlins test' on the Internet. It's very easy to make a mistake if you are hasty, so you just need to concentrate. They give you time to test for about an hour max.

For those who don't know the English language so good, my little advice on how to learn it faster—watch a couple of movies with English subtitles and listen, read and remember as much as possible. Also, pay attention next time when you are listening to some songs with English lyrics.

As for what positions there are on the ship and for which exactly you want to apply, it depends on your previous experience, but here are all the departments that exist on a cruise ship: Spa and Beauty Jobs (massage therapist, hairstylist, manicurist, etc.); Casino; Bar; Restaurant; Medical staff; Salesman; Computer technician; Galley Jobs (executive chef, sous chef, cook, etc.); Pastry and Bakery; Guest Service Jobs (Receptionist/Concierge, Night Auditor, Butler, etc.); Housekeeping, Photographer, Entertainment Jobs (Cruise Director, Stage staff, Host/Hostess, Dancer, Singer, Musician, etc.); Child Care Jobs, Sport and Fitness Jobs (Fitness Instructor/Personal Trainer, Yoga/Pilates Teacher, Sports staff, Lifeguard, etc.); Shore Excursions Jobs, Administration Jobs, Engine/Technical Jobs, Deck Jobs, etc. Each of these departments is divided into a couple of positions for which you can get more detailed info at the agency.

When you pass the English exam, the last and most important step to secure a job on a cruise ship is an interview that is in the English language, of course. The agency gives you the date of the interview, and you need to come on that day formally dressed to have an interview with certain people from certain companies. The interview lasts about 15 minutes.

Usually, they ask you questions such as where have you been working before and for how long, which kind of experience you have, and why you want to work on a cruise ship. Don't even think to answer something like 'because I want to make money and see the world'. The most important thing in the interview is that they feel your positive attitude from the moment you walk into the room. To convince them how much you want a new opportunity and a new experience in life. That you are ready for this kind of challenge, and you are a real team player, always ready to do your job the best as possible of your ability.

Another very important detail is that from the moment you enter to the moment you get out, wear a big smile on your face. A smile is something that every company considers a very important factor in employment. Why—you will understand once you get on the ship.

4. *I have all the documentation, I passed the English exam and interview, what now? How long does it take for me to finally go on a ship?*

When you do all of this successfully, what you have been waiting for is coming—embarkation day. After the interview, the agency will let you know the exact boarding date as well as flight details. Your waiting time could take a while so just relax. Could happen that your embarkation day is for a few months or you just get really lucky and embark already for a few weeks. In my case, from the moment I applied to the agency until the moment I stepped on the ship—six months.

One important detail about flights—some companies pay for your flights and the night at the hotel before embarkation day (if it's necessary), while some other companies don't cover your first plane ticket for the first contract. Contact the agency for more details.

5. *What do I have to take with me?*

One suitcase and hand luggage are enough. Check what exactly you are allowed to transfer on the plane because if the security finds something they shouldn't, your excuse 'I didn't know' will be of absolutely no use to you. Plus you will have security controls many times and pretty much everywhere. To find out more details about what is allowed to bring on a plane, you have Google. As for how many clothes to bring, I wouldn't recommend dragging something too much with you because you'll always go out and shop somewhere at the ports. My recommendation is that the most important thing to bring in your suitcase is hygiene equipment because for some things it is better to have it from the beginning of the contract.

Regarding luggage, it would also be good if you stick the address on it. That could be the address of your hotel where you will stay overnight (the day before embarkation) because sometimes happen that the luggage gets lost. If you are flying from Europe to America for boarding and having connecting flights, in most cases you will pick up your luggage at the last destination, but still, check it at the airport when checking in. Also one more thing about luggage, I recommend that you do not buy a cheap one. Buy good quality—strong. Why? You will understand my point when you meet with your luggage after a couple of flights.

I strongly recommend that you have all the necessary documentation with you in your hand luggage (papers from the company, passport, wallet, mobile phone, laptop, etc.). Take care very well of those things because those things are the most important for you, not your luggage with clothes. Also, it would be good for the start to have at least around 100–200 dollars in the wallet because you never know when you will need it. If dollars are not used as money currency in your country, leave everything but dollars at home or spend it because you will not need it on a ship.

### 6.  *Embarkation*

As I mentioned, there is a big possibility that you will stay in a hotel the night before embarkation. In this situation I advise you the moment you leave the airport and head to the hotel, if you do not have a free transfer offered by the company or hotel, do not take a taxi at the airport because it is too expensive. Avoid any taxi drivers who will jump on you and offer a ride from the airport to the hotel. Take a walk and check a little bit outside of the airport (if possible), and you will come across quite cheaper offers of transportation. When you arrive at the hotel, you should have a paid room, dinner, and breakfast. The next morning, after breakfast, comes the transportation that will bring you to the ship, and from THAT moment, you will dedicate your life for the next 6–8 months to the work on a cruise ship.

When you embark, everything is organised so you don't have to worry too much about it. You will get a contract with a starting salary that you sign right away and after that, you go to your 'new house'—a cabin that you share with a few other crew members. You'll get a little time to organise your things, but shortly after that you will need to go grab your uniform and after a couple of hours you'll start to work. From that moment, your life adventure begins—full of good, great, but also bad and sometimes really difficult moments.

*7. Do I have the right to refunds?*

About that—Yes and No. Every time I boarded the ship, I always brought with me all the bills from everything spent—from the medical examination, the visa, and even to the bills for the food, I bought at the airport while waiting for my next flight. Keep everything you think is useful to keep and the first month onboard you go with all that into finances and already they will tell you that refunds will be given to you, which one not. The bad news about this is that I've heard that some companies from 2017 will no longer do a crew refund but that still doesn't mean you have to throw your bills right away in the trash. Save, ask, see.

*8. Adjustment*

That's it, your desire to work on the ship came true. As everywhere, the beginning is difficult, and so it is on the ship. The first few months (depending on the person) are a brutal adjustment to the schedule, food, sleep, roommates, catching free time to go out in the ports (that's always present), and for the 'happy end'—training. From the first day, you will have the obligation to attend all possible types of training. Of course, I don't mean the physical part, at least not at the beginning. Once you sign that contract, you are a member of the company, and you are treated like a true professional, first and foremost for reasons of your safety and the safety of your guests but also for your better progress of career on a cruise ship.

You have different types of training—from safety training, list of secret signals that present danger, first aid, knowledge of how to survive at sea alone, learning about any survival equipment and even learning about your tasks during an emergency drill that is done once a week on each cruise. I'm sorry to have to say this but you need to expect a very difficult adjustment. Just when you have a break of a few hours to rest in the middle of work, you will have to go to training. The company needs to make sure that they can count on you to take good care of your guests or in case of extreme emergency (God forbid).

You will also have exams that you must pass. Take this dead seriously because such things are no joke and can save your life or the lives of others if you find yourself in a tough situation. In case you fail the exam a couple of times, the company will send you home. But again, not everything is as scary as it may sound, these are all simple but very important things. As soon as you solve all these things (after about a month), no one bothers you anymore with training, and you will get more free time.

My advice on this topic is that no matter how hard (and it will be hard), don't give up on anything. Be persistent, patient and don't allow yourself to be annoyed by the slightest nonsense or some little things like 'waking up before you lie down' create some pessimism and a life without hope just because it is a little bit hard. You asked for it and now you deal with those things. In other words, now you will only see for yourself how far you can reach your limit of stability, patience, self-confidence, the ability of resourcefulness and everything else that will be in your way. Don't give up and just be brave, fight for your spot.

After my first three months, I got a promotion opportunity that I refused twice because I was afraid of bigger responsibilities. In the third contract, I accepted the re-offered promotion and the results were outstanding. After only two months, I received an award for one of the employees of the month with some other awards and everything went very well for me. I even got the opportunity to work the rest of the contract in one of the best restaurants onboard where it was a much better schedule, payment and conditions. The point of my story is, of course, don't be afraid of any better opportunities offered, just because it sounds 'too big, too demanding and too difficult' at the beginning. Just go ahead.

*9. How often do we have the opportunity to go out in ports?*

Only one thing depends on it—your schedule. Sometimes, you will have the opportunity to go out several times in the same port and sometimes not so much, but the good thing is that you will come to the same ports so many times that you may already get bored. The cruise ship has certain destinations that must be kept for a while. After a couple of months, destinations change, and so on.

*10. What else do I need to know about the ship to be considered important?*

My two golden rules that are very wise to remember:

Rule # 1—Don't trust 100% anyone (except the safety officer). The crew is filled with about 60 different nationalities and let that be your school from the very beginning. There are people of all kinds and that's why this is not a place to talk about everything, especially more private things. There will also be people who will want to provoke you just to set you up out of jealousy. Don't be fooled by their amateur tricks. From the beginning of the first working day, listen and do everything you are told.

After a couple of weeks when you figure out who you really need to listen to and who you don't, make sure you still stay OK with everyone. Avoid any conflicts because you never know who could have some…let's say, 'hidden privileges' which could cost you consequences. If you don't like someone, just keep your opinion about that person for yourself and simply avoid him/her as much as possible. If you run into someone who insults you and disrespects you, there are always people with whom to talk about such things and solve the whole situation.

Rule # 2—Wherever you go out in a port, never but never go out alone in some suspicious ports. One example from Honduras: Two crew members came out in Honduras and moved further away than they should from the ship. They ran into some criminals who robbed them and killed one of the crewmembers. The other one managed to escape.

Central America is very dangerous in these circumstances. Always try to go out with someone, preferably in a group, and stick to locations where most people gather. Watch out for your wallet, cell phone, and other valuables, and if you see any suspicious situations, get out of there as soon as possible. I don't mean to discourage you but that's the fact of what kind of things happen and of what you need to be always aware of. Simply find your team of friends and wherever you go out, stick together and enjoy.

I wish you good luck and a peaceful sea. ☺

# 1.2 My side of the story about ship life: An introduction

*Hello,*

*Could you please tell me what are the requirements for working on a cruise ship? A friend of mine gave me your reference.*

- An email I sent on 28 June 2012 at 10:23 a.m. An email that started to change my life without me being aware at that moment of how huge a change would hit me.

10 minutes to noon, I got a reply that honestly, I didn't expect so quickly. How lucky I am about sending emails, usually a couple of months pass when someone answers me, and in many cases, the answers very often don't even come.

Until recently, I didn't know about one fact between 28 June and my birthday, which is on 6 July (1989). Since I'm a person who likes to be sometimes very curious, literally even in the smallest things, I realised that those dates have the same day—Thursday. From the day I was born until the day I started the 'ship adventures', 23 years passed, and it turned out to be the same days. This doesn't have to mean absolutely anything, but I will still take some credit for this because the beginning of the story sounds more interesting to me and my life has never remained the same after that.

The response to that email was my miserable resume, which was only a page and a half. I remember filling it out on the way where I left quite a few blank lines between the contents just to make my CV look as big as possible. No matter how 'poor' that paper looked at that time, I was not afraid of anything because I knew what I wanted and for that, I was 100% sure of this kind of decision.

After a couple more exchanged emails, four days later I received information and conditions, which I had to meet, such as knowledge of English (communicating, reading and writing) and a minimum of 70% to pass the exam. Under American law, to be over age means to be at least 21 years old, to know how to work with people, behaviour, manners, to be able to pass all exams onboard such as the basics of survival and safety, first aid, etc.; to be able to work 7 days a week, be adaptable and tolerant in a small space such as sharing a cabin with other crew members, be present at all the necessary training that the company requires from you (about work but also general basic things when it comes to working with people), being always in a friendly mood and pleasant in the company of guests or crew, a fixed-term contract (in my case seven and a half months) and finally, what is probably of interest to many—the starting salary. And of course, all the obligatory attached documents such as a passport, certificate of impunity, a picture with a smile and a recommendation letter in English. They also sent me a link to one YouTube video.

Since my CV was 'doctoral' rich, the only spot I could get on the cruise ship was in the gastronomy, more precisely, in the restaurant, department. But I was not complaining either for a second because my only goal at that moment was to get on a ship. The video of 20 minutes they sent me was an introduction to gastronomy from one of the Cruise Lines, which, on this occasion, I will call Cruise Line No. 1, since my agency was preparing me for that company. When I started to watch that video, my eyes stuck to the screen. I absorbed every word spoken, every picture, I admired the interior of every room on the ship and even the crew cabins that looked so small (because they are).

I was simply fascinated by everything I saw and heard. I don't have to mention that I watched that video a couple of times and started to feel that life adventure that I didn't intend to miss anymore. My dose of excitement and curiosity grew day by day.

**Friday, 20 July, 4:22 p.m.**

*Please come to the agency for the English exam, bring 20 €, and a brief preparation for the interview.*

As soon as I read this, I started to get nervous. I thought, *Oh dear mother, this is getting really serious. English Exam? Interview? What interview, I'm not even halfway…*

I got an example of an English exam from a website called 'Marlins test' which I reopened countless times. I found all possible ways to learn English as soon as possible, but I can say that of all the 'crazy' methods, watching movies was the most useful for me. I watched a couple of movies with English subtitles and thus listened, read and charged my memory card in my head. More or less, I improved my English knowledge that way and the next thing that is about to come—Monday. Let's give it a shot, I told myself.

I took the English test on a laptop. After about 30–45 minutes, they came to ask me if I was done with the test. After that time of brainstorming English, I pressed the final step, when the results appeared -77%. *What now?* I asked myself. I see, the line is green, it should mean something good, and I remembered then that 70% is the minimum required to pass. Wow, it's good…

The next thing they sent me during the week was the email I was waiting for. An email that has the most important information of all emails.

**Thursday, 26 July, 1:24 p.m.**

*The interview for Cruise Line No. 1 is being held tomorrow at our agency. From 10:00 a.m. to 3:00 p.m. when you have time. Be sure to bring a SMILE FROM HOME!*

When I read that, I didn't know whether to jump for joy or run to the toilet out of nervousness.

The more I became aware that I had an interview the following day, the more excited I was but equally terrified. That's how it looks like when you're suddenly hit by a wave of mixed emotions that I'm sure everyone has felt in life.

So the first impression was an 'attack of emotions', the second thing I thought of when I see the time, with the note *when you have time*. What when I have time! OMG, you are waiting for an interview like crazy and then they write to you *when you have time*. I'll be there at 7:00 a.m. if I have to, not *when I find some time*. And lastly, *be sure to bring a SMILE FROM HOME!* And it is written in capital letters. My dear brother, I will lie down smiling today, sleep all night smiling and come to the agency smiling from ear to ear, just to make everything go well!

**27 July 2012—Interview for Cruise Line No. 1**

From the moment I woke up, I started with some fear and nervousness in my head. At least 20 of us came in front of the agency and since there were so many of us, everyone had to wait for their appointment. And to kill the time we sat down somewhere nearby for a drink. Everyone ordered some strong shots—to kill the nervousness, but I only had coffee. Me, who was there probably the most nervous and filling up the underpants, ordering to myself a cup of coffee, which by the way I drink very rarely. O, dear mother of God, I should have ordered something stronger too, I thought all the time during drinking my coffee.

When a few of us were invited in for an interview, you think here it goes now… but of course, a little bit more of waiting and sitting followed. The longer you wait, the worse it is. I was spinning English sentences in my head, such as

21

how to say where and what I was doing, why I want to go on a cruise ship, etc. Everyone who walked into that interview room came out smiling carrying some papers. It was finally my turn, I came in, sat down on a chair, and in front of me was sitting a middle-aged man. I will never forget the look in his eyes. I felt like Satan's servant was staring at me.

The big sclera (white part in eyes), some short haircut-almost bald, big dark bags under his eyes, and a deadly serious face that gave me more of an impression like I came to my own funeral and not a job interview. That first impression of his completely ruined even this little bit of my confidence, but that was my first mistake, to allow something to affect me that doesn't really exist— fear. But come on, calm down, I told myself.

He started with the questions I mentioned earlier and my second mistake was that I fired my two sentences like from a cannon. Simply, my answer was way too fast. On that, his eyes didn't even blink, which was the cause of even bigger nervousness and distraction for me. Then he asked me once more the same questions but also he told me to explain a little bit more. At first, I thought 'what the heck is not clear to you now' but a second later, I realised his point—the point where we are coming to a very important conclusion of each interview. No matter which company or person from that company, honestly they are not too worried about your work experience and the reasons for going on the ship.

Do your answers influence the final decision—definitely, but what I want to emphasise is how much more important to them is listening to your English. Quite simply because for that reason they, according to their experience with people, get the whole picture of you as a person. Your 5–10 minutes in English is enough for them to evaluate whether you are or not for a cruise ship. Of course, regarding this, I don't think that's the case for every department you apply for. If you are applying for higher positions, it is logical that your work experience has the same role as your English knowledge.

And of course, after his repeated question and the 'gentle' look, my thoughts sank more and more into huge negativity and my mind was simply blocked to the limit that I could not speak a word of English anymore. I was only able of repeating the same sentences, like some pirate parrot, hoping to get out of this trouble.

After that, a few seconds of silence and suddenly he just thanked me for coming, which was a sign that I could get up and leave the room. When I got up and realised that he was not handing me any papers, it started to bother me even more about what will happen now after all this. When I left the room, a man from the agency immediately noticed me, approached me and curiously asked how it went. He was surprised when I came out empty-handed. Nothing was clear to him at that moment, and he just told me not to worry, that they will find out what is coming next and let me know.

After all, when I met my mother who was waiting for me since she was my support and transportation, I was cut by a feeling I had never felt before. So many negative emotions were running through my head. I didn't know if I was going to vomit or pass out. I was not able to eat a piece of bread or drink water, nor relax without thinking about what would happen… it was quite an unpleasant and indescribable experience, I can tell you that. It's only been a couple of hours, no one has called me or sent me an email regarding the interview.

You can only imagine how I felt minute by minute, waiting for some positive response. I couldn't take it anymore so I sent an email to the agency to hear where was exactly my place now after that disastrous interview. I sent an email at 4:33 p.m., just a minute after I sent it, I got a reply:

*Unfortunately, the person who interviewed you thinks that you need a bit more practice with English. We will stay in touch.*

What was obvious but also what I honestly expected. Part of me already knew. *It's okay*—I told myself and tried to calm down. My contact from the agency calmed me down as well in some way and gave me new hope and opportunity. I was told that the new interview would be in September, which later turned out to be in late October.

In that period, from my failed interview for Cruise Line No. 1 until 27 October, I was quite busy with some more documentation, attended two seminars in Zagreb (where we were advised about the work on a ship) and of course, I don't have to describe how much I worked on myself when it came to English. That failure, actually benefited me a lot, more than I could have imagined. At least I thought so until the next interview. Do you know that feeling when you prepare to the maximum and think that nothing can surprise you anymore, so when all of a sudden—a new shock!

The same day we finished the seminar, I was called from the agency and what followed I would call it literally a change in life guidelines. Namely, when I came in, and we started to talk about a new interview, I got a date (that 27

October) but not only that, the interview will be for, let's call it the CL2 company (Cruise Line No. 2). I thought, *which CL2 now? What happened with Cruise Line No. 1?* All my thoughts and preparations regarding the interview were exclusively focused on Cruise Line No. 1.

I was pretty interested in that company and learned everything there was to know about it when now, all of a sudden, CL2 showed up as my second chance. That moment, I heard the first time about that company and didn't know absolutely anything about it. I remember in that conversation I even asked for a new interview with Cruise Line No. 1, but today I have to say that I am very glad that I didn't get a second chance back then with Cruise Line No. 1. Until today, I believe it was God's will.

I have read a few times how God answers our prayers in three ways: 'No'—because there is something better for us; 'Wait, not yet'—because it is very important to be patient and believe in His timing; and 'Yes'—when He knows you're ready.

Through the first contract on the ship, I understood all three answers more and more, and the picture of the whole situation became clear to me. Of course, that did not finish there. Our whole life, we receive these three answers from God, but only if we strongly believe in Him, in different circumstances and situations that we encounter every day. But there is also a fourth answer that dear God has for us and that is the way He shows us how to solve a problem that would mean in other words—sometimes we, ourselves, are the answer to our prayers. We always want a God who will solve all our problems immediately, but in most cases God wants us to deal with our problems because that is how He gives us the necessary wisdom.

*God helps those who help themselves.*

Benjamin Franklin

This time, as soon as I found out the date of the new interview for the crucial CL2, I became aware that I was missing just one more personal thing. I had to do something about my self-confidence and mental strength. There is always a reason why we meet some people even if only once in a lifetime.

A week and a half until the new interview, it was interesting that exactly in those days, I met a person who opened to me a new way of thinking and advised me how to control my self-confidence—for which we must not allow for all possible negatives to fall into our mind in the most important moments, what happened to me during the first few minutes on the Cruise Line No. 1 interview. The first step was to implant calmness in my mind and at the same time throw it out—to abandon every version of nervousness and fear, and I succeeded, believe it or not, through meditation.

I put on some relaxing music for meditation, lay down on the bed, closed my eyes, took a deep breath and began to go deeper and deeper into myself. It felt like that kind of music was guiding me on a safe and peaceful path and starting to build brick by brick of self-confidence and positive character. I really started to feel a lot better and safer. I repeated such a process a few more times and felt ready.

The second step is to stick to that path and not allow neither a second to turn on the wrong side (your thoughts)—a side that will destroy in a few minutes what you have been creating for hours or days.

What I am trying to advise you in this situation is when you have an important moment in life where you know that you must not lose concentration, just follow your knowledge, be confident in yourself and do not allow yourself a second of any doubt because if you do, it will jump even bigger and stronger doubt and all that negative energy I'm talking about starts to grow and grows until you lose complete control of your mental ability.

The same thing happens if you think positively. If you stick to that direction, your self-confidence will grow and grows to the point where absolutely nothing can draw your attention to a bad way of thinking anymore. I am truly grateful to that person with all of my heart for teaching me and opening my eyes to some important things because I have to say, that help was a crucial key for my next interview.

## 27 October 2012—Interview for Cruise Line No. 2

Here's my second chance! This time my CV didn't look so poor. The two-day seminar prepared me well for this day. To be honest, I changed my resume a bit, so instead of working for a month in a 'fast food restaurant' in Varaždin (a city near my place), I turned it into two years of work experience. I'm not proud of the fact that I lied, but it's important that the paper you use to present yourself to the company looks good because the last thing you want is that as soon as you enter, they look at you hopelessly after they take a look at your CV. After all, most of them did the same. These are not big things so it's not like I cheated and applied for high positions. Anyway, later, once you get on the ship, that paper means nothing because everyone there (your supervisors) evaluates you well and which kind of person you are, with working habits.

This time the interview was held in the same hotel where we had the seminar. There were a lot more people waiting but this time my confidence was in the right place, and I didn't allow the situation to find a chance and stab me with some doubts or nervousness. Although there have been such temptations, it is only necessary to control and keep the right way. When it was my turn, I entered with high self-confidence and on the other hand thought like I was going for a casual conversation with a friend. Already, the first minutes of this interview were completely opposite compared to the first one.

I was talking to some dear lady, an American, and as I said, from the beginning I felt a positive and good mood between the conversation. I remember that moment, in the middle of the conversation, in my mind flashed, *Man, this is the easiest thing I'm going to do*, and it really was that way. The conversation went great, my knowledge of English met the required criteria, my body language was pleasant and accommodating and that was it. Before I left that room, I knew I had passed. This is proof of how much positive thinking can change a person's attitude.

Or as a friend (my future colleague from the ship) said later, about the interview:

*You have to beat yourself that day—your mind, you have to destroy the nervousness*—which I completely agree with.

Since it was Saturday, I received an official email on Monday.

*Congratulations, you passed the interview.*

Here it is, that's it! I knew I could! A little more and the life adventure begins!

After two months, on 8 January at 11:09 a.m. I received information that made my eyes shine:

*Dear CL2 future crew members,*
*Your boarding date is on 24 March 2013, on the ship—let's call it Aries.*

Below the message was a list of five people. One girl and four guys. Two of us are from Croatia, one from Serbia and another remaining with the girl in our group from Bosnia. We had all applied for the Restaurant Steward position.

Since I'm not mentioning the real names of the ships, I choose the names of Zodiac signs for the first two ships while for the third one I choose freely.

The next thing I remember doing, the very same minute I read that email, was that I jumped quickly to Google and typed the name of the ship. When pictures of that ship appeared, I think my eyes looked like they were in cartoons, full of glitter and rainbow colours of joy.

That *Aries* really impressed me at first, plus just the name of the ship sounded to me like some hidden reason waiting for me to step as soon as possible on this marvellous thing.

*Aries* was built in 21$^{st}$ century, although it was constantly renovated until today. (A huge detailed reconstruction was made almost two decades later.) These renovation things are necessary first of all because of logical safety terms. Just imagine having a huge ship where around 10 thousand people pass through in a month. The capacity of this ship is more than 2,300 guests while the crew is around 1000. The length of the ship is almost 300 m and the height around 30 m.

For the first time, I think that this ship would seem huge to everyone, and there are even bigger ones.

The next step after a successful interview and observation of the *Aries* was a detailed medical examination and a D1 course—a basic safety course for seamen that lasted only a few hours and cost me 140 €. About the medical examination, they tested the blood for all possible things. I remember getting even a couple of vaccines against some diseases to protect myself and not get infected; after all, I will travel all over the world and be in the company of different nationalities, on and off the ship.

They were also checking the hearing, sight, lungs, heart and some other organs. I also found out the blood type that I never knew until those days. As soon as I found out that, I felt somehow even healthier than I was.

When I could leave it all behind, the only thing left was a visa.

The C1/D visa is a type of visa exclusively for Seamans and for issuing that visa, I had to make an appointment at the US Embassy in Zagreb. I was scheduled to issue a visa on 6 March 2013, at 8:30 a.m.

Since I applied for this type of visa for the first time, I only got it for a year. Later, when I finished my first contract, got off the ship, and before starting the next contract, they extended that visa to five years, plus I had the right to apply a second time for a tourist type of visa B1/B2 as well, which was also for five years.

I became so indescribably excited that even the last month I was sleeping only six hours, intending to start to get my body used to the huge change that was waiting for me. Actually, I advise this as well to those who decide to go on this adventure. No matter how well prepared you came, once you get on board, you'll realise how much more you've come unprepared.

As soon as I found out with whom I share the same future destiny, I tried to get some contact with my future colleagues, but out of four of them, I managed to contact only one, Sasha from Serbia. Since we were going on the same ship, I assumed we should also meet somewhere on the way there. If not at the airport, we should definitely meet at the same hotel, the night before boarding.

As soon as we started contacting each other on Facebook, all kinds of topics started to open up. When I opened the conversation history to write this book, I really had something to laugh about when I read it all over again.

We met in mid-January and from then until the last days before going on the ship we talked constantly like little curious children.

We questioned each other a lot. We started about the interview and lying to a resume (in which case Sasha was even worse than me, he talked in an interview about how he worked in a luxury restaurant and served famous singers and actors from his country—no comments). Then about a trip from our home to the ship, who will fly from which airport and where, how long we will need to wait at the airport, what about our luggage, how much weight is allowed for luggage, how from the airport to the hotel and of course do we have to call someone or will someone be waiting for us? (this question was the most common). After these first—turbulent topics for us green beginners, once we opened the way to curiosity, it only continued growing. The main topic began—the ship.

We talked about the ship and what awaits us. We studied the routes and destinations we will sail on, but the most common topic about the ship was a mystery to us—what kind of people are on board? What kind of crew and what nationalities will be present in our circle of socialising and how much we will get along, what kind of guests are onboard… really anything.

As I mentioned at the beginning, I am a very curious person, sometimes too much than I should be. I don't even know how many pages I read in those countless forums on the Internet on the topic 'Working on a ship and experiences'. After that, we began to be really aware of what we were getting into. But again, I lost a little bit of control of my emotions and because of those other people's experiences, I created unnecessary worry, nervousness, and fear.

This is very important for anyone who decides or has doubts about going to work on a cruise ship and doing the same thing as me, reading unnecessary pages or to put it simply—nonsense on the Internet.

Understand one thing—each person is special in their own way, which means that all people are different! Everyone accepts (and tells) things in life in their own unique way, no matter are those working habits, love and friendship relationships, or adapting to all the circumstances that come our way to achieving our goals and even our biggest dreams.

Don't, I repeat! Do not follow others, what they tell you, what they have gone through, that you will go through the exact same experience because you will not.

Advice is always welcome and should be remembered for sure but one thing is when someone wants to help you, as I am in this case and the other thing is when someone tells you stories where there is only a little bit of truth, a truth hidden by fabricated lies just to make the story sound the more creepy it is and fills your head with worries *'how am I going to do this, how am I going to do that?'*

It is also very important from whom to take advice. If you don't know a person and listen to how he discourages you because it's hard, you don't know the circumstances in which that person was raised. Whether humbly or is it some spoiled brat who fantasised only about how he/she would come to enjoy the ship, see the world, and save a mountain of money with hands in pocket and once he/she realises the reality of the ship life, suddenly will be everyone's fault of everything, only he/she miserably and innocently suffer injustices and makes excuses for every situation that appears around the corner, deeply disappointed gives up after the first month and goes home crying and as the biggest critic.

I mention this because it is one of the examples that is happening. Some people gave up even after only a few days! Hello! The ship has not yet made its weekly route to return to the same place from which it sailed away and already crying 'I want to go home!'

I'm not claiming now that these are the only reasons people leave the ship before the contract is done. There are countless of them.

Understand it this way: In the beginning, a ship is a place that forces people to make a brutal adjustment and change, which can make a person very strong in many ways. Of course, as everywhere, at the beginning is the most difficult, so the first few months spent on board it is as well. But trust me, once you catch the rhythm, everything will seem like a game to you, and even those toughest jobs and responsibilities that if you heard about it now, would sound absolutely abnormal to you. It will just all sit down in some natural way, you just have to be brave and not think about giving up because trust me, you can and will regret it as soon as you get back on the plane returning home.

Just for advance motivation, if and when you will feel discouraged and with doubts, remember that main reasons you had for going on the vessel! Was one of them the economic situation in the country where you live? Was your personal desire to help financially and provide for your family? Or was it just an undiscovered adventure that you seek so long for? Do I need to continue?

Different people experience everything in different ways. You will experience your adventure in your own unique way and thus create your own experience and journey. So go ahead and how our dear mothers always saying: **'Be careful!'**

And when comes a little harder rhythm in your life, just remember:

*'If you can't, then you must, and if you must, then you can!'*
Tony Robbins

I learned and understood this very important experience in the first few months spent on board. The only reason why I was reading a bunch of pages on the forum was that I wanted to prepare as best I could. But the good intention was one thing while the true result of that was another thing, which appears as negative and filled up with a lot of worries. Once I clearly saw my circumstances and the situation on the ship, I wished to beat myself on the head, how stupid I was for believing in all those sentences I read and wasted my health on my nerves and time for nothing.

But let's go back to Sasha, me, and our many hours of conversations.

After all sorts of comments from the forum, we were both half-and-half how things will be, but regarding a couple of things we were sure, we couldn't go wrong, such as climate adaptation and dietary changes. We were also right about two things that will change once and for all and that we will never look at the same again, once from the moment we step on the ship:

1. Once we see what this life experience is like it will be very difficult not to come back.

2. We will never be sure where we can be greeted by a special and better opportunity, on the occasion of a career or love so that life can bring us somewhere else.

Both of these things have happened to a lot of people, so the only thing I can say about this is:

*Life is full of undiscovered surprises. So travel as much as you can, as far as you can, and as long as you can. Because life was not meant to be lived in one place.*

Lifehack.org

After all kinds of discussions in the end our answers for all questions and worries were—we will see. (laugh) ☺

As we totally immersed ourselves in all these topics and life changes, on both sides we could feel a slight nervousness in the air that was getting bigger day by day when suddenly, the time to spend at home was less and less.

Since we were more than aware of that, we tried to calm each other down because we realised we exaggerated a little bit with the nervousness so we tried to distract ourselves for a while from these things. We started to talk about my favourite topic—football (soccer), football players, and clubs. An interesting fact at that time was that on 22 March 2013, were qualifications for the 2014 World Cup between Croatia and Serbia. Exactly the same week when we were supposed to start a great life adventure. My country against his. Luckily, we had the opportunity to watch the game and everything finished great for us Croatians. We won 2-0 that evening and the next morning a special destination for me—the airport.

***

But before I start a new page of a completely different life, let me briefly describe to you a few things that are better to know now, as this will be followed up later in the book.

I finished high school in my born city Varaždin, a career as a carpentry technician designer. I graduated in 2008 and after that, for 4 years I was looking for any normal job, but as you can guess, it was unsuccessful. I even completed courses as a computer service technician and web designer, for which I completely lost even the little desire I had. Simply, you know that feeling when you are 100% sure that something is not for you at all? Well, here I am with web design. Congratulations to those who love this kind of job, but I simply couldn't have found myself in it. Neither I had enough desire nor patience.

Anyway, since I am quite interested in sports, I tried to get into a three-year part-time college that was just preparing to be opened in Čakovec, a city that is quite close to my town. I wanted to apply for a fitness trainer but due to the insufficient number of applicants they simply gave up on all starting this three-year college. I also worked for a very short time in a metal factory. And the last thing that I did for only a month was what I mentioned before, making and selling hamburgers in a fast-food restaurant.

I think my final conclusion was (to confirm to myself that there is no future in such circumstances) when the boss mentioned to me that I would have to work for Christmas Eve, Christmas Day, New Year's Eve, and New Year's Day. The schedule was from 5:00 p.m. until midnight considering that I do not count the time for a short break, cleaning, and preparation for the next day. Talking about salary—Thank you very much, I wish you nice holidays!

In the end, I wonder again, but I also believe how much God has influenced all these situations of mine, how He found some mysterious way and every step of the way brought me to what changed me and my life for the better. God is always working on His plan for us, and it is up to us to trust Him firmly, no matter how hopeless everything may seem.

What I have important to mention is that from the beginning of my childhood until the day I stepped first time into the airport, I always fight and struggled to make my soccer dream come true. I didn't grow up in the best environment that was without the right and necessary conditions to realise that dream plus my self-confidence has been countless times the target of temptations and underestimations by others. Throughout that period, I had some semi-chances that didn't bless me with enough luck. I went to try-outs in Austria, I was waiting for my promised opportunity to join the training back then, a professional club in Varaždin that I did not get in the end, and after that, I was a member of three different clubs in my region, in lower local leagues.

My dose of persistence and strong desire was never in question. The passion I share for football (soccer) is the most important thing in my life. I was often made fun of for being seen many times in different weather conditions during 'lonely'—individual training, but I didn't allow something like that changed me for the worse because then that wouldn't be me anymore. As a player I was average, but who knows, maybe just back then there was still no time for me to mature into a better player… either that or that kind of environment affected my emotions too much. Did I keep dreaming, find out a little bit later in this book.☺

## 20 March 2013

An email has arrived with:

- fly details,
- Cover letter from Cruise Line No. 2,
- information about the hotel where we will spend the night, and
- information about baggage conditions.

What can I say now about this… I'm looking at those old emails and reading the details of the flights… and simply even today I get the same chills as that Wednesday, 20 March 2013.

I don't remember because of the excitement, the order in which I did the following things, but after I jumped from the chair like thunder, ran faster than the antelope to inform my family, sent a message to Sasha if he also received such an email, started thinking how to begin packing my luggage, not forgetting to stick the address of the hotel, to crack 'like a rifle' in the purchase of clothes, hygiene items, nonsense… here we go! The explosion of excitement erupts. Just a few more days!

Flight details:

Departure is from Zagreb, 23rd (Saturday) to Frankfurt at 6:55 a.m. while arrival is scheduled at 8:30 p.m. At 10:15 a.m. from Frankfurt to Atlanta with the arrival at 3:40 p.m. The time difference is taken into account (to which it was unusual and very strange for me to adapt for the first time). From Atlanta, it is the last flight to New Orleans at 5:25 p.m. and arrival in the city of boarding around 6:00 p.m.

From the last airport, according to the information we received, we have transportation to the hotel with a paid room, dinner, and breakfast for the next morning.

## 22 March—Friday

After a super detailed purchase of everything I needed, I started to worry that my luggage did not pass 23 kg because for the first time you are not overly sure whether you will have enough of 'this' or 'that'. Excitement and nervousness fight in my head and make a mess. You don't know who will win because the fight is uncertain, which was the reason for me during the day, visiting the toilet to 'throw out' all that burden. (laugh)

I said goodbye to my friends, only I'm still waiting for a tense match of Croatia (to divert my focus and relax a bit) and my bed and its beautiful size, which I will not see for more than half a year.

## 23 March 2013—Saturday—Aries, here we come!

Good morning! Great morning!

Before leaving my house, I said goodbye to my family members and got in the car with my parents. With some heavy look, I greet my dear home until next time.

On the way to the airport in Zagreb, I was spinning countless things in my head. *Did I bring this? Or that? This paper? That paper? Do I have this thing and that thing with me? Did I put it in my luggage...* you know already, this and that. I had such a check even before I got in the car. But this is all the chemistry of excitement when you become aware that there is no going back after that and that your life has officially changed.

Because of such stress in my head, I said to myself all of a sudden:

*'To hell with everything, I just need papers, a wallet, a cell phone, and a passport! And amen more to that stress! I don't care even though my luggage gets lost and travels to Africa, I can do without it!'*

As soon as I said that to myself, there was peace in my head until America.

Here we are at the airport! I made check-in at the Air France counter, issued luggage that I will not see until Atlanta (I needed to take over there by myself) and waited for boarding time. I spotted a couple of the same age as I and assumed it might be my future colleagues. And it was like that. We were introduced with those looks in our eyes *'I can't wait, to what everything will happen?'* Sasha told me, a few days ago, that he will fly from Belgrade. Now our next guess was either we would meet him in Frankfurt so we all fly together (the four of us) to

America, or we would meet with Sasha at a hotel, which it was in the end. He arrived at the hotel just behind us. There was a special case with the other Croatian future crewmember, his flight was cancelled. I don't think he embarked until the following year.

The hour and minutes have ticked, it's time to go!

We said goodbye to our parents, and even though we were 99% focused on the next 8 months yet the person catches a difficult moment and emotions when it comes to leaving for so long. There is no doubt that it was not easy for our parents to send us into the world miles away, but in those moments we became more and more aware that we are facing a big life exam in all areas where a person learns, sins, and even forgives.

Zagreb (Croatia)—Frankfurt (Germany)

First, we went through security checks which I assume that more—less is familiar to everyone. Cell phones, laptops, chargers, any devices from hand luggage, keys, and other things from your pocket, all shake out in front of them. If you wear a metal belt, remove it as well, just be sure to avoid any inconvenience and treat everyone there with your underwear.

While all your luggage is going through an X-ray scan, you go through a metal detector, pick up your things and look for a boarding gate, in our case, we wait for the bus, which took us to the plane. When we got on the bus, didn't pass either a few seconds, I saw the former Croatian national team member Dario Šimić who was also boarding our plane. He was only a few feet away from me while on the plane a couple of seats away. *Boy o boy, I wish you could arrange me some soccer try-out*—I thought to myself when I saw him.

When the plane took off, my eardrums almost cracked from the pressure. That first experience of flying was weird for me, but after a few minutes was OK. The thing is that that was just something new for my body that was adapting to new things. I also felt some dizziness at that moment, something like a hangover.

Frankfurt (Germany)—Atlanta (USA)

O dear Lord, help us! The airport is huge! The fact itself says that after we landed, we drove to get off the plane for almost half an hour. We looked at the time and start worrying about not being late for catching the next flight. We were like: *'Come on, Mr Pilot, find some side parking already because we need to run!'* When we finally got out of one of the terminals, we had about an hour left to find our next terminal but before that, we had to do an immigration check (since we were flying from Europe to the USA) and that always takes some valued time. Basically, we ran pretty much already in Germany for the first time. Thank God we got on the next plane at the last minute.

Since we weren't sitting together this time on this flight of 10 hours and 25 minutes, I got a seat in the middle of the plane at the wing right next to the door that only opens in case of (God forbid) an emergency. I haven't sat down and made myself comfortable yet, already some nice lady—stewardess was asking me if I know English. I don't know why, but when I heard that question, I felt like I start sweating already with the thought: *'What the heck? Even here I'll get an English exam? Do I have to go through that again to make it sure?'*

But as soon as I answered her nicely: *'Yes, I do'.* she handed me a guide that I had to study carefully (because my seat was at the exit) how to open the door in case of an emergency. What a wonderful welcome, ma'am! Especially for me, who is flying across the ocean for the first time. After studying how to open the door in case of an emergency and all that introduction by the flight attendant before the flight, when I finally relaxed, I wondered what I was going to do 10 hours on a plane?

I noticed that my seat has a small screen on which I had the opportunity to watch movies, listen to music, and follow the flight path.

Next to me was a middle-aged lady who was breathing like a vacuum cleaner, but OK, we are all humans. From her left side was a window, through which one I was looking countless times. Throughout the whole flight, I enjoyed and relaxed. We got food, drinks, snacks… they were passing with the 'bar' countless times. I managed to take a nap, but a couple of hours before landing, my screen blinked and turned off so I couldn't use it anymore until the end of the flight. Since that moment I had more fun watching a huge teenager of 2 metres sitting to my right across the 'street'. It took me a while to figure out what he was playing on the laptop. The guy was driving harvesters and tractors on a farm around pigs and cows.

With the last 45 minutes left, I hope the airport in Atlanta is smaller than the one in Frankfurt.

Atlanta (USA)—New Orleans (USA)

The airport in Atlanta looks even bigger than the entire Germany! Due to the time difference, we were gripped by indescribable fatigue. We felt like they had kept us locked up somewhere for three weeks and made us run a marathon. Oh, my dear mother, I was wondering what is this now, and we haven't even started working on the ship yet! Which kind of tiredness will wait for us there?

After a 'little bit' of more waiting, we got on the last plane and again I sat down next to the exit, again I'm in charge of opening the door in case of emergency, God forbid.

Arrival in New Orleans

When we finally got out of the airport, I will never forget that climate. Literally, for the first time, we felt the American air full of steam and heat. We had more clothes in our hands than on us that evening, leaving from cold Zagreb in jackets. When we found our transfer to the hotel, finally after some 14 hours of overall flight plus time spent waiting and some security checks at the airports, we had a chance to freshen up and take a shower.

Our colleague is coming too! *Sasha, brother, here you are!* We were all incredibly exhausted but the dose of excitement didn't drop a bit. We went to dinner, (I even remember the seating schedule of the four of us) and went to sleep for the last time on the land before boarding the Aries.

# 1.3 Cruise Line – Aries

### 24 March 2013—Sunday—BOARDING THE ARIES

We were not the only crew members in that hotel so in the morning around 9:00 a bus picked us up and took us to the boarding place after only 20 minutes. How excited and impatient we were to see the first pictures of the *Aries* from the bus.

Huge beauty of the ship! Wow! The first impression really attached to my memory was a wonderful feeling of joy. In front of the ship, we were greeted by a dear young lady from the Philippines, who was in charge of us 'freshmen'. The first thing we had to do was to go through a short paperwork procedure. As soon as we were done with it, it was time to get on the vessel.

As we all began to step toward it, my eyes flashed all over the ship. From our angle, we couldn't even see where the vessel begins and where it ends. It was huge!

I still remember, as if it was yesterday, that feeling that overwhelmed me that day as we approached the gate. If I had to choose, out of all three contracts I've done for a CL2 company, definitely I'd choose this day as the most exciting and emotional.

Of course, the other days were not less valuable, but still, this was the first 'sailor's step' for me. With so much indescribable excitement, when I suddenly realised I was in front of the entrance, I looked once more left and right across the ship and heard a strong voice in my head: *'That's it! My life has changed!'* and entered the Aries.

As soon as we entered and passed a short check by the security guards, that nice Filipina took us to a restaurant where we finished all the paperwork and the official signing of the contract. The moment I passed the security check, a few metres away I saw a person sitting on the stairs, kind of looking like without hope and exhausted. Our eyes met for a few seconds, as we (fresh crewmembers) passed through that hallway, and already back then, from the very beginning, after entering the ship, I was pinched by a small dose of mystery about that lonely girl on the stairs.

In those seconds, inexplicably questions came to my mind, would I see that person more than once because she looked like she needed someone to talk to, and she seemed to be waiting right there sitting that someone who might be able to help her. Because of a bunch of duties, which was still waiting for us that day, my thoughts were on that path. Just a few hours later I remembered those first scenes again after entering the Aries.

Why am I mentioning this now? Why is this so important, just because I saw someone sitting on the stairs? I mean, how many times in our lives do we pass by others without paying any special attention? You see someone and simply walk past him/her with the thought of seeing that person only once in your life or not even that.—Don't ever have that way of thinking about others. Life is truly full of surprises.

That person I saw with some not excessive curiosity, was one of the first people I saw on such a huge ship. That person was sitting on those stairs right where we were passing, that person today is my wife, Elizabeth! If I had tried to come up with a better scenario regarding my life and the ship I would not have succeeded. God had already anticipated my life in this because He had His plan for me.

I wouldn't call it 'love at first sight' because it wasn't back then but later, as the days went by, time and circumstances on the ship put us on the same path.

After we signed a contract at one of the restaurants, we met David, the safety officer who gave us a tour around the ship. He showed us everything and anything about safety. From the fire and watertight doors, various lifeboats, equipment intended for emergencies, hidden sound signals that only the crew knows what they mean, procedures in case of abandoning the ship, and quite a lot more…

That day the only thing we didn't see was 'the Bridge'—the main place that is run by many officers and a captain. Due to extremely high and strict security measures, going to see the Bridge was allowed only in a very small group, of course, accompanied by officers and only if the tour is part of the training. That day we got a bunch of information, a 'manual' to learn everything as soon as possible.

After this 'first day at school', we went to the Crew mess (a canteen for the crew) to eat something and as soon as we finished, a new challenge already arrived—Self–coping.

The four of us held together that day as a child for mom's hand when it's unsafe not to get lost in the crowd. Fortunately, for a start, our rooms—cabins were not far from each other. It was only a little bit creepy that our cabins (and a lot of others) were two floors below the water level.

My roommates were two Filipinos, one Indonesian, and one 'Rastafarian' from Jamaica. After we quickly made ourselves comfortable in the cabins, we had to be, according to the instructions, at a certain time in a certain place. The good thing and advantage were that on the port side (left side of the ship) in our crew area is the main corridor we called I-95. Why so, I have no idea either until today. In other pictures, I-95 was the main road from which you turned into all the side streets. Such as in our case cabins, laundry rooms, crew gym, storages, pastries, bakeries, garbage room, and I do not remember anything else, except of course the entrance and exit of the ship to the ports. Everything else is above.

All the way forward on the vessel from I-95 we went to pick up a uniform, which included a few pairs of pants, a shirt, a tie, an apron, and a pair of shoes, which were incredibly uncomfortable. Then again running to the cabin to change and again to the personal office where we got some more paperwork and NameTag (name, position, and flag) which we were required to carry at all times no matter whether on or off duty. Only we didn't need to wear it in the case when we were in the cabin and going out at the port for a few hours. Otherwise, if you refuse to carry the NameTag in your free time on board, and even just for a quick 'jump' to the Crew mess for a while, to get a movie or to buy something in the crew shop, you could get a warning from your superiors that could cause even bigger problems due to indiscipline. Wearing that NameTag is a strict rule and our main identity.

When we more-less put all the dice together, it was the final time we got to know our work environment. The four of us Balkans went to the Restaurant Manager's office. He (Malaysian) wished all of us a nice welcome and explained a few things. He sent three to the huge Buffet on the 12th floor and one to the Crew mess. You can guess who was that lucky guy to work in the Crew mess.

I don't know if I got the Crew mess because I was standing last in the office, I might have left some bad impression or it was just bad luck. Basically, me going down, my colleagues up. At the Buffet at that time, the Maitre'D (the supervisor) was one crazy guy (in a good way), let's call him El Colombiano. This man is a real comedian but in a serious way. I will get back to him later.

My superior in the Crew mess was Ronnie (Indian), with the position of Assistant Maitre'D. The thing with these supervisors and their assistants is that there are quite a number of them on board since there are many restaurants and wherever they send you to work, you listen and adapt to their requirements, in 'their field'. That was the rule anywhere.

What also does not fade from my memory are my first working hours. My job description was refilling food and drinks in the Crew mess, cleaning, and maintaining the working areas. Nothing overly complicated, at least not until you catch the right rhythm. They sent me at one point to pick up some vegetables that were on a deck below. I was so lost and spinning in a circle as if wandering through a maze. I knew that everything was close, but I couldn't simply find a way to the pantry. What went through those few hours in my head was how the company would send me home in a couple of days because as soon as people started communicating with me more and more often, my mind was blocked again because of the English language so I struggled with composing sentences, to answer correctly. But in the end, that was just a short phase and an illusion of fear.

Since it was our first working day, they let us go a little earlier from work, to rest and recharge our batteries as much as we could. Because for what followed, for the next almost eight months, those batteries were very much needed.

What I can't possibly promise you about this book is that I can't describe every experiences and emotion that happened exactly each day. You can't even expect that because there were countless of all these mixed adventures and experiences. Actually, I regret that I did not keep a diary and notes every day, but again this was impossible because there were days when you want to see your bed as soon as possible how tired you could feel or get out of the ship fast as possible to see the place where you dock. But luckily, I kept some notes I loved to write down when I caught a few minutes of time.

*Ship's Itinerary (24 March–21 April)—Gulf of Mexico*
*Sunday—Embarkation day—New Orleans, USA*
*Monday—Sea day*
*Tuesday—Costa Maya, Mexico*
*Wednesday—Belize City, Belize*
*Thursday—Roatán, Honduras*
*Friday—Cozumel, Mexico*
*Saturday—Sea day*
*Sunday—Disembarkation/Embarkation day—New Orleans, USA*

## Day 1 Aries

I started quite early but got up an hour before work to study well and to adjust a crew area. The way from the cabin to the workplace took me a while to learn where each place was. In all aspects, I was giving my best from the first day. No matter was work, study, exams, cleaning the cabin, taking care of my clothes, etc.

After a couple of working hours, we had a safety exam, already the second day onboard! This is no joke by any means and should not be taken that way. An exam of almost 50 questions about the things we had to learn in the free time we got on the day of boarding. But I don't want to scare anyone about this now because it sounds that you have to study like in five-year college. Not at all.

This is all very simple but crucial information. Honestly, I don't think most of our group even looked at those papers (I mean who would already the first day onboard?) so all of us were trying to solve the exam based on what we heard and remembered from David on the tour and classroom lectures the day earlier. My only enemy at those moments was lack of sleep (like the most). It is like that for everyone's first week. If you are coming from Europe to the USA, you are first killed by a time difference that you are not used to (especially if it is your first time) and a moment later, work schedule, and training onboard. So I have not yet completely recovered from the flight, not to mention a new and completely different rhythm of living than I had so far on land.

I just don't know how to explain those hours how I felt. I didn't know was it worse when I was trying to hold my head with one hand, so I don't smack with head on the table from lack of sleep, or reading questions on English language and translating in my mind from English to Croatian—my language, and in order to find the right answer, back again in my mind translating from Croatian to the English language. Really, what a brutal challenge in such circumstances.

Everyone was already done and left the classroom only I was left behind, thinking all the time that I would fail this test. David, who is a former UK Marine approached me, sat down next to me, and asked if I needed help. For that I was so grateful as a street dog you throw some food at. He helped me with about two, three questions and after that, I finished with the test. He immediately checked to see results, while I was waiting and burning from inside, did I pass or not…

I was 99% sure that I would not pass the test, all because of an incredibly difficult struggle with myself, when the next scene, David put a paper on the table and told me with a big smile that I had passed. Wow, I was exactly on the edge to pass the test. God for sure loves me, so He helped me, I thought at that moment! Must be that because for sure, I don't remember even today how I succeeded to pass an exam in that kind of version of myself—so sleepy and deconcentrated. After this drama, I ran to the cabin to sleep for maybe an hour or two and go back to work.

Already the next day spent in the crew mess was somehow easier. I started to catch that kind of starting routine. The thing I remember on my second day on board was how I almost served raw broccoli and cauliflower to the crew, but thanks God, some Jamaican chef stopped me on time!

*'Yoo Yoo Maan Yoo!'*

**Day 3 Aries**

Since we were in Mexican waters, due to the time difference it changed one hour back. Of course, I didn't know that so I woke up even two hours earlier than I should. Amazing! Next to all this exhaustion and not enough sleep, I make it even harder for myself where I shouldn't. A really idiotic move from my side. But things come like this when you are in the progress of learning many new things so let's please, forget my stupidity and take it just as a way I intentionally want to strengthen myself. (laugh)

We had a training tour again, but this time we discovered the real luxury of the Aries. There are at least 12 different restaurants full of different specialities and 'cuisine' from all over the world. The huge Buffet that I have already mentioned, Laguna (fast food) which is open 24/7, an Asian Restaurant, Pool Bar and Grill, two main complementary and largest restaurants of huge capacity Vermilion and Royal Blue, and speciality restaurants with extra charge a Brazilian Obrigado Churrascaria, Italian Sienna, French Opéra, Japanese Nigiri, and the famous American Burgundy Steakhouse. As for the bars, there are over ten different bars. Without a pool of course a cruiser would not be a cruiser. One large outdoor pool featuring a huge variety of slides and four Jacuzzis on each side. Even we in our Crew zone had a Jacuzzi located all the way forward. *('I'm the King of the world!'* or?)

A huge beautiful gym and next to it a Spa with a large selection of everything. My biggest mystery, since the days I find out I will work on the ship was does the vessel has an area where we could play football—soccer. When suddenly behind the corner on this tour, beauty, and medicine for my eyes! Quite a solid field for soccer, basketball, and even volleyball. There are even small golf courses nearby. As for recreation, my favourite part about the ship is the outdoor jogging track, around the entire vessel.

There is nothing more beautiful than getting up before dawn and running a couple of laps overlooking the ocean illuminated by the sun's rays. About this part, I totally mean on guests, not myself, or any other crew member, although I admit that I ran a couple of laps a couple of times in the afternoon.

The cruiser also includes numerous shopping malls, souvenir shops, jewellery stores, and watch shops. Internet Café, Video-game room, Wine Cellar, library, entertainment centre for teenagers and children aged 3–12, a huge theatre (where we all had a Captain's meeting once a month—a meeting with the entire crew) and a small 'Las Vegas'—popular Casino.

Yes, there is a lot of things on board. It can be freely called, not only this but any other cruiser, 'a city on water'.

We finished the tour around noon and according to the schedule, I was free until 5:00 p.m. Great, I thought. I had time to get some sleep, but then my colleagues reminded me that we have to write our 'Escape Route', which was supposed to be from the cabin, but also from the workplace to our assembly station (this is necessary for every crew member, to know their own fastest route to lifeboats in case of emergency). If we don't solve this and hand it over to David as soon as possible, we can forget about going out to the ports. As I said, security measures were at the highest level, as they should be.

There were three of us left who helped each other because for us beginners everything was difficult but doable. For each door we passed along our route, we had to write down their numbers so in the case of emergency we are familiar with the route. When we finally finished with that, here comes another shock. Just enough time left to prepare for work that means no sleep for me at all. I worked until 8:30 p.m. and had a break for an hour and again work until 1:00 a.m.

The good thing is that I didn't start the next day until 9:30 a.m. I felt like it was my holiday because I would have a chance to sleep seven hours straight. Of course, it wasn't like that at all since I had beautiful roommates. I tried to make some contact with them in those first days, to see 'what I'm dealing with' in the cabin, but they didn't talk much. Kind of strange but OK, I haven't had any major problems with them. Except that they didn't really bother to have so much consideration for others because of the noise they made in the room while others slept.

That night when I was hoping for a seven-hour sleep, of course, I didn't get it because this 'rasta' from Jamaica was cleaning the cabin. It sounded like he was cleaning with a bulldozer and not a broom, but I didn't dare complain to anything because cleaning the cabin was partly my duty as well. We had a Cabin Inspection once a week and the purpose of this was to keep everything disciplined, tidy, and clean to prevent and spread any bad bacteria and diseases. But that night I was totally exhausted and didn't have the strength for anything.

## Day 4 Aries

I haven't had water in the shower since last night. Thought OK, by the evening someone will notice, report, and fix. At work literally, I run like crazy and almost smoke went out of my shoes. Ronnie noticed how I worked hard (what was my goal) and called me for a moment. He told me that all this is great, that he see how I'm trying and working more than enough and good, that I should just continue like that, but in a lighter rhythm. I will never forget his first piece of advice: 'Don't work hard, work smart'.

I understood those words best after some time at work and what exactly he meant, you will find out a little later.

During that day I received the most important thing—a Visa credit card where I was getting my salary.

When I came back to the cabin from work dead tired, first I went to check if there is water. The next thing that happened was my report about the water situation in cabin 2729. Next to those boneheads, roomies who were longer than me on the ship, and who knew a lot more than me, it turned out that was my move to go to report this problem. I was still waiting for a while that someone comes and fixes the water problem, so I didn't need to wash like the previous night, only with help of the sink in this 1 square metre bathroom. Even Louis XIV would envy me.

## Day 5 Aries

It was my first Boat Drill that day. As usual, that first week I was lost but still manage to finish the drill, with a daily dose of fatigue. After that, our five minutes of glory finally came. Opportunity to go out in the port for a couple of hours in the beautiful and hot Cozumel, Mexico. That was my first 'going out at shore' since embarkation day!

Because of the work schedule, I went out only with Sasha. We walked around the tourist area and kept as close to the ship as possible for the first time. We sat in a bar called 'Señor Frog's' and took a breather with one of the famous Mexican beers 'Sol'. Truly, it was incredibly good. Was it because of the heat? Was it because we came from work and some mental break came off? Or it was just simply that beer was really good? I think there were all the given reasons.

I will never forget that our first going out, brother! We laughed enough for the next week. The moment we were thinking about where to sit and have a drink, we saw that 'Señor Frog's' which looked more than good to us, so I said let's go. In that bar, you could already see a group of guests from outside—Americans from the cruise ships having fun. Their table was full of chips and salsa, nachos, quesadillas, tacos, fajitas, enchiladas, and some 'liquid material' such as various Mexican beers, margaritas, cocktails, and of course traditional tequila. From the content, you could assume that they were more than in a good mode.

Anyway, we sat down and enjoyed our beer when suddenly a waitress appeared out of nowhere with some liquor shots, exchanged a few words with Sasha, and without hesitation, she shoved it, one of the shots, in his mouth. At that moment Sasha was looking at me with this 'what a heck is just happening' look, not blinking and drinking that shot from the waitress's hands. After he emptied it, we thought, OK if she came to us like that offering maybe the first one is for free, when suddenly she put the bill in Sasha's hands. We just looked at each other even more confused. I mean, OK, it wasn't some big money to pay, but again… man should beware of such traps. But like I said, we laughed pretty well. What's pretty cheap and good in Mexico is food and beer. Ok, it depends on the food, but the beers are super tasty and cheap, although I'm not a professional user of 'Cerveza'.

**Day 8 Aries**

I haven't even turned around yet, already it's been a week. What can I say, what are my first impressions after the first week? I manage every day and learn more and more.

We will soon have training for waiters, which includes quite many necessary things but we start with the basics such as waiting for guests at the entrance with a welcome and escorting to a certain table, proper technique of carrying a small tray, on one hand, a large tray on the shoulder (can have a maximum and up to 12 plates), proper table setting, proper serving from the right side, in what order and which way always approached at the table, questions that must be asked before serving food or beverage, to have extensive knowledge to describe the menu and to know how to offer a recommendation, way of talking to guests, etc.

Good and bad things so far? The bad things are you don't get too much sleep (average 5–6 hours) but I've already started to get used to that rhythm. From the beginning, I was firmly aware that I came to work and needed to expect the worst, and when you have such an approach in life circumstances (in general), then everything is somehow easier to bear, and sometimes you are even surprised that it is not really as bad as you may have thought at first.

I'm still struggling a bit with the search for a good signal for the Internet when I go out in the port, but in time that will also find the way.

The good side, for now, is that a positive atmosphere is always created onboard wherever you are. I meet people of different nationalities more and more every day and it is a good and valuable experience.

My stupidity of the day was when I was filling up my working hours and did that correctly just for the fourth time. Luckily, Ronnie is a man of patience. Finally, when I was done with that, I just needed a signature in a couple of places. I signed and everything looked great until I realised I had signed in the wrong column. My dear mother, what is wrong with me, I thought! But Ronnie surprised me once again with his patience and sorted it out.

Thank God I ran into such a first boss. Ronnie was the type of person you could constantly joke with and talk about different topics. He was more than a boss—a friend. But something warned me in my head in those moments and even though I could look at him as a friend and talk about anything, I did not allow myself to change my attitude towards him (in the way to take advantage of some things) and like that maybe damage his authority. I remembered that my parents didn't raise me to take advantage of people whenever I got the chance.

Like any other, as a crew member and as an employee, we must be aware of our limits and keep that professional distance between our superiors and ourselves.

It's past 11:00 p.m., I'd rather throw these shoes out the window, how uncomfortable they are, but luckily I don't have a window in the cabin. I'm going to kill the bed of sleeping, since waking up the next morning is at 6:00.

**Three weeks later, Aries**

Last night we had a first aid test. A colleague and I were on the edge of falling asleep. We were looked at each other with that question in our minds: *'When will come to an end to this, how much more?'*

For the first month when you are required to do all possible training, this incredible fatigue is a common occurrence. You come from work for a lecture or a test, and you fight in your head with a concentration on all that while your brain shouts from the inside: *'Sleep! I need to sleep! No matter where, how, when... right now and here! Zzz...'*

But that's why our superiors were so kind that they woke us up the same seconds every time we fell asleep for 86 milliseconds. You pull out your hair, you bite a tongue or hands, fingers, you slap yourself... you do all that just to try to stay awake. Finally, when that 'submarine phase' passes you, and you are more-less OK, in the next scene the officer turns on the video projector and turns off the light. Do I even need to talk about how many of us fell asleep again for a moment? Simply, a challenge and a comedy. After this, you go back to work a little more. But it's OK when you move and work, you don't feel sleepy. The problem is once you stop, sit down, relax, and your eyes just shut down.

I discovered the whole department that is just for the crew (where we live). For I—95, I have already mentioned, as well as for the small Jacuzzi, which is located all the way forward, and the laundry room. We also have a gym that looks more than solid. We have our small video library where we can borrow movies and books to read, board games but also Internet access on computers, which, of course, we need to pay if we wanna use it. Actually is quite expensive not to mention how desperately slow.

If you are at the port and use the Internet after 2:00 a.m. the price is half cheaper. Sometimes, you can't go out in the port and sit down somewhere for a drink to take advantage of the Internet there, to talk a little with the family so for those reasons I took an Internet package a couple of times. Oh my dear gosh! It takes an eternity to connect and when you finally have a chance to talk to your family, it's like a broken phone game. The conversation could be a few seconds late.

While I was talking about one topic and my family about another and in the end no one heard the whole sentence or understood anything. When we finally somehow find a way of understanding this kind of line, after the conversation, a couple of times happened to me that I forgot to log out. Wonderful. Just wonderful. It's not enough that I waste precious minutes already on connecting and log in, but I have to lose as well the remaining minutes because I forgot to log out. This was already a common thing among the crew. So much about the Internet from the ship.

I think the most visited room in the Crew area is a Crew Bar.

No matter how tired people are, they always have time to stop by for a beer or wine and talk about the daily funny and unreasonable questions and scenes they have heard and watched from guests during the day.

Drink prices are of course cheaper than usual. At least some stronger advantage for us crew members (laugh). So beers cost a dollar, two to three, while bottles of wine are five to some ten dollars. Not as wide a selection as in the bars above for guests but at least something. The crew has the right to organise their parties often as well. By that, I mean 'Latino party', 'Indian party', 'Indonesian party', 'Filipino karaoke' and even in my contract I experienced the 'Balkan party'.

There are more, it all depends on the ideas of the crew. However, we also received the right from the company to larger organised parties in disco clubs (without guests of course). Parties such as 'One Colour Party', '80s Night', 'Halloween party' and 'X—mas party' are some of the most popular. All parties were only allowed up to 2:00 a.m. If you intended to continue to party, forget it because security is already waiting for you at the door at two o'clock, which, by the way, 99% of securities are from Nepal. We often joked with them that Nepal is the safest country as it has so much security.

But let me tell you what was happening that day!

Finally free for a couple of hours and it's time to head out to the beautiful port of Costa Maya, Mexico. I arranged with Elizabeth to go out together.

One evening in the canteen she came with a friend. I was standing behind the buffet counter and heard her first question addressed to me. She was looking for some honey. Because of the way I was standing, I couldn't see her head. She is 1.50m tall but as you can see, the high counter of the buffet was as well. What can I say about that… It was a funny scene.

In those days, we start to talk and get to know each other more and more. Namely, one evening I was supposed to get help in the crew mess and Ronnie teased. He noticed that I liked Elizabeth, and he sent her, as if 'by accident'. Almost every night, she ran from the restaurant (where she worked) to the crew mess to 'quickly' drink water. While I was cleaning the ice cream machine, she was drinking that glass of water, well brother to brother... those 'few minutes' was up to ten minutes, sometimes even more.

My schedule matched with this port, which is more than good since it's last week in Mexico, and the next one we're sailing to Europe. I will sail across the ocean for the first time. If I flew over it, let's sail across as well. As for work, I had some compliments from colleagues. Obviously must be a good sign. We got five new workers, which means giving me the privilege of teaching novices, of course behind Ronnie and his right-hand man, let's call him Gustavo (Colombian). Gustavo worked with us in the morning or afternoon shift while in the evening he worked in the restaurant.

A middle-aged man who loved my work habits and thus trusted me more and more day by day. Somehow I had a feeling they could move me to a better place soon but let's be patient with the fact that now I look even better next to these novices who seem slow and inflexible, no disrespect. Some were fast and even like old turtles that I looked at as a big advantage because they can make me stand out even more with my hard work. Now training is waiting for me again and after that, I'm running outside to the beach.

Later that night before bed...

Yes, you can imagine how much fun I had. Let's look at the whole picture.

From 5:30 a.m. to 9:30 a.m. I was working for breakfast. This is followed by a break that of course was filled with training for about an hour. I had doubts, does it make sense to go outside from 11:30 a.m. to 1:30 p.m. because they put me another wonderful training lecture in the middle of a wonderful free time. After much hesitation, we decided to go anyway. After all, we were last week at that port. So we run as fast as possible to the nearest beach, swimming for about 20 minutes, ate something, drank Corona, and again ran in a taxi to drive us back to the vessel, hoping to catch my training. I have to mention how fascinating this sea is! Beautiful colour with even better temperature. It is very refreshing to take a swim, even for such a terribly short time, on such a hot day.

I arrived for training at the last minute. Of course, I didn't mention it before about training. If you're not punctual and on time, there's no entry after the officer. Okay, he looks through his fingers once or twice who comes in a second after him but then locks the door and since you can't get in, you're in trouble later because of the delay.

I sat down on a chair still in wet shorts in which I swim half an hour earlier. And again—relaxation as soon as you sit down and an attack of fatigue follows.

Fighting with myself and wondering when the training will end so I run to the cabin to get some sleep. Training is over. Great, I have time just to take a shower, come to my senses, and get to work. Amazing rhythm, full of speed.

I was supposed to finish at 8:30 p.m. but why, when it's better to stay half an hour longer! I was in charge of cleaning the ice cream machine (which I mentioned earlier) and since it was a special procedure, and I was the only one who knew it and did it right, at least I got more compliments from Ronnie—which means a lot. Next to that, I had as well coffee machines at my care. Actually, I did prefer cleaning that part of the crew mess better than the one where the buffet is. After 9:00 p.m. a little break and night shift until 1:00 a.m.

Yes, a brutal adjustment in the beginning especially if you lived a life of 10 to 12 hours sleeping before boarding like me. Hard day, but seeing and feeling that beach for half an hour was really worth it and thus overshadowed most of the day.

*Ship's Itinerary (22 April–7 May)—Crossing the Atlantic*
*Monday, 22 April—Sea day*
*Tuesday, 23 April—Embarkation day—Miami, USA*
*Wednesday, 24 April—Monday, 29 April—Sea day*
*Tuesday, 30 April—Ponta Delgada, São Miguel Island, Portugal*
*Wednesday, 1 May—Friday, 3 May—Sea day*
*Saturday, 4 May—Dover, England*
*Sunday, 5 May—Sea day*
*Monday, 6 May—Helsingborg, Sweden*
*Tuesday, 7 May—Copenhagen, Denmark*

I saw Miami for the first time but only from the ship. It looks pretty nice.

When they filled the ship with all the things that would supply us to Europe, my first cruise across the Atlantic followed. In the meantime, I spent a pleasant evening with Elizabeth in the Brazilian 'Obrigado Churrascaria' where I was surprised by the rich food. As a crew, we had the right to go to restaurants for dinner but of course with the approval of superiors. It was our first dinner on 27 April 2013.

What I also felt especially during those days was that feeling when we crossed the Atlantic. Usually, on a break, I would always sit by the window and watch the ocean full of waves and particular blue colours. This brought back to me that feeling as in the beginning when something deep and loud from inside tells you that things in your life will change a lot and nothing will be the same. Elizabeth admitted to me that she often found me like that, deep in my mind, staring through the window, and recognised something special in me. Something that I think every person has in their own way.

A ship is truly a special place where things go through your head that you never thought you would think. There was always a piece of mystery hiding around the corner that gave me some explosive positive energy and hope for something, even though I didn't know back then what but I was looking forward like never before in my life!

I was very surprised when I suddenly realised that we were going to visit the island of São Miguel, which belongs to Portugal. I had a chance to go out, and I can say that the climate was quite good and the place was also interesting. In Dover, the next port was rainy and a bit cold—typical for England. Nothing particularly interesting except the old fortress for which we did not have enough time to visit.

Helsingborg is a very nice city, but the bitter taste was left by 'Irish coffee' which I could barely drink. This 'Irish coffee' was far from the original. Literally, they just put whiskey in the coffee. They did not heat the cup before serving, nor added sugar, and let me not start to talk about the most important part—the top. How do I know?—In the third contract, we were visited by a lady from a company that has many years of experience with the bar. Our bar manager was a little baby compared to her. Since I was working in a special restaurant at Burgundy Steakhouse at the time, she came to teach us a little bit about wines, aperitifs, cocktails, and other drinks that we had to know to combine with a different food for better recommendation to the guests. On one occasion, she made the famous 'Irish coffee'. The ten of us stood with our superior and admired her the way she did it. When I tasted that 'Irish coffee' it was really special. Amazing taste! Wonderful connection of hot and cold, alcohol, and coffee.

Not that I knew how to recognise the original 'Irish coffee' in Sweden because I didn't know it until the third contract, but to be honest, everyone would be horrified by that coffee I had, which is neither coffee nor whiskey. But it's totally OK. Everything is fine, we cannot expect to have the best time in every port we visit and that is completely normal and realistic.

Costa Maya, Mexico

Costa Maya, Mexico

Elizabeth, in Roatan, Honduras

First dinner with Elizabeth

Costa Maya, Mexico

Helsingborg, Sweden

*Ship's Itinerary (7 May–20 September)—Baltic Cruise*
*Ports: Copenhagen (Denmark)—Disembarkation/Embarkation day*
*Warnemünde Rostock (Germany)*
*Tallinn (Estonia)*
*St. Petersburg (Russia)*
*Helsinki (Finland)*
*Stockholm (Sweden)*

**Two months on the Aries**

Time flies, especially when you work at this pace and look at the clock only when you go to work. What to say after two months. The bigger and bigger image is opening up. Many, many unreasonable people, no matter what I mean on guests (although I'm not yet in that working area) or the crew, which leads to the consequences of strengthening and testing patience to the limit I didn't even know I had. I got another supervisor, which is happening due to the introduced rotation of employees towards a certain job. This means the work environment changes every three months.

In a little while, it will be my turn and the end of this 'initial hell'. Truly is. From 5:30 a.m. to 10:00 p.m. or sometimes even with nightshift until 1:00 a.m. When you put it all together, you only have a couple of hours off all day, and at that your free time you are still required to attend training plus studying and tests. Exactly those training makes you even more exhausted, (like a schedule itself is not hard enough). But that's the way it is and unfortunately, it has to be, but it's a good thing that such a rhythm we are passing only once. It's really true when people say: 'The beginning is always the hardest'.

I have to mention during this occasion, how much it actually helped me that I often trained and kept fit for months and even years before the ship life. I strongly recommend those preparing for a cruise ship job to do the same. Work out, in the gym, run in the parks, bike, do any recreation. The stronger the better for your body because you are somehow preparing it for the difficult new adjustments that await you on board. Your body will be more resistant to some things, your immunity will be ready for that difficult start that awaits you. We don't have a gym on the ship without meaning, but for such reasons.

Also for me one great mental strength that I drew from my own cell phone. A power without which I might not have endured. I will not forget how much it meant to me when during short breaks, I sat down and watched on the iPhone all those videos of soccer skills and magic that gave me some indescribable hope, by which I felt I was still somehow connected to my dream that kept me 'alive' and gave me all the strength I needed to continue the day. I did my best to keep that dream alive in my heart but also in my mind even when everything, in my situation back then it seemed totally hopeless when it came to soccer. I'm not sure how much you can understand me during this story, but let's put it in other words;

In life, it's very important to create motivation because it's necessary to 'survive'.

What often happened to me was a shocking awakening in the middle of sleep. After finishing work when I came to the cabin, took a shower, and went to bed, finally 'all four in the air' after a couple of hours of sleep I woke up suddenly, around two or three o'clock in the morning. This was the most confusing part of the contract for me. The reason for waking up was no noise from a roommate or 'neighbourhood', but the reason that my body simply woke up with countless questions in my mind. Can you just imagine what it's like when you lie down after 14 hours of work and wake up in a couple of hours terrified with dozens of questionnaires over your head, questioning yourself if *I'm done with the job? Did I maybe jump to the cabin, lie down for a while, and fall asleep? Am I late for work now? Did I clean that part? Did I prepare this for tomorrow? Did I... Did I...?*

And the funniest thing during that moment, I don't know where I am or how I got here, what and why... total hardcore confusion. This can be understood only by those who have gone through such situations alone. After a few minutes when a part of my brain began to slowly awaken my entire memory, the next words to myself were, *'Come on, you lunatic sleep! You have 6, 7 hours to sleep, and you are now burdened with unnecessary nonsense! You know you always get the job done and no one has ever complained about you! Sleep!'*

I think that on the other hand, this is a normal phenomenon since you are still in that beginning phase of (pre) excitement where everything is still new to you.

One day the crew mess was visited by the restaurant manager and some other supervisors I don't remember. They noticed my efforts, and I was left with only their compliments with the promise that I would soon go upstairs to the restaurant, which means a promotion for the Assistant waiter. The schedule is much more acceptable. As exciting as I was about it, I was just as scared. Why? I don't know, just when images started flying in my head about how I would take care of the guests because of some things I heard how guests complain sometimes about the service. That thought somehow stopped me, and I started thinking in the wrong direction.

After about a month, I also started a relationship. A relationship I didn't know how and in which direction it would go since we are from different parts of the world. You guessed it, it's about a cute little Peruvian, Elizabeth. I don't know if I found her or she found me.

When we crossed the Atlantic, I finally played a bit of soccer as well. I was overjoyed to be on the field with the ball again, in this case, the ship's field. Here you go, even this I experienced—playing soccer on a cruise ship in the middle of the Atlantic! Well, who can only wish for something like that!

But due to not training for a couple of months, logically there are consequences. The next morning I had muscle soreness from the heel veins to the hair on my head. That feeling when you return to physical activity after a long time—just priceless. But I would have been even in worse shape if I hadn't lived in training before the ship. After that soccer, I moved a bit like an old granny, but after one ibuprofen pill and a 45-minute sleep, I was ready to go, almost like new.

Since already I mention sleep, I think I broke some records. Once, of 47 hours I slept only two and a half hours (and maybe here and there taking a short nap of about 10 minutes). I know it sounds completely unreal, but trust me, if someone had mentioned to me before what is waiting for me on a ship, I would very likely call him insane and mature enough for a mental hospital. I might even drop the application. Luckily I didn't, although it was brutally hard I don't regret either a second!

## After three months on the Aries

Because of a very busy and heavy schedule, I ended up in quarantine for four days. While I was working my ass off (apologies for my expression) a fever, sore throat, and a total drop of the immune system were present for some moments. But before I explain this situation to you, I think I can describe in this section one important detail that has affected my health in such a strenuous rhythm.

**Crew food**

The food is wonderful! We have everything the guests have and if they wandered into the crew mess by accident, they wouldn't even notice any difference. And one more thing, I hope you liked this joke.

I simply have no comment on the food in the crew mess. We had some vegetables, fruit, meat, and fish. It would be OK if they weren't put chicken and fish mostly in some creepy sauce from which peek some horror, and not meat. Soup too. And rice, oh my dear brother… *'No rice, no power!'* is a famous quote. But that comes more like sarcasm than in a good way, depending on who says it. There are tons of this rice.

Every day I filled that rice with two large deep table pans and as soon as it ran out, after two seconds they were already whining: *'No rice! No rice!'* and I said, *'I'm going, man, relax!'* In addition to this, there were pizzas, French fries, and some chemistry of desserts. The best scene in the crew mess was when it opens for dinner and the place is full of Filipinos and Indonesians where all of them taking almost the same meal—shovel of rice and a bit of fish or chicken soup with a piece of meat. From cutlery like is mandatory for them to take only a spoon and fork. God forbid they will use a knife.

In all my three contracts that I went through, in 99, 99% of cases I saw that Filipinos and Indonesians eat only with a spoon and fork. However, they have their own eating technique with this set of cutlery, which I admit is quite interesting and even I eat like that sometimes.

Once during a break, I put some ketchup on the rice and everyone looked at me like I had killed someone. I was like; *'What? Did I commit a crime or something? Are you going to throw me off the ship now because of that?'*

Anyway, to finish this topic, for now, the food is not fabulous, but it's OK. There were days when we got good food but it was in case of holidays or some celebrations.

As I started talking before, I ended up in quarantine for four days. How?

Simply. Because of not enough healthy nutrition and such a hard schedule, your immunity must fall once. It wasn't so much the sore throat or fever that bothered me, but the lack of sleep as you might have guessed. Being awake from 5:00 a.m. until 10:00 p.m. and having a three-hour break during the whole day is something that the human body simply cannot follow in the long run. A friend advised me how to pull out the small trick and get some time and rest to sleep. I went to the ship's doctor and lied that I had pain in the stomach, in other words, diarrhoea. It may sound ridiculous now, but trust me it wasn't back then.

People who really do get that, need to stay in quarantine for a few days for safety reasons so they don't jeopardise others. After three months I really couldn't keep up that pace anymore. With the fact that I was every day working my ass off, I decide to do that 'fake move' and to get a few days locked in a room only with the intention to get some better rest and sleep like a normal person. The only bad thing because of my fake diarrhoea was that I was on a special diet. They only brought me damn crackers and toast. It was like a holiday for me when I got sometimes a banana, some rice, and a glass of juice. But, how much I slept, dear brother, too much. I was most of the time just sleeping and watching movies—things I desperately needed a short but worthwhile break.

When I came out of quarantine, I worked another week in the crew mess, and after that got a call to the restaurant manager's office. They offered me a promotion and a new job, in a very luxurious restaurant on the sixth deck, which I kindly turned down for the second time.

For future sailors, learn from my mistakes! Never but never refuse a promotion and thus fear more and more responsibility, as I did.

Somehow those days just bothered me if I would have the opportunity to get out in the ports since we were doing a Baltic cruise. The salary was bigger but I admit that I was scared when I saw how much and at what pace the restaurant was working, so I asked to be transferred to the night shift at the Buffet area, with the excuse that I would work through training another job and change department. There is this option, if you like another job, you can only go there if you work through training. Usually, these are just certain jobs like photographers, receptionists, excursion teams, gift shops, entertainers, or working with children and teenagers. It first occurred to me for a photographer (I have no idea why exactly that direction). The restaurant manager was quite disappointed with my opinion (how could he not) and gave me a night shift but also from that day a different attitude and look.

After that, every time he passed by me, I greeted him while his first and only words were, in a rude way: *'Clean this or that table'* (pointing with finger). Until the day I changed his opinion of me, he always sympathised with me and looked in a positive direction but after that day it was the totally opposite story. But after that, I actually realised how hypocritical and rude he really was. After only two weeks he put me on a day shift at the Buffet. He was just 'playing' with me in a psychological way. Shortly after that, he was fired because too many crew members and even some guests complained about him. At least that's what I heard, but all I can say about him is that something came back to him from everyone and that 'something' is karma. I have always believed in karma.

If you do good things it will come back to you one day. It's the same for bad things as well. They took me back to the night shift that isn't that bad at all. I started at 6:00 p.m. until 10:00 p.m., four hours break, and then follows the night shift from 2:00 a.m. to 7:00 a.m. The only disaster was when I had training around 10:00, 11:00 a.m. because at that time I was deep asleep. But it's OK, I will survive a few more training that I was obliged to do.

But once, while those training came to an end, I had half a day off, which was exactly what I wanted—the possibility of going out in any port and going often to a gym. I did not allow myself to lose all my fitness, so I tried to maintain it as much as possible in those conditions. I remember preferring to sleep an hour and a half less just to get to the gym. Logically, you would think, why even force yourself in the gym now, as 12 hours of work a day is not enough?

The thing is, if you do more extra recreation sometimes, you really feel more energised. Here comes what I mentioned before.

As soon as my schedule changed, so did the opportunity to go out to the ports.

In early June, Elizabeth had a Sign off from the ship after she finished her contract, and her next one started in early August. When you finish the contract you get two months off if you want to go back to a new one. I didn't think too much about her coming back. I left everything to God's will. Until then, when and if she returns, I spent an unforgettable fun time with my colleagues Sasha, one Bosnian, let's call him Edin, and many other different friends.

*** 

My first time going out on this Baltic cruise was in Tallinn, Estonia. The first impression remained somehow special to me because we saw from the ship, the city that was foggy and looked mysterious, which gave a very interesting and some specific atmosphere to the whole environment, but in a positive way. A Bosnian colleague and I went out together to find out what was hiding behind this fog in Tallinn.

Here are a few interesting facts about the second-largest city in Estonia:

- There is a labyrinth from the seventeenth century under the Old Town, secret passages and tunnels that were later used during the Second World War; it has been open for tourists since 2010, with 380 passageways.
- Tallinn has its famous sweet liqueur 'Vana Tallinn' which started to be produced during the '60s (unfortunately I found out about this information too late so I did not have the opportunity to taste it).
- Tallinn's first name was Reval.
- The famous TV tower *Teletorn* is the tallest building not only in Tallinn but also in the whole of Estonia, tall 314 metres.
- The oldest city Café place is *Maiasmokk* (translated as *Sweet Tooth*) which was opened back in 1864 which's interiors have not changed for almost a century.

When Sasha, Edin, and I went out to Warnemünde Rostock (Germany), we just came across great shopping with big discounts. That was nothing else but pure luck. I bought the original quality of clothes for about 120 Euros, which in Croatia would cost around 250–300 Euros. It's also one of the inevitable things when you're working on a cruise ship and just travelling the world, you're constantly coming across something new and it's almost impossible for you not to buy a few things. These 'few' things can exceed your luggage weight, which I will talk more about at the end of this contract. Also one of the other things I will not forget in this place is when the three of us spent about 150 Euros on chocolates, chips, cookies, juices… I mean, really nonsense! But what to say, some things are fun only once.

I can say that we went out often in Rostock. Even when our 'battery' was in reserve, we follow the motto: *'I'll be OK, we'll be back earlier and I'll have time to sleep and be ready for work'.*—Yea, you can only imagine that it was like that. We always arrived exactly to have enough time to take a shower and eat something. It's just like that. Either sleep or use your free time to go out. You think, *'Well, I'm not here or there every day, I'm going out, I can manage!'* And then after work instead of going straight to bed you choose the opposite option! Like You have to see who is in the Crew bar because you 'accidentally' passing by and when you 'unexpectedly' run into some folks with who you constantly hang out and who become like family to you, you have to drink one beer, two, maybe three if is not already 2:00 a.m. Then suddenly you remember you are breakfast off (not working in breakfast shift) OMG, there comes your new temptation! The four of us run to buy a few more beers or bottles of wine seconds until the crew bar closes and the next stop—cabin party. Yes, that ship's life is hard, no joke! ☺

I did not mention how much we lived in delusion during the crossing of the Atlantic. When we realised that we were going to visit Russia, our first thought was who would even wanna go out in Russia where it is probably very cold. No, we don't wanna go wandering around the city in such weather, we thought. The closer we got to St. Petersburg, yet we decided to go out of curiosity. We were already preparing in the cabin and dressing as warmly as possible and when we got to the gangway and saw people outside in short, we just looked at each other and went back to change. I will not forget in that city when we travelled by subway going downtown. To reach the surface with an escalator in the subway downtown took forever, really like all eternity. Quite a long route in which you question yourself about six times, whether you are going in the right direction or you have turned somewhere and is taking you into the universe.

Now seriously, no joke! The city surprised me big time! There are so many things to see. And yes, it was really really hot! After all, we came in the middle of the summer season.

Here are a few interesting facts about the Russian metropolis:

- City of St. Petersburg changed its name three times (St. Petersburg, Petrograd, Leningrad) and finally returned the original historical name in 1991.
- The famous Alexander Column on an even more famous square weighing around 600 tonnes and stands for more than 180 years on its own weight only.
- It could take 'only' 10 years to see the whole Hermitage, it's that 'small'.
- One of the deepest Metro in the world is located in St. Petersburg, 86 metres underground (no wonder it took an eternity on escalators).

Just two days later, on my birthday (6 July), we were walking through Finland. Helsinki is an OK city that looked to me with an extra lot of traffic. We looked at a couple of sights, parks, whatever was in our way, and after so much walking we got hungry. We weren't too picky so we immediately turned into a McDonald's (only healthy choices!) which we spotted as soon as it started screaming out of our stomachs. We ate those burgers faster than when we waited for them. Each of us made calls, to our families, so they could hear that we are alive and still crazy. We didn't feel it so much full from these burgers, but I said, let's go. After a few minutes of walking, one of us saw a restaurant with a buffet and a very reasonable price. We stop there and looked at each other a bit and after a short philosophy discussion, we went in and ate half of the buffet.

When we returned to the ship, I remember as if it was yesterday when I checked in the cabin once again messages. I received another message from my far Croatia. It was a picture of relatives wishing me all the best for my birthday. What's so weird about that now?—Well just that fact that I literally couldn't figure out at least five minutes minimum, where that picture was taken. When I finally realised, other than that, I also realised at that moment how much the ship and this environment confused my memory. OMG, it took me a few minutes to figure out where my relatives were photographed. It took me a few minutes to recognise behind them, the terrace of my own house. Really, I remember a lot of things from the past but something like this has never happened to me before. Here unfortunately I have to express one of the worst sides of the ship—which is the lack of sleep. It wouldn't be so bad if I often kept to the rhythm of only working and sleeping. Then everything would be OK. But it is almost impossible not to go out, drink or eat something, maybe buy a souvenir or a piece of clothing and all that affects you and your free time.

The worst consequence of this is your memory, which suffers and does not 'clean' the brain from sleep, as has been scientifically proven. I'm not claiming now that you're getting so forgetful that you don't know where you were last week because just take me for example, I'm writing a book about the ship I boarded in 2013 and disembarked in 2016 and I remember quite a lot of details although I could have remembered even much more but only of course if I had slept more. These 'confused' five minutes that I needed to recognise my own house is one bigger example. Later, once you anchor ashore and live a normal but sometimes boring life, it will happen to you that you will forget the little things you had before in a little finger. But that's nothing terrible, so don't be scared.

Having already mentioned the memory, you are totally lost on the ship as far as the day of the week is concerned. You don't think that day is which port, you're just used to being guided only by ports and Embarkation day. Tuesday, Wednesday, Friday, weekend, etc. means absolutely nothing to you. Your whole contract is only Monday and when you go home then you take it as you finished working hours that day.

I also have to point out another bad thing that happened to me on my birthday, which I believe everyone goes through a nostalgic moment. You have a birthday and everyone congratulates you, wishes you the best and that's all great but when some pictures from memory take you for a moment when you remember how you celebrated every birthday with your family and friends at home, with homemade food, it's hard to hold back a tear in the eye.

I think this is the most normal thing and that there is no person who has done a contract on a ship without shedding a tear for the memory of their own at home. Unfortunately, that is the price of the ship. But come on, my comforting birthday present was when we played soccer the day before my birthday. Later after work, when I had a break, I went to the crew bar and buy some drinks to treat some friends.

After these adventures in those cities, I remember one from Denmark.

It often happens that the port is located outside of the city's downtown, which is logical. So Veljko (Serbian) and I took the subway to see a little bit of that city. I had an obsession everywhere to buy postcards and souvenirs, which I think is one of the most exciting things in the first contract for a freshman. When I took a couple of postcards and a magnet souvenir there, I can say, it cost me quite a lot. I'm not trying to lie or something but if my memory serves me well, I think it was around 15–20 €. It's awful that kind of prices are there. Standards there are so high that is simply amazing. The whole of Scandinavia!

We had a good laugh, especially when you have such a special colleague next to you when from most things he sees, he comments in some confused ridiculous way, which sounds like a total parody. After hilarious tours of the city (which I must mention is very disciplined neat and clean), when we were returning by train to our 'home', we talked deep into some topic, that we almost forgot to get out at our station. What a hilarious scene was that. We were sitting so relaxed, looking out the window and talking about I don't know what.

When the train stopped at our station, we didn't realise. We were still sitting relaxed and talking. When at the last moment I realised where we actually were, I exclaimed, and we both jumped in half a millisecond from our seats to the door, which was still closed. Veljko froze completely, he didn't know what to do next, until I saw a button with light and thought: *'That must be for the way out, let us out of here man, so we don't get late for the ship!'*

It wouldn't be terrible if we went to the station further, but the thing was that we were already too short with time, and we would be late for the ship. Thank goodness we arrived as usual, at the last minute.

Interesting facts from Copenhagen:

- Copenhagen and the whole of Denmark, in general, presents itself to the world as one of the most desirable places to live, due to the generally very friendly mentality, Danes are considered one of the happiest people in the world.
- Similar to the Netherlands, more than half of the population in Copenhagen goes to work by bicycle, it is not said in vain that in Copenhagen you have a better chance of being hit by a bicycle than by a car.
- Walt Disney was inspired by the famous Tivoli Gardens, which is also considered to be Copenhagen one of the main sources for inspiration for fairy tales.
- Copenhagen shares rival with Stockholm, as the largest cities in all of Scandinavia.
- The flag of Denmark is the oldest flag in the whole world if we take into account all the independent countries, and it began to flutter in the wind back in 1219.
- Copenhagen is one of the safest cities in the world.
- Most famous Danish beer is *Carlsberg* and yes, I had the opportunity to taste this one. ☺
- Copenhagen is at the very top in terms of the greatest cleanliness and tidiness in the world.
- The origin of the famous LEGO toys is Denmark.

Tallinn, Estonia

Warnemünde Rostock, Germany

Welcome to St. Petersburg, Russia; somewhere between Estonia and Russia

On the square and Cathedral St. Isaac, St. Petersburg, Russia

Hermitage, St. Petersburg, Russia

The Church of the Savior on Spilled Blood, St. Petersburg, Russia

Helsinki, Finland

Helsinki, Finland

Helsinki, Finland

City Hall, Copenhagen, Denmark

City Hall, Copenhagen, Denmark

Sunset

I also managed to change the cabin with Sasha and the rest of the Balkans. There were five of us in the cabin. Two Bosnians, one Serb, one from Grenada, and me. What can I say about that—comedies from dusk until dawn, which on the other hand was necessary to have so you don't become depressed about things you miss. I don't think we'll ever forget when one morning a cell phone alarm rang and the three of us woke up confused asking each other, *'Is that my alarm or yours?'* Speaking of the alarm, I won't forget the Bosnian who slept on the bed below me. He had a whole song for alarm and when his alarm started to sound, he couldn't wake up.

I mean, literally, he kept his cell phone right next to his head. Of course, the rest of us woke up but not him. We shout Edin, Edin!—Edin nothing. Well, is he alive? Does he breathe?—we were wondered, while the alarm almost played the whole song. Finally, when this one opened his eyes, he turned off the alarm and went back to sleep. God forbid, how he got out when he was late for work, we don't know until today.

On this occasion, I must also mention that our people are the greatest comedians on board. Bosnia—Croatia—Serbia together in the cabin is priceless! I started realising that later. In the second contract, I didn't have our people as roommates while thank God in the third I did. It's not that the rest of the nation doesn't have a sense of humour because it does indeed but yet our language with three different accents is sometimes hilarious to listen to. Once a restaurant manager (the one who was fired) wanted to separate us from the cabin, but we 'did not allow him', in a decent way. Best describes this situation when one of us mentioned that it has probably never happened in our history that a Croat, a Serb, and a Bosnian hold so tightly together. I guess you can't go against ex Yuga, whatever you are.

There's also one video I shot the day before the cabin inspection. This video, still today when I see, I cry of laughing.

Sasha, Edin and I were in the cabin, talking casually, watching TV, listening to songs on our cell phones… when suddenly one of us remembered that the cabin inspection will come the next morning. When we realised with the looks around us how much cleaning we had, we all started laughing like we were drunk. Right away I grab my cell phone and start recording this unforgettable evening! I started recording all the possible mess in the room. From clothes scattered on the beds, garbage on the floor like chocolate wrappers, cans of juice and beer, empty yoghurt glasses, a table full of the whole world, a bathroom where you need to search for toilet paper on the floor, same for towel, but the top was a huge garbage bag that we had forgotten about since the last inspection, which these two crazy ones hid.

During the filming, I spilt a little beer on the carpet when in the next scene, Sasha takes an expensive perfume (which by the way was not his but Edin's) and tries to hide the smell of beer while the two of us laughed non-stop. All of this may not sound so funny but trust me, for us, it is very much even today!

Let me tell you a little bit about work and the work environment.

The team from the night shift was crazy and completely awesome. I have to mention that in addition to going out with Balkan people, an equally great part of my first contract was my night shift with this team. Do you remember El Colombiano? I mentioned it at the beginning. In the meanwhile, he went and came back from vacation. During my time at the night shift, he was back at the Buffet area. With him, things were even funnier.

But once I was upset with him because after my shift and breakfast, when I was already asleep, he called me on the phone after only an hour in the cabin. I had to come and sign some paper, which turned out I could sign also later at work. Since I couldn't sleep anymore that day (yea, I know, sounds weird), I headed to the gym, after the gym took a shower, and napped until 5:00 p.m.

About the phone in the cabin—you do not have it for the reason that you could order food and room service but to call your family back home, other crew members, or have your supervisors calling you when you fall asleep and are late for 'check-in' before working hours. But such situations can be tolerated very rarely. If you are a person who has a frequent problem with being late for work, the company will not keep you for a long time, and you will be fired for being undisciplined.

What else to say about El Colombiano, the funny guy…

From 6:00 p.m. to 10:00 p.m. I got a special part of the job, unlike the others. Namely, the ship contained at the front, in the middle, and at the back on a couple of decks pantry rooms, where a crew from the room service brought dirty plates, glasses, dishes, and everything else that is cleaned with room after guests order room service. My task was to take the trolley and pick up everything from each pantry and bring it all to the dishwasher for washing. Very simple job.

I didn't even think I was actually going to enjoy it for a while because what I liked was that I had my peace of mind and time to do it. Of course, in the beginning, when I was just starting, getting to know these pantries, it took me four hours to finish everything. El Colombiano didn't bother me for the time I took for the job. He didn't keep an eye on me very often. The only thing he expected from me was when I finished each pantry to call him from the phone and let him know, which one was cleaned. Sometimes, I didn't have the habit of doing that either (laughing).

Sounds ridiculous because I am currently laughing when I think back to those days, but pay attention to this—if you work logically, things on the ship will be easier for you, I guess that's the case in life in general. I remembered those first tips from Ronnie when I was back at crew mess: *'Don't work hard, work smart'*. And of course, when I caught a fast rhythm, I finished my job in just two and a half hours. But El Colombiano's timing was still four hours for my job. Certainly, I didn't call right away that I was done with work but left my trolley near my staircase and went to the cabin to sleep for an hour or so. I had everything planned in my head even if they caught me, and they never did. It lasted for a while which was good for me. Half an hour of sleep means a lot on board, not to mention a full hour or more than that.

On the other hand, this character from El Colombiano seemed to us like a person who doesn't care too much about some things. It's a kind of phlegmatic person as we say. He performed his duty well, but everything else remained as a comedy moment for everyone.

The people I worked with on the night shift were also very funny. It was like they escaped from cartoons. We were six on the night shift team, but only four of us hung out the most and performed all the time crazy stupid nonsense.

Let's call them Leyton (Grenadian) and two Indonesians Tarjo and Putu. Leyton was in charge of the coffee station where he had a lot of work—cleaning coffee machines and preparing for breakfast. Tarjo was the one who always brought things from storage and filled the cold room and controlled everything while his compatriot Putu was in charge of cleaning the floor of the entire Buffet area (mopping and vacuuming).

And me? I cleaned the juice machines, refilled them, filled the station with glasses and cups and some other little things. I know I've mentioned it a couple of times already but I have to repeat, how great times we had on the night shift. There were no supervisors, we had our peace of mind and also finished work in just a few hours, as well as with the pantry and the rest of the time messing around until the early hours before the Maitre'd arrived.

One very special part of the night shift that has left its mark forever on me is all those beautiful sunsets and sunrises. Part of the work I did outdoors, next to the pool is also a buffet that I prepared for breakfast and never missed the beautiful sunrises of the early morning sun. In the evening, the Maitre'd sent me often to the pool area, where are about twenty tables. Dear readers, there are no such words, no language in which to describe these beautiful images of nature! Either on the open sea or near the coast, each sunset and sunrise made me feel touched every time. It gave me a special peace of mind and strength in my body. What I am incredibly sorry about is that these pictures from the paper can't be explained in the way how I felt there. Truly the best part of the day and night in the whole contract!

If you ever decide to cruise no matter if as a crew or as a guest, by no means do not miss that! If you have the opportunity, use it! Because once you see that, you will understand my point but also find some version of yourself at that moment. Nature is amazing! People are not aware of what is given to them in today's world.

From the days when I often trained, before the vessel, I was going for a run to a hilly vineyard where once you get to the top, you feel blessed when you catch a sunset full of shades of red, yellow, and orange. Since then, I've realised how much I love that part of life.

August is approaching, which means that Elizabeth is coming soon. Although even we did not know where to go with our relationship the day she left the ship, we stayed in touch and who will say, God obviously wanted her back to me.

Stockholm was the only city I always kept on the 'scales'. Why?

The thing was that a couple of us as a group went to Stockholm (a little outside of downtown) to Kaknäs where we played soccer on a beautiful pitch. That pitch belonged to one club but for our crew, I think it was always organised. We got the equipment, jerseys, and soccer boots, all for soccer. Very often we played in the hot sun, later we could eat something and after an exhausting running, going back to the ship. On this occasion, I would like to thank on behalf of the crew, once again to the wonderful people from Kaknäs—for being so kind and respectful allowing us to enjoy at least a little bit of soccer but the nice company as well! I would like to visit this nice place again one day and play a few more games on that pitch and with that to awake these beautiful memories.

We also played a couple of tournaments with other teams from other ships. And that was that 'scale'. Every time I came to Stockholm I thought about either going to play soccer or exploring the city. Of course very hard sometimes, I couldn't miss not seeing a little bit of a city that looks really special because makes you think—*we've been to that Stockholm so many times and now I won't see the city at least once or twice, no matter how much I love and want to use every opportunity for soccer?*

Interesting facts from Stockholm:

- The Swedish capital is situated on 14 islands connected by 57 bridges so no matter where you are in Stockholm, you will always be close to the water; the city also has 96 beaches.
- Since 1901, Stockholm has been the permanent hosting place of Nobel Prize ceremonies.
- In Stockholm, fishing and picking berries and mushrooms is allowed everywhere—even on private territories, to own a boat or small motor ship you won't need any permits; no license is required to steer a ship, either, and you can even build your own vessel anywhere on the shore; the people of this city own around 20,000 boats.
- Stockholm is one of the world's cleanest cities particularly because they don't have heavy industry.
- The Swedish motto 'After work' usually is implemented as 'Happy hour'

*...Well, after more than half of the contract I have to mention something outside of this book. When I started writing this book, I was very excited and impatient to share my experiences as soon as possible and open up a few new pictures in people's life. But I didn't count on one thing, and that was my lack of conscience how much would be difficult for me to write a book like this. Why and in which way difficult?*

*To have a little harder time remembering some adventures it stands but they weren't so crucial now that I couldn't start writing a book. What I mean by 'difficult' is once I immersed myself in all those adventures, emotions, pictures, friendships, and even the bad experiences... I actually realised then how much I miss ship life. That feeling of nostalgia is so strong and great, literally indescribably powerful even to the point that I paused for a moment and began to question myself about returning back to the ship. I even talked to Elizabeth and discussed the advantages and shortcomings that we would gain and lose if we decided to make a big comeback.*

*It cannot be explained to a person who has never tried and worked on a ship. Simply this now dealing with the most beautiful memories in life is not easy just to put on paper without emotions. I also talked to a few friends, some of them are still on board while some are anchored like us. For those of us who have left (or at least tried) the ship behind, no matter how hard that rhythm of work was and a little of free time we got, without any doubt I can say for sure that we will always miss it. As sailors would say, you can take a man out of a ship but you can't take a ship out of a man. Real truth.*

*But don't you worry I'm still here, I'm still trying to finish the book and will I go or not back to the ship, I think you'll get the answer to that question towards the end of the book. What I just wanted to let you know is that this writing woke me up and shook me up a bit, and I just described half of the first contract. How I will just feel then when I finish the book with three contracts…*

## 20 September, Aries

Last time in Russia, a couple of days ago we went out; Elizabeth and I took a look at a little part of the city that we haven't yet. Orthodox churches and cathedrals were an interesting experience. After that, we sat down somewhere to eat something, and I have to praise that restaurant, which name I, unfortunately, don't remember, for delicious food and refreshing cocktails.

What I feel obligated to mention about St. Petersburg (perhaps more because of myself than for you my dear readers) is how I felt those particular days.

I went out in front of the cruiser, (just in the terminal) and found a spot, a more secluded place by the sea. I sat down on that metal thing to which the ship was moored and with headphones in my ears and a song in my head asked myself questions for which ones the answers would come a quite good year later.

Has there ever been a moment in your life, those few minutes to really ask yourself what your life will look like? Will you succeed in the things you dream of? How do you know you are on the right track? Will you get that 'calm' peace of mind and finally say one day, *'Here I am, and I did it! That inner peace means more to me than any other kind of happiness'.*

That moment hit me hard, especially a song whose lyrics strike right in those places where emotions are strongest. If you are interested, listen to *Todor*

*Kobakov—Lost in the All,* and you can imagine a scene sitting by the sea, listening to the song, and looking for what is hidden in the depths of your heart. Trust me, you will get tingles all over your body.

At that moment, I held the rosary tightly, which I pray regularly, and asked God for life guidelines and to never leave me blind. It would be my biggest lie to say that on that day, that moment, those few minutes, I didn't feel God's presence. In fact, when I think about it, I have never felt a stronger force before in my life than that day. It was a force of faith.

I don't think people often talk about such experiences but they should.

I don't believe at all that I am the only one going through such emotional stages. I have often seen, by chance, supervisors, and officers, or any other crew member, alone on the open deck, looking so deeply in their thoughts staring at the ocean, very likely going through such 'blessings and enlightenment'. At first, it was weird to see such scenes until I went through one of them myself and now I can say I understand what they are going through.

***

We got a new Maitre'd at work because of the rotation we are now listening to, let's call him Bastián (Chilean) which marked a big change. When we met, he initially seemed like a great person to us. I remember he even invited the whole night shift team to the crew bar and treated us to one round of drinks. He may be OK in society but as a supervisor, he is pretty strict. He took one guy from our night shift, so with one person less, we had to make up the job for the person who left plus he assigned us a couple of more jobs on the side. We did not understand this way of managing the Buffet area the best, but what it was, it was back then.

In those days, the mystery of some questions, and the sadness of missing everything at home began to catch me again. Halfway through the contract, I started already to think whether to return to the ship or not after this contract? If yes, then maybe better to another department, if yes again, to which one? I even started with plans for the option to try a job somewhere in the USA and for that the visa created difficulties, I'm all lost, I don't have as much time as I wish for the gym or my favourite soccer. What disaster days were. But that's how it comes and goes, it's just short phases that you go through when you're on a ship.

On this Baltic cruise every week on a certain day, we had a particularly incredible amount of work due to the organised evening for guests called 'Choco—night'. The entire Buffet was filled with hundreds of chocolate desserts. I was obsessed with chocolate-covered bananas. On one occasion I took a whole tray of these bananas and brought them to the cabin for my crazy Balkan friends. If Bastián caught me back then, I would definitely get a warning. You get a warning when you do something more serious against the rules. If you get three of them, you fly out of the ship. But you can also get only one to kick you out in case there are some illegal things in question, fights, etc. I thought, who cares! Let them give me a warning for this little robbery because these bananas were just too good. Elizabeth was an assistant in that organised crime. (laughing)

*'Take it now or never!'*—Elizabeth's words to me in the crucial moment ☺

Baltic sunrises and sunsets – priceless!

Baltic sunrises and sunsets – priceless!

Baltic sunrises and sunsets – priceless!

Living the moment, Kaknäs, Sweden

Stockholm, Sweden

With Veljko, a colleague from Serbia

Stockholm, Sweden

Stockholm, Sweden

On the way to the Norway

*Ship's Itinerary (21 September–6 October)*
*Ports: Bergen (Norway)*
*Ålesund (Norway)*
*Lerwick—Shetland Islands (Scotland)*
*Tórshavn (Faroe Islands)*
*Reykjavík (Iceland)*
*Oslo (Norway)*
*Ponta Delgada—São Miguel Island (Portugal)*

Beautiful Norway, incredibly cold Scotland, interesting Faroe Islands, and surprising Iceland.

We are approaching Bergen, it will soon be seven o'clock in the morning, the sky will soon dawn, in that still semi-dark dawn only lights from the mainland can be seen, something that will remain as a particularly nice picture for me. Another one like that will appear in the last contract. Anyway, let me share with you some interesting facts about Bergen:

- Bergen is the city which is surrounded by seven mountains.
- Population of this city is around 270 000 which makes it the second biggest city in Norway.
- Bergen is one of Europe's rainiest places with an average rainfall of 231 days per year.
- In the year 1986 – edition of the Eurovision Song Contest was in Bergen.
- Bergen became a member of the UNESCO Creative Cities Network in the Gastronomy – Category since 2015.

This Ålesund is also fascinating. When we arrived at the main viewpoint, the view of the city literally looks as if buildings and houses are standing on the water itself.

I don't know if we just hit the wrong weather or it's normal there however I definitely recommend if you have a desire to visit Scotland, don't come in mid-September (not to mention even later). Or if something simply just pushes you to go there at that time, make sure you dress very well and keep warm because back then the blood in our veins froze. Scotland is quite interesting, it has beautiful hills and valleys and specific green areas, old fortresses and houses, but the dear mother of God, it's so windy here. We were just followed by some icy wind all the way wherever we went.

Few facts about this cold place:

- The name Lerwick was taken from the Old Norse word 'Leirvik', which means 'muddy or clay bay'.
- In Shetland Islands the fish industry is bigger than in the whole of England, Wales and Northern Ireland together.
- In 1625 Lerwick was punished and almost disappeared in a fire.

Tórshavn (Faroe Islands) we didn't have much time to explore but that grass on the roofs around the houses as part of the decoration left an interesting impression. Even we didn't catch quality time for exploring this area, we heard a few amusing things about this place from our colleagues from the Shore excursion department.

- Fishing is the islands' most important industry. It provides more than 90 % of all exports, and astonishingly tourism as the second-largest industry.
- There is no prison on the Faroe Islands and for any long-term prisoners will be send to Denmark.
- The Faroese language, is very similar to Icelandic, English is also over all spoken
- The Faroe Islands were elected by the famous National Geographic as the world's most appealing island community, out of 111 island destinations worldwide, also they are very recognized for their kindness and friendliness.
- Streymin bridge (connection between Islands Streymoy and Eysturoy) is the only bridge over the Atlantic Ocean in the world.

I must say that I really never hoped or thought I would visit Reykjavík. This was a very full day of events like no other.

Until then, breakfast usually opened at the Buffet area at 6:00 a.m. Just because of that port, that day opened half an hour earlier. Since it is a very special opportunity to visit a lot of things at that port and with the fact that we didn't stay there for long, you can only imagine how crowded it was for breakfast. It wasn't even 5:00 a.m. yet, I remember already a large number of guests were coming. Just 15 minutes after opening, the Buffet area is on fire! We are under attack! We had a feeling like these guests were coming from other ships, dear mother of God, we didn't even know that this ship could accommodate as many guests as suddenly appeared. People came to help us from all sides, supervisors send help from every restaurant that was open back then also for breakfast. The whole restaurant department has risen to its feet!

What was a bit funny to see, that even the highest superiors of that department such as the Restaurant Manager, Hotel Director, and F&B Manager (Food and Beverage Manager) ran and helped in all directions, which is, of course, a very rare occurrence.

We from the night shift had to stay until 8:00 a.m. After that extended night shift because I was very interested in that Iceland, I had only two options that you can already guess for yourself—either to sleep or to go out. At 11:00 a.m., the bus leaves the port for the 'Blue Lagoon'. I have three hours left for breakfast and some sleep.

Horror, but as it goes, 'I'm not here every day!' and in my first contract, that Iceland was visited only that time. It took about an hour to reach Blue Lagoon. This is a place of Icelandic springs of hot geysers. Outside was probably 5, 6°C, and we bathed in warm water. It was a very interesting experience that, honestly, was enough for me to have only once.

On the way back to the boat, some sleeping time on the bus, (at least as far as you got to catch), one quick shower, dinner, and *Rock 'n' Roll*—ready for work!

After the day shift, break for a couple of hours and *Ready to Rumble* at night again. Wow, how much I get tough and stronger from that crew mess before that I didn't feel overly tired, even after a day like that one in Reykjavík.

What I wished to see a little more of all these ports is Oslo. It looked to me like a very interesting city full of stunning architecture and delicious food. But, maybe next time.

And that's all about the European adventure on the ship Aries.

After that, we turned to the Atlantic, on our way back to America we visited the Portuguese Ponta Delgada once again, and then a week filled only with the ocean, and a few more beautiful sunsets and sunrises followed.

I didn't mention an important detail when we headed to Europe and that is the time difference. There was a 'weekly killing' when we moved the clock forward every night, while on the way back you turn the clock back every day and wish to do that the whole contract.

Alessund, Norway

Alessund, Norway

City and fort Charlotte, Lerwick, Scotland

Blue Lagoon, Iceland; interesting houses on the Faroe Islands

Source of hot water, Blue Lagoon, Iceland

Oslo, Norway

Ponte Delgada, Portugal

## The United States Public Health—USPH

When a cruiser sails American waters, there are detailed inspections, which means that very often cleaning and disinfection actions are carried out on all rooms and work surfaces. It was always frustrating and irritating to us whenever we heard an order from our superiors *'Deep cleaning'*. Literally, very deep cleaning because the ship must be prepared constantly and maintained under American regulations, where at any American port can be surprised by the inspection of all inspections—USPH!

At first, I kept thinking about how these Americans exaggerate and behave with all these rules like some arrogant and spoiled brat. How everything has to be above perfect, to satisfy the American standards.

Today I understand the point of all this, and without any doubt and with a clear conscience I can say firmly, clearly, and loudly with certainty that I support all these laws 1,000%!

More experienced colleagues have always told me that once I return to the mainland and start another life there, only then I will realise how clean the ship actually was (in comparison to most of the places on land). That's living truth that I wish badly to pursue again. About these standards, Americans are totally right! Today when I see any places where gastronomy moves, 90% of them would not pass the USPH inspection for sure! The vast majority of them are not even aware of how wrong they are doing some things, which leads to an even bigger problem—the consequences. I won't mention many examples just one of the biggest ones that were during my stay onboard—We once received information that about 300 people get infected from another company, I will not name which ones. So I say no, the USPH does not exaggerate its regulations that need to be followed and taken seriously.

Once I anchored after the ship's life, I found the first job in a private hotel (three stars, although refused to have four) and after a week I realised how much the place lags behind at least the minimum necessary conditions. In order not to judge the mainland because of only one hotel, I talked to a couple of friends who work in the same city as us, but also elsewhere in the world, also in gastronomy in a couple of different and powerful locations, only with the intention to find out better information and comfort myself how much I made the first impression wrong. Unfortunately, from reliable sources, the information was not too far from the one at the beginning.

Not only is this city where we currently live like that but you have bad places everywhere in the world, unfortunately, that will always be the case. You don't believe me?—one of the most respected names in the kitchen is the British chef Gordon Ramsay. I saw him the other day on TV where he has his own show. And I'm not talking about cooking. He randomly checks restaurants where he reveals to people who can't see and don't know, in which kind of a mess and unhygienic conditions these restaurants serve food. If you haven't, watch at least one show, and will be enough for you. I hope that now you can better understand the truth I am talking about.

It is certainly not easy to maintain and control this type of work but everything starts and arises for a single reason and that is staff training. If every staff in every place had half the training we did on board, I'm sure the change would be noticed quickly. As for those things and cleaning, everyone on board really did a perfect job.

From experience, I advise you, wherever you go for lunch or dinner, even if only along the way something quick to snack on, always pay attention to details. Especially if you are travelling as a tourist. These are just a few of my tips that are well-intentioned and don't take them for granted. I believe that most people (who work in gastronomy) will agree with me. Whether in the city centre where you live or in a tourist destination where everything is crowded with people, avoid any restaurants and 'fast food' in that good circle. At least some 200–300 metres from the core is a solid option either in terms of price or quality. When entering an interesting restaurant, pay attention to the cleanliness of the tables and details such as pepper and salt bottles, oil, and cutlery (if set) while waiting to be escorted to your table.

If everything looks neat and clean enough, that's a good start. Next, pay attention to three things about the staff, i.e., the waiter. The way they speak, body language and the neatness/cleanliness of the uniform are the biggest indicators of what kind of person and place will serve you. You can easily find out all this in just a few minutes while having a conversation deciding what to order. If you are interested in something about food or drink, ask. The longer you talk the more you learn about the quality of the waiters and the place i.e. the way they work, of course, I am still considering talking for just a few minutes, so no hassle, please.

If possible, pay attention to these details when serving others. (How is the guest treated, whether the food is creatively served on a plate or just 'forcibly' thrown away, etc.) If you are all right until then, you have no reason to get up and leave the restaurant.

These are some tips that can open your eyes better when it comes to hygiene while when it comes to food quality and preparation we can't know until we experience that food in our mouths. But let's get back to the topic of the ship.

It wasn't easy to stay an hour or two longer at work because of all that cleaning. How much I just listened to that *'Three bucket system'* (three rules of cleaning). If one cruise lasted a week, out of seven days we had a six-day inspection so you can understand how serious this is taken. In Europe, we had a little less, maybe once-twice a week while the USA was a completely different story.

## LIFEBOAT DRILL

This is something necessary and without that, a cruise would not have been approved. There are no jokes here because human lives are at stake. More than known, the Lifeboat drill is conducted obligatorily once a week or once in a certain cruise route with the proviso that the exercise is carried out when the ship is anchored at the port, never during the voyage. The meaning and goal of such exercises is to prepare, introduce, and teach the crew and passengers about escape routes, i.e., evacuation in case of real danger.

To give you a little clearer picture of how seriously all these regulations are taken, try to understand this from the following example.

What was unfortunate on 11 September 2001 (attack on a WTC in New York) on the land, the one incident of the ship from one company was on the sea. After that attack on New York, the authorities tightened the security and security rules that make a massive change since that attack. Same thing with the 'sea incident'. After those disastrous images from 2012, the seaman's book was gaining weight to implement even more detailed and stringent safety measures.

Each lifeboat drill starts at around 10:00 a.m. with an alarm on the PA system from the captain's 'bridge' (control centre). Now, what types of alarms and security codes are, all dependent on the company. The four most common alarms (which we had) were a first aid alarm, a fire alarm, a man overboard alarm, and an alarm for safety reasons such as ship damage or spillage of hazardous chemicals. All these types were determined by special tones and names. After we would hear the alarm for the lifeboat drill, everyone would take their card, which has a personal number, the station number you have to go to, and other necessary instructions that of course, you have to know by heart.

It is strictly forbidden to use elevators during every exercise, especially in case of a real emergency. When you arrive at your station, there you perform your duty to the passengers you evacuate in groups and wait ready to enter the lifeboats if you receive the last instructions from the captain. The alarm indicating the Lifeboat drill sounds with seven short and one longer tones while the alarm of all alarms, which God forbid anyone hears, is one uninterrupted longer tone which means *Abandon ship* or how we would say *run for you life* (but in that case, where?)

Usually, for guests, this drill is carried out the same day after boarding, while we as a crew have once again during the week, which lasts up to an hour, an hour, and a half. So two lifeboat drills per cruise for us.

In case a crew member misses the boat drill, he receives a warning (verbal and written warning). The only reason he can miss is from two cases. Either he is recovering in medical (quarantine) or he is an exception, so he stays to work because how would it look like everyone goes to the boat drill to the last and no one works for breakfast in a huge buffet.

Another thing on board in terms of security is the modern technology used by officers. If you are afraid of cruising because you think you could be hit by a very bad storm, that's just your fear. You have no reason to panic because cruisers have so much advanced technology that you can't even imagine. As for natural disasters in the oceans and open seas, this type of technology helps them a lot. They can find out in advance a couple of days if not more, where there will be some awkward storm and bypass them with maximum caution in a wide arc, so you have no reason to kill your nerves with such worries. In the three contracts I've done, the worst storm we've had was a little stronger rough seas, but again not to the point of losing control of everything.

Even if you decide a ship's life for a longer period of more than a couple of years, you are more likely to encounter minor accidents and damage to the ship that very rarely occur in the ports themselves, such as situations where cruisers hit other anchored ships because they sailed with a little uncontrolled speed into the port.

All in all, at the end of this topic I just want to assure you that you really have no reason to worry and fear as far as your personal safety is concerned and know that the people responsible for safety on board do absolutely everything to avoid even the slightest inconvenience during any cruise.

Boat Drill

With David (Safety officer); trainings on the ship are no joke

Crossing the Atlantic

Crossing the Atlantic

*Ship's Itinerary (13 October–10 November) – the last month*
*Ports: Miami (USA) – Embarkation day*

> *Cartagena (Columbia)*
> *Panama Canal*
> *Puntarenas (Costa Rica)*
> *Puerto Chiapas (Mexico)*
> *Huatulco (Mexico)*
> *Los Angeles (USA) – Disembarkation/Embarkation day*
> *Cabo San Lucas (Mexico)*
> *Puerto Vallarta (Mexico)*
> *Huatulco (Mexico)*
> *Puntarenas (Costa Rica)*
> *Panama Canal*
> *Cartagena (Columbia)*
> *Miami (USA) – Sign Off = END OF THE CONTRACT*

Here we are again in America. Arrived and 'parked' in Miami. We had a feeling the cruiser could hardly wait to replenish itself with everything it needed. Do you know the feeling when you drive a car with the last drops of fuel, to the nearest gas station and pray and hope that your car will last so that you can 'overeat' it with fuel in the next few minutes?

We had that feeling too when the cruiser in Miami was gaining weight once the loading and unloading started to arrive.

But while they were 'feeding' our cruiser, I noticed that I didn't mention and talk too much about the crew on the ship, so let's go, I think it would be quite the final time to do that.

**ABOUT THE CREW (from all three contracts)**

I mentioned that on the ship work about 60 different nationalities. That number tells you everything, how many different races, cultures, customs, ways of behaving, etc.

In order to avoid a case like 'a dog and a cat in the same cage', it is necessary to have, especially in addition to so many nations, strictly disciplined regulations according to which each crew member must adhere. Everyone to the last, from the dishwasher to the captain.

Logically, no crew member should have any contact with any drugs, be aggressive and provoke others and be prone to fights, verbally insult or underestimate anyone based on religion, race, culture, appearance, and sexual harassment. When such situations occur, that person is fired and disembarks at the first next port no matter where he/she is. In the case of a couple of days of sailing at sea or more (such as crossing the ocean), that person is locked in a cell on board (if necessary), until arrival at the first port. Yes, you read that right, we also have a jail on board. One cell for guests, one for crew members. We just have to have it because it often happens that you have someone who doesn't know how to keep order and discipline, and you can't just throw him off the ship in the middle of a cruise (although for some 'species' it would be desirable but insufficient).

There were also cases when crew members were caught with drugs in the Caribbean and Mexico and, in addition to being fired by the company, placed in their prisons because since you break the law in a certain country, you are obliged to serve a sentence according to their laws. I think there was even one case in the newspaper of Balkan people about how they were caught with drugs and placed in a prison in South America.

So it is very important to remain a good friend with everyone as much as possible. There are no limits to human intentions, so there have been cases of planting illegal things on innocent people. My intention is not to scare you, future crew members, from going on a ship, but to warn of such situations that are very rare but still present because as I said, you can't trust anyone 100% and you should always be aware of that.

Of the crew, the most numerous nations are the Filipinos and Indians. There are more than half of the crew for sure. Behind them, in terms of ratio in third place, I would put people from the Caribbean, such as Nicaragua, Jamaica, Dominica, Grenada, Saint Lucia, etc.

The rest are Indonesians, Croats, Serbs, Bosnians, Macedonians, Romanians, some Ukrainians, Bulgarians, Poles, and well-known Latino populations such as Mexico, Peru, Brazil, Colombia, and Argentina, while the smallest number come from other developing countries. I will try to describe each nation to you in a few words.

Filipinos and Indians—for me personally, I didn't like working with Filipinos because you can't expect some solid teamwork from them and help when you need it. I don't believe Indians are any better at this. In terms of behaviour and character, I did not experience most of them as a social group of people, while a few of them are very easy on the trigger and ready for belligerent discussions. But I must mention that in every nation as well as with them, there are exceptions that can become your best friends and it even depends a lot on which part of the country they come from, something I noticed.

For example, when I started working in the crew mess, in the pot washroom was working one Indian, who was a very modest and kind person, very friendly and radiated that peaceful positive energy. I could always talk to him about soccer, players, clubs, etc. While one such Indian does one of the quite bad jobs for a lower salary than mine, you have other Indians working in restaurants in much higher positions and filled their character with some arrogant attitude. But such a case is present everywhere, no matter which nation it is. For example, in the third contract the Restaurant Manager was an Indian who helped me a lot and was a person you could learn from.

I recently found out from a friend who is still working on a cruise ship, that my former CL2 company stopped hiring Indians due to too many cases and intents to get to the ship just to get out in America and never return to the ship. In other words—immigrants who have used a slightly more efficient and resourceful way to get to America.

What to say about crew members from the Caribbean? Believe it or not, I've been thinking about the answer to that question since the beginning of the book. If I would describe them in two words I think the best picture that describes them is: Aggressive and hilarious.

I don't know if it's because of such an environment where they come from or it's just in their genes, but their aggression is really too sensitive. I must mention that this refers more to the female population (at least onboard). I don't think there is a crew member who hasn't had a conflict with the 'Caribbean girls' at least once. These are the types of people who find it too difficult to do something here and there for others (I'm talking about the restaurant department here).

Once I needed a plastic bin in which we collected dirty plates, cups, etc. and since there were no more of them in the dishwasher, I saw one of the stations full of these bins so I thought to go grab one from there. Of course, a conceited female head from the Caribbean was working at that station, and as soon as she saw me approaching the bins, she asked me in a very arrogant and high-pitched tone what I needed (if she had something to shoot me with, probably she would). Of course, she didn't give me at least one of the 6–8 bins she kept hidden because that would mean an incredibly hard job for her to walk some 20 metres to the dishwasher and take a new one when it's washed. That's just one of the examples.

What is not exactly right sometimes is, that with this kind of attitude they manage to scare assistant Maitre'ds, which leads to that they either do not dare to deal with Caribbeans or simply do not want to bother with such people and have any further problems. There have been plenty of cases where people from the Caribbean have been fired for such a form of aggression in excessive amounts.

The other word as I described them is hilarious. The male population predominates here, but the female population should not be neglected either.

As much as we laughed just because of them, it really was one of our main valves to relax in addition to so much stress with all sorts of people on board. What makes them so funny and special that they are different from any other nation? Well very simple—their way of speaking English. They have that one as we called 'broken English'.

When you start listening to them I don't think even a doctor of English grammar would fully understand them. If you've ever watched a documentary about Bob Marley (if you haven't I definitely recommend it), remember how Mr Marley spoke and in what way. Truly this way of expressing them is fascinating and unique. When I remember how much it made me laugh I really miss listening to them live again. In the older movie *Cool Runnings* when I watched it, I thought those Jamaicans were intentionally acting out such an accent, but I was actually convinced that it wasn't acting at all. They really talk like that!

Of course, some of them talk nice and really fluently and understandable English, while most of them are the opposite story.

In the third contract, we played soccer on board with them quite often and that was the highlight of their comedy. When you look at them, total anti-talents who missed an empty goal from an impossibly close distance, and when they started arguing with each other, we burst out laughing from the side. Of course, it wasn't that aggressive quarrel I mentioned before but one that shows funny sides. That quarrel in 'their language' remained one of the funniest memories for me. Who hasn't experienced it doesn't know what I'm talking about and who has, he literally laughs even now reading this and remembering words like 'bomboclaat and Babalou' language.

But what most of the male population of the Caribbean is doing is unforgivable.

As soon as they see new crew members, they chase naive girls until they get what they aim for so that later in case the girl gets pregnant, they leave her and never call back. It was the same with one girl from Europe who fell in love with one of these, got pregnant, and got hope that they would live together and raise a child, but that never happened. The guy probably promised her everything she wanted to hear at those moments and after that he never contacted her. This is a very common case with people from the Caribbean. What to say except for young girls who decide to board, to watch out for such situations.

I got along best, of course, with Balkan people, the Latino population, and the Indonesians.

I really sympathise with Indonesians and the way they live is amazing. Most of them have a very calm peace in them and it is almost impossible to annoy them and start an argument. They are very friendly and willing to help you with everything even risking to the extent that they take it away from themselves, just to give you more.

I hope one day to visit Indonesia because they have beautiful beaches and ambience. The culture of the people is also very pleasant and modest. Throughout my three contracts, I have had a large number of supervisors from Indonesia, and I really can't remember that any one of them leave me a bad impression.

Either way, the contract would not be the same without Bosnians, Serbs, Croats, here and there some Macedonians, and some lost Montenegrins.

But CSB (Croats, Serbs, Bosnians) were at the top of the fun and socialising. When I changed the cabin in the middle of the first contract and shared it with Bosnians and Serbs, we all laughed in that contract probably more than anyone by itself at home before. In the third contract the same thing. I have to admit, I also came across a couple of very rude and arrogant people who are only similar to our mentality.

And best for the end—Latino population. Shortly—very sociable, funny and real party people. The dance floor and drinking alcohol are in their blood. Speaking of the Latino population, do you remember 'Gustavo', Colombian from whom I listened and learned in crew mess when I started? I didn't mention it but in the meantime, he finished his contract and travelled home. When he came back, who would say, they put him in my cabin, my last month onboard. What else to say except that it was fun with him in the company.

Here are a few more humorous things about the crew. Terms most commonly used among the crew and understood only by them—

Crew Dictionary:

*Taka—taka*—when someone talks, gossips or says meaningless things

*Cacaria*—an expression they use in the context when applying some new rule that is actually meaningless, type more in a political sense

*Next Cruise*—a term intended for a crew member who is late or unable to join others in the elevator due to insufficient space

*Washy—washy*—(washy washy, happy happy) is actually a song that we sing to the guests when they enter the ship, buffet, restaurant, etc. with the aim of disinfecting their hands

*Plenty like rice*—a sarcastic expression used when we express that there is something in large quantity, always reminiscent of a crew mess where rice is served three times a day which would mean that there is a lot of it

*No rice no power*—without rice there is no energy (obviously)

*Run like chicken*—when you literally run loaded with plates, glasses, etc.

*Bomboclaat*—an expression that comes from Jamaica which would mean a surprised or shocked reaction

*Babalou, Dopi, Malaka*—stupid, idiot

*Paisano*—friends who are of the same nationality as you

*Mafia*—to me one of the best terms used for a group of people when someone helps someone with things that are hard to get and in a way makes their life onboard a little better (things like food from a restaurant, alcohol from a bar, when someone wants to move a friend to a certain cabin, etc.)

*Banana*—when someone like a supervisor calls you for a talk because you did something wrong so you have to listen to 'sermons'. Believe it or not, this expression still comes out of my mouth even today when I comment on something while others just look at me strangely, not knowing of course what I'm talking about.

*Day off*—we use it in a sarcastic context

*Batty boy, Chi Chi man*—another term used by Jamaicans for homosexuals

*Cheapatone*—an expression for stingy guests who don't want to spend money on almost anything

*Mamacita*—cute and pretty girl

*Playing fool fool*—when someone pretends to work and just walks around

*Ayayaiii*—another reaction of surprise or shock

*Basura*—means garbage

*Boom Boom time, Pum Pum*—when it's time for... um... let's call it 'physical connection' ☺

*Chop Chop*—in terms of a hurry, fast

*Kaputt*—comes from the German language which would mean when something is broken

*Mama/Papa*—Girlfriend/Boyfriend


*Big time; Calm down; Easy tiger; Good life; Hard time; Let's go, man; Maricón; No problem; Pagulong; Brate; Pare; Respect; Tranquilo; Too much drama; Why like this; Yah man; How come; Chicki chicki; Disaster; Konju; Monkey Business; Kuku; etc.*


Regardless of the relationship with any nation, in the end, there is only one word that binds you—**the team**. I wouldn't even be wrong to call it another family. When you work and live in such an environment every day for more than half of the year it would be simply unnatural if you wouldn't feel much sadness over the parting of your best friends. More about this topic in the last days of this first contract.

What I think is important to note also when we talk about different nations is that these people of certain nationalities are not the same onboard and ashore. What do I mean by that?

The ship truly deserves a special and thicker chapter for every person who has worked on it. If I only had five minutes to recount life on board, in the first sentence I would mention to you the two biggest benefits and experiences you can get while staying so long on board.

The first one is to learn to 'read' people.

Up to a few thousand people of different nationalities and cultures take turns every week, and you are the one who works with these people in order to meet their expectations on their pleasant holiday. No matter which department. Whether it's a restaurant, a seller of watches, souvenirs, photos of guests or excursions to the ports, whether it's working with underage kids or teenagers, spa departments or even a casino, really it doesn't matter because people are always there, coming and going. They always leave a part of the experience to us workers from which it is already natural for us to get the best out of it and thus enrich our lives not only in terms of career. Once you return to the mainland, although your 'traffic' will be drastically reduced, you will read people like a kid working colouring book.

When I started working on land again, I realised in the first week of each of my colleagues what they were like, but I still kept those opinions to myself, and only then I realised this advantage of the ship I am talking about.

Another thing I would cite as also a golden experience is to learn things you would very likely never learn on land. If so, these are really rare cases.

To teach you everything about work (even a little wider) is from the first to the last day, but what indescribably strengthens you and sharpens your resourcefulness and flexibility is that you are 'baptise by fire' from the very first days. There is no learning at a slow pace, step by step, then a break, then we go back a little to repeat the knowledge, etc. There is learning 10 steps at once in the first 15 minutes. The best I understood this part was when I started working on the third contract on my own, at the Officer's Mess, but more about that a little bit later.

Before making the book, I googled a bit the experiences of other sailors and people who worked on cruisers and the only thing I can say about it is what I already confirmed at the beginning—every experience depends on the person's character and traits.

I have noticed that most have presented their experiences literally like the worst things that exist in this world. It's not true!

Yes, it's hard. It's very difficult, at least at the beginning. And there may be too often injustice when we talk about promotions in a short time but don't allow yourself to be distracted by a few words from amazing lessons and above all phenomenal adventures.

One should be aware that the persistence of good work habits is crucial and that the day will come when you will be noticed by someone important and given an opportunity to take a step further in your career.

I dare to say that this kind of experience is better than most schooling and studies. Why? So because here you are immediately confronted with a harsh reality and it depends on your will and the strength of your desire how far you want to go and progress. Here we open those true and deepest qualities of a man! What he is really made of, and how strong he could be, in both ways, physically and mentally. Here come all those most important life tests for which there is no time for preparations but only actions.

You are not sitting at a table for five years learning about things how to prepare for them. Not to be misunderstood, I am not emphasising the lesser value of study and college, but highlighting perhaps better options to broaden a person's horizons to life situations. People can always come back and continue or start studying but I think then they will have a totally different, stronger, and more mature approach.

Many say you have no life on board. I'm not saying the opposite, you may not have a life but your life changes for sure.

But I ask them what exactly do they mean by 'having a life?' Is it sleeping every day and up to over 10 hours? Is it working 8 hours and the rest of the day doing shopping and supplementing the feeling of satisfaction with material things? Is it perhaps to have a good time every weekend either for the young or the elderly? Is it maybe starting a family life?

Yes, all this is waiting for us again one day, but until then you have a different life and not 'having no life' as many express themselves.

Until then, you have a life filled with perhaps the most valuable experience this opportunity can offer you. You travel the world, discover unknown and unseen places, meet people from east to west and from north to south, taste different traditional food and drinks from certain destinations, work at an incredible pace from 10 to 12 hours, sleep only a few hours but never, you will never ever feel more 'alive' than back then, in those moments!

That is something I can guarantee you with my life! And I honestly believe that in the same way think those who most of the experience from the ship look at it negatively.

That's why I put such a book title because it describes <u>life on a ship</u> = a different type of life!

Whenever I meet one of the sailors, we always talk and express to each other the necessary dose of respect for everything we went through because after all, it is what binds us, all sailors, what they have in common no matter on which side of the world they drop anchor.

Once you start living on land again, no matter what job you have, there will always be that good old saying: *'If you survive a ship, then you can survive anything!'*

There is great truth in that.

*Ship's Itinerary (13 October–10 November)—the last month*
*Ports: Miami (USA)—Embarkation day*

**Cartagena (Columbia)**
**Panama Canal**
**Puntarenas (Costa Rica)**
**Puerto Chiapas (Mexico)**
**Huatulco (Mexico)**
**Los Angeles (USA)—Disembarkation/Embarkation day**
**Cabo San Lucas (Mexico)**
**Puerto Vallarta (Mexico)**
*Huatulco (Mexico)*
*Puntarenas (Costa Rica)*
*Panama Canal*
*Cartagena (Columbia)*
*Miami (USA)—Sign Off= END OF THE CONTRACT*

Back to Miami. The cruiser is full, both with food and new guests, the occasional and some new crew member. We are ready to head towards Colombia to the first port of Cartagena. This cruise lasts two weeks, through the Panama Canal all the way to Los Angeles. Same thing on the way back to Miami.

My last month in Aries has been full of mixed emotions. Similar to the first time I found out the boarding date. I was still just as excited to visit a couple of new ports that we hadn't before, but that same energy was present on the other side as I was already eager to go home.

When we arrived in Cartagena, not far from the port was a very interesting place. I don't know what exactly to call it so let's call it a green park. That park was filled with greenery on all sides. From palm trees, various shrubs to all sorts of mixed flowers. Now you've probably thought, so what if I was in a mixed plant park, it's everywhere. Is there really such a thing?

That park was full of different animals. Like a zoo, just open to animals' freedom.

Monkeys climb and jump on trees, peacocks and flamingos walk around like at a fashion show, even those huge iguanas were next to them (OMG they are ugly, no offence to those who love them), birds of different colours fly very low, almost so that some kamikaze flew into my head. The parrots walk where people pass by while my sweetest moment was when a little deer approached me. Amazing how domesticated these animals are.

When we got into a taxi to take a short drive to town, the first thing the driver warned us to do was not to keep our hands with cell phones and cameras out of the window so that the other side of Columbia wouldn't steal from us. Unfortunately, South America is full of criminals and thieves who look at most tourists as their targets. We came to a square, took a walk, sat down, ate something, enjoy a bit with a Colombian beer, and here the time passes, we went back to the boat. The amazing thing that happened to me on the way back was when we were walking through that park full of animals again. I saw two colourful parrots sitting on a bench and asked Elizabeth to take me a picture with them.

Everything would have been great if I hadn't leaned my hand on the bench when one of the 'mobsters' pecked my finger with his beak. Eli shot the picture at the perfect moment—the moment of my reaction in pain, which, without a joke, was not small. How even could be, when these parrots have so sharp beaks. Anyway, I catch some interesting facts about this place:

- At the end of 2015, near the coast of Cartagena, an over 300-year-old Spanish shipwreck San Jose was found, containing over 17 billion USD in treasure and gold.
- The Rosario Islands are located around 100 kilometres away from the coast of Cartagena, also known as a National Park of Colombia with a purpose to protect the coral reefs and ecosystems
- Around the city of Cartagena is a wall which was built to help and protect the city from pirates in the sixteenth century

The next day we pass through the Panama Canal.

Well, there's a lot to see here. Since this famous Panama Canal was dug and a special system for crossing to the other side was installed, due to two different sea levels, this process takes up to half a day especially for large ships like our cruiser. At the time we went through all this, 90% of the guests watched it all on the open deck, only the hungriest ones stayed in the Buffet, which meant that there was not too much work for us. Actually, even we watched it all through the window or from the open deck, and because of such a special case, our supervisors did not forbid us, but they joined us.

It was an interesting experience to see and pass that canal, especially when we noticed a crocodile on the shore from the jungle on one side.

After that canal, we passed under the Panama Bridge and next to the city of Panama. Unfortunately, the city of Panama was not on the cruise schedule to visit, but that doesn't mean I can't tell you a few things about this Canal:

- As we know, Panama Canal is a shortcut to the other side, it takes about 8 hours to cross the Canal's 77 km (50 miles), otherwise, forgoing all around South America it would take to pass nearly 20, 000 km (12,500 miles).
- The Panama canal is more than 100 years old, in 2014 was the 100th anniversary of the opening.
- Twenty-five-thousand people lost their lives during building that Canal.
- Since opening in 1914, over 1 million Vessels have crossed it.
- The price for transit it for the largest cargo ships can run about $450,000, while Cruise ships are paying per person, for example in 2016 was $138 per person

Next destination Puntarenas—Costa Rica

Honestly, this port shocked me. I don't know why this place is on the ship's itinerary but what we saw was nothing special. If there are, most likely the only good locations are miles away but since we didn't have time for those miles, we walked a good part of the place, and you know how it goes already—sat down, had a drink, and went back on the ship. I remember like yesterday that on my way back to Miami, in Costa Rica, I got blisters just because I didn't wear socks but only soccer sneakers, which is my favourite style of footwear.

Puerto Chiapas—Mexico

The place does not look bad at all, quite a relaxing atmosphere with lots of greenery but unfortunately again for better locations you need to travel for which we did not have much time.

Huatulco—Mexico 22 October

This port will be remembered! Unforgettable moments that every crew member should go through at least once (I mean more than once of course). ☺

Sasha from Serbia, Edin from Bosnia, me from Croatia, Elizabeth from Peru, and one guy from Poland, who hung out with us and was 'part of the gang'. His name is Lucas and his character was quite similar to ours so he fits in well. We went out to the beautiful Huatulco beach which was literally next to the cruiser and saved us a lot of time and money so we didn't have to take it anywhere further by taxi.

The place is truly beautiful and relaxing as you only see on TV. Beautiful clean beach, next to the bar with cheap prices and those natural umbrellas. From the beach amazing landscape, with one side of the green forest, and on the other side our cruiser. That view is memorable!

After a short swim in the incredible water of perfect temperature, we spotted on the beach Jet—Ski and our views did not philosophise for long, so we said 'let's do it!'

Although they were not cheap to rent, sometimes you can't just look at the money. Yes, the money should be kept and saved, but also we should live! The money will always come and go but the experience of enjoying life will not always be there (by that I don't mean any illegal actions).

It was a phenomenal feeling to ride that Jet Ski on the water next to and around the cruiser. But at first, we had a good laugh as we needed to get some practice on how to drive it as well. It wasn't exactly like riding a moped on the road, it's the water that easily deceives you. There were scenes like from the movies when Sasha and I flew from Jet Ski to the sea. We had so much fun.

After this adventure, we sat under those natural umbrellas, joined a few other crew members, but also guests who invited us to join them already at the beginning. Ice buckets full of Corona on the table (famous Mexican beer), 'Mariachi' played the famous Canción Del Mariachi from Los Lobos in the background with awesome company and environment. Everyone was relaxed and had fun, the sun was burning while we were enjoying cold Corona in the shade.

While Edin is photographed with a snake on him (there is no chance that I will ever do that, and still pay for it!), Sasha and I were thinking of riding another tour of Jet—Ski. It wasn't as fun as the first time but there was no lack of fun either. I'm writing to you with a sad heart that this was the last time that this gang had so much fun together and spent time out on the port. I miss those great times, and I believe, everyone else as well!

Los Angeles—USA

We arrive at the great American name Los Angeles or as some call it the city of angels.

If you were expecting a great story from this city, I have to disappoint you because it wasn't there. I have no good memories of Los Angeles. Since I was only once, on that occasion in Los Angeles, I doubted whether to go out or not. None of my team was free to go out, and it took at least 45 minutes by taxi to reach downtown if my memory serves me well, but with such traffic there it will take even longer.

While thinking during breakfast in the crew mess whether to go out or not, I was joined by one Ukrainian and a Bulgarian who was definitely planning to go outside but only by foot, until the first shopping because one of them wanted to buy a cell phone. This was actually the only possible option for me because I actually had to buy headphones, which I used to talk to my family after my old ones 'retired'. Okay, I'm going out with them.

We walked about 30–45 minutes to the first store. Since I was with them, I didn't pay too much attention to the details of the way we passed. The Ukrainian bought the phone while I had to wait to pay for the headphones (which cost as if they were made of gold, for God sake with prices) because there were some complications with the cash machine (of course, that machine seemed to be waiting for someone with bad luck like me). I asked these two dorks to wait for me outside, that I would join them as soon as possible I sort this out.

*'Yeah, we'll wait for you just hurry because we're going to be late for the ship'.* Great, I'm thinking, those two are waiting for me while this salesman in the store reset the whole system on the computer. Wonderful, we're a few minutes late, and they can't fix that computer. I explain to them that I will be late for the ship, and they keep telling me how everything will be ready to proceed with payment very soon. *'Now will be, now will be... WHEN IS THAT NOW?'*

After 15–20 minutes when they finally fixed it, I went out of the store and couldn't find these two idiots anywhere (I apologise for the expression). Now we can go back to that part where I talk about how to never trust anyone 100% because it's one of those situations.

When it hit me that I was completely alone, more than half an hour away from the ship for which, by the way, I needed to board in a little less than 30 minutes, no taxi in sight, no bus, and I have no idea where I am in which part of the city. Now, what?

In that so-called panicked situation, I just took a deep breath, took out my wallet in one hand, cell phone in the other, and start to run like a maniac. That looked something like when you wait for the last minute on Friday before the weekend, to run home from work as soon as possible. I ran like never before in my life! Maybe I broke some record, who knows. I rested for only 15 seconds at the traffic lights, although in that situation I was ready to run through the red. Why such panic and force? You'll find out a moment later.

As I mentioned before, I didn't pay too much attention to the route we took to get to that store, as I thought we will go back together, but no. Why would it be that simple, let's make things a little more interesting!

I didn't remember the whole way, but here and there some small details such as some special signs, advertisements, and one small chapel that was at an important crossroads, which somehow remained the most in my memory. I wasn't even aware of how much those little details actually saved me at that moment! Or to put it in other words, in the same seconds you remember and learn everything when the life force presses you.

Only dear God guided me that I returned to the ship at the last minute. Although I was without breath in that hot weather and appeared all dehydrated, I arrived on time—yes, a great experience from L. A.

What happens if you are late for the ship regardless of whether you are a crew member or a guest?

The ship is not waiting for anyone—simply and briefly.

Boarding times from guest or crew ports are determined by the time of arrival and departure to the port itself. In most cases, the time to return to the ship was between 4:00 p.m. and 5:00 p.m. When entering and exiting the ship, you always go through the security who swipes your card for checking in the system. For example, when the guests come out, the safety officer can see exactly in the system who has not returned.

If that person or group of people does not return on time, they may wait for them for a few minutes, but then the door closes. If you are late in that scheduled return time but arrive in those last minutes as a crew member you get a warning while for guests such a situation is not known to me. Luckily I didn't get any warning because usually, the last return of the crew member is half an hour before the last return of the guests, so I arrived on time (how could I not from that 'Usain Bolt—run').

The ship has an organised schedule and time for all routes it sails and everything must be perfectly accurate as planned so that there is no room for exceptions such as waiting a couple of hours for someone who is late and thus disrupting the entire schedule. On the other hand, there are also finances in question, since we can't even imagine how much the company pays per port and how long it stays there, which again varies from certain destinations.

What happens next to those who are late and fail to board the ship, I do not know nor do I think I ever want to know. If anyone is willing to go on a cruise or work on a ship with the intention of being late once at one of the ports, just to see what will happen, feel free to let me know so I can ask if it was a nice and enjoyable experience.

After a 'great time' in Los Angeles, the cruiser returned the same route to the other side via the Panama Canal to Miami. My last two weeks on the Aries!

In those days when I was spinning the whole contract in my head and became aware that there were only two thin weeks left of almost eight months of life on the ship, at that moment it seemed inconceivable that such a long period simply flew by and when I remember how much we thought on the very beginning: *'Omg, how long this contract is!'*

Life is really terribly short when more than half a year actually flies by in a few blinks.

What made me a little nostalgic again was that I missed the birthdays of my loved ones at home and my favourite grape harvest (which is traditional in my region—Zagorje). Unfortunately, that's the price of the ship. You miss many things that to you used to be quite normal, and you actually learn the value of it only when you are not able to have them again (at least not that moment). I missed my brother's and father's birthdays, as I will miss my neighbour's wedding whom my brother, and I grew up with all our childhood. Of course, it was even harder for me to have information in my head that my brother would be the best man at the wedding and that I would not return home until just two weeks after my friend's wedding.

In addition to such situations, you start to miss the feeling when you learn to appreciate the mainland. It's all a great adventure when you visit so many different places but what I want to point out is that actually when you don't unconsciously appreciate some things and only when you get to a chapter in life where you can't have most of those things, only then you do realise how much you enjoyed those moments. And it doesn't have to be some big things but the simplest ones like in my case running in the park, soccer with my friends, chores at home like mowing the lawn and arranging the yard, helping my father with stuff at home or even helping my mother to water the plants, visiting grandparents and listen to their stories from younger years, visit the vineyard and admire the nature of my region, etc. These are all moments that remain in a person's memory as the most desirable.

Most likely, most of you maybe would not understand me about this so I'll say again that you can't have absolutely any knowledge about something until the moment you don't go through it yourself. But I need to stay calm and strong, do my best knowing that I will soon have a return flight to Europe, parents at the airport, homemade food, soccer with the home friends, the most beautiful day of the year—Christmas, and endless sleep. Wow, dear brother, I'll sleep for half a month!

From L. A., our first port was the Mexican Cabo San Lucas. On the way to that place, I caught a couple more beautiful pictures of sunsets. Truly amazing what a mix of natural colours it is!

Only Elizabeth and I went out to Cabo, took a short walk, and sat down in a nice restaurant. The waiter was very kind and offered us before the main course, back then one of the newest produced tequila which was quite strong and rich in flavour. If fate or desire ever takes you to Cabo San Lucas, I highly recommend this restaurant called *La Taverna*.

Our next Mexican port was Puerto Vallarta. We had a couple of free hours there, but somehow we didn't wanna go too far because of the rainy weather, so we just walk nearby. We visited a shopping mall where I bought some sportswear and on the way back to the ship I stopped to look at one of the souvenir shops and jewellery nearby. Something called me and drew me there. When I suddenly saw a beautiful cross, an inner voice was telling me: *'Take this cross now and give it to your wife one day!'*

I kept that cross until the day Elizabeth and I got married and gave her that gift that evening along with the story I kept from the day I took that cross. It was 30 October 2013. And by that, I remember Puerto Vallarta the most.

The third port on the Mexican surface is again already known from before, Huatulco. Here we went out again but only Elizabeth and I and captured the last moments of Mexican magic. Beach, sun, sea, cocktails, relaxation, and fun. When we sat down and decided on cocktails this time, as I looked at the list of all the cocktails they had on offer, by name you don't know if you're reading a list of cocktails or movie titles of different genres. I'm not quite sure what I ordered, but it was something similar to *Long Island* as it contained three types of strong alcohol—vodka, rum, and tequila. The glass was interesting—a coconut with probably half a litre of cocktail in it. The taste was indescribably strong made up of all that alcohol and just a little bit of sweetness from the juice they added. I thought if I drank all this, I wouldn't be able to get to the ship or see it, which was only about 100–150 metres from us.

After the coconut—cocktail relaxation, two more well-known ports followed, Puntarenas (Costa Rica) and Cartagena (Columbia) while between them was again that popular Panama Canal.

That last week, I was fiercely confused by some emotions again.

I no longer knew if it was happening to everyone (who was near to the end of their contract) or just to me. As I worked in the early evening outdoors, next to the pool and that environment, I heard a song in the background that somehow plunged me into the depths of my life questions. Holding that moment, watching the place where I gave a piece of life, the sun slowly sets and casts its colours in the sky, a pleasant breeze follows all that and this song in the background seems to want to give me the answers I'm looking for in some way.

It was also the last evening Elizabeth and I spent together at the French restaurant Opéra. She left the ship a week after me because of health reasons.


## 9 November 2013—The night before Sign Off

Incredibly, last night at the Aries!

While I am packing my suitcase in which I have stuffed half of the world, *Wiz Khalifa—Young Wild Free* is playing in the background. Somehow that song stuck in my very special memory of that moment. It was as if the rhythm of the song and my parting from the Aries coincided. I wasn't the only one packing that night. Sasha also left the same day with me, since we started the contract the same day.

Because we had a Sign Off the next morning, we were released earlier from work, at around 9:00 p.m. I had to take a couple of pictures with my supervisors and colleagues who truly made up my contract filled with a great dose of humour.

The last week before disembarkation we got a new crew, to whom we had a duty to teach our jobs, as we were leaving and someone had to replace us. When I saw these recruits being lost and a little scared, I saw myself from those first days. But we did not make fun of them because the rule of morality is in respecting one's neighbour, no matter what position he held. Being always fair to new members is necessary because, above all, we were once at that difficult beginning where all information is important and useful to us. And what else to say without being said in the first contract? I really don't know anymore, I can only tell you that the adventure continues after only two months from the end of the first contract.

**10 November 2013—Miami, USA—Sign Off = END OF THE CONTRACT**

It's over! The first contract is done. We didn't get much sleep from the excitement but I think it was a normal occurrence on that occasion. Saying goodbye to everyone as far as we got, I said goodbye to my Elizabeth, hoping and intending to meet again one day, and here we go… that's it.

The last thing we did before leaving the ship was to hand over the NameTag. That NameTag that was our identity on the ship, which we wore every day somehow marked us, and I can't claim, when we took it off, that it was easy for us to remove it. A man is simply too attached to some things he does every day for such a long period of time so that could mean even a piece of plastic with his name, national flag, and position. When you throw that NameTag in the basket and hear that sound, then you fully become aware and realise that you are done.

Very similar to the feeling when I took my first steps towards the ship knowing then that I was opening a new chapter in life. Part of you is filled with sadness while the other part is filled with joy. Indescribable.

When we boarded the bus that took us to Miami Airport, we followed the last glances towards the Aries—which definitely changed our lives because nothing has been the same since.

There were five of us leaving together that day. Three girls, Sasha and me. Since we had a couple of good hours until the first flights, we rented a room at the airport where we left our luggage and headed to the popular 'Dolphin Mall' shopping centre which was only about half an hour from the airport. We didn't buy anything, just went for it to kill the waiting time until the first flight. When the last hours and minutes ticked by, it was time for another farewell.

Everyone went their own way, to home, and family. At that moment, I was indescribably sorry that Sasha and I were parting. First of all for that reason when I remember how we met when we had conversations on Facebook at the beginning—and before boarding, the days when we went out together and shared amazing adventures, fulfilled the contract with daily laughter to the point of unconsciousness—in other words creating unforgettable memories while sadness for another reason that I simply knew we would not meet anymore after that day even though we have remained in contact to this day. Either way, good luck to you my brother wherever life has taken you.

Before boarding the plane, due to my overcrowded luggage that looked on the verge of an explosion, I had to pay $100 due to being overweight. Later I found out that I only needed to show the seaman's book which would exclude me from this additional payment (at least it was like that back then, I don't know now).

From Miami, I flew to Paris and from Charles de Gaulle to my homeland.

It's an amazing feeling when you step on your ground again after almost eight months. As soon as I stepped out of the plane onto Croatian soil, I knelt and touched the ground with my palm, so I could somehow 'feel' Croatia again, while my family was impatiently waiting for me at the airport.

Miami

Cartagena, Colombia

The moment with the deer, Cartagena, Colombia

No comment, Cartagena, Colombia

Cartagena, Colombia

Panama Canal

Puntarenas, Costa Rica

Near one church, Puntarenas, Costa Rica

Huatulco, Mexico

Huatulco, Mexico

Weird stuff at sea; Beautiful nature

With first supervisor (Ronnie on the left side) and last supervisor (Vikram)
night before sign off; Going home

# 1.4 Two and a half months of rest (10 weeks)

Before we arrived home, we stopped along the way, at a famous restaurant for lunch, to celebrate my return and after that here I am, again at home!

I was exhausted to the point of unconsciousness but I had another 0.09% battery to say hello to the rest of the family. Around 8:00 p.m. I went to bed and woke up the next morning as early as 7:00 a.m. It was a very strange feeling when I woke up. At first, it took me a few minutes to realise that I was at home in my room, and then from there some feeling as if everything was something new to me. All in all, it's nice to be home again. For the first time that I was so long, those almost eight months away from home, from family and friends, from Croatia!

What comes in such a situation, once you return after such a long time, they 'attack' you from all sides. Everyone is calling you to see you, to hear experiences they haven't had a chance to listen to live before. Thousands of questions!

*'What is it like working on a ship, how many hours did you work, were you able to go out, where did you like the most, how are these people of other nationalities, which kind of bosses did you have, is it a good salary, did you have a storm, how is this, how was that...'* really an attack!

It took me the first week or two to normalise and get my body used to the time difference and everything else. As for the food, I loaded it like with a shovel because of course, you crave homemade food after such a long time not to mention after that lovely choice in the crew mess every day. Everything was really as ordered! I arrived home at the perfect time – preparations for Christmas, finally playing indoor soccer with the team, spending time with family, hanging out with friends, watching movies, playing FIFA, sleeping... all in equal amounts. This time I could even afford what I had long wished to have. My first and probably only tattoo. Those so strong and powerful words that motivate me but humanity in general as well.

After about a month I received an email from Cruise Line asking me to confirm my return to the ship but not on the same one. This time the challenge invited me to Cruise Line—the Aquarius.

I was pretty lost with all that situation. These months have flown by in the blink of an eye. I knew that if I started with a new contract, I would have to miss the upcoming World Cup in soccer, which took place in Brazil, and that was somehow the most difficult for me. I was very hesitant whether it would be worthwhile for me to do only half of the contract and then return home because in those moments it would be inadmissible to miss the biggest possible soccer event for me. Plus, if I would resign, I will need to pay for my own ticket back home for sure.

In those days, I also talked to Sasha, who was tormented by the same thing. Somehow we had enough of the ship those days after we realised how nice it is to have a little more freedom back again and enjoy other things, but that I would just call it the current situation of reckless decisions.

At that time, while I was still at home, I sent about a dozen letters to the USA to numerous sports colleges intending to get the opportunity to study and at the same time play sports, in my case soccer of course. Why the USA? Simply because I like their mentality, I like to speak English, and they have a lot of things well organised. I don't know why I pinned some hopes in that direction, but again maybe it better that I wasn't destined for this kind of journey. Sasha decided to do another contract and finish the ship life while I was still in doubt trying to figure out which way to jump. When I remembered again what binds the ship, which adventures, this time new ports and countries. Since there will be no old friends this time, new friendships would be waiting for me again on the new contract.

I wasn't even sure what to do and how with my relationship back then, I didn't want to disappoint Elizabeth but again we weren't even sure if we would get the same ship… everything was somehow upside down and confused. But after all, when I look at the whole picture of Croatia again and think, what am I going to do here again?

At the end of this drama of mine in making the right decision, I was helped by my mother who advised me to try at least one more time so I will see how to continue after all. However, it would be too early to give up then. And so it was, I left everything in God's hands and began to do a little research on the ship Aquarius until I ran out of some of my free time at home.

When I typed the name of that ship into Google, I was shocked! Until that moment, I knew absolutely nothing about that ship, but once the pictures appeared, I thought… well… I could say everything. If I called the Aries a marvellous thing, I really don't know then what I would call Aquarius.

Aquarius, which sailed for the first time just a few days before the start of my first contract, with an incredible guest capacity of nearly 4000 and a crew of more than 1500.

Length more than 300 metres; width around 50 metres and 19 Decks (floors).

Her home port (Embarkation day) was New York, for which it was registered as one of the largest cruise ships anchored in the Empire City back then. Amazing, what a tremendous ship.

My new big adventure starts on 19 January 2014.

I can't say, that I didn't have a pretty similar sense of excitement as on the first time.

Yet that first feeling—the experience is original and unique while now this one, is a little bit already 'readout' version but even though this time I already had a big picture more-less of everything, again my inner instinct gave me another side because the truth was that in some way I was starting all over again—on a new different ship, crew, ports, and new mysterious experiences.

# 1.5 Cruise Line — the Aquarius (4 months)

Here we are for the first time in New York! I never thought that all this adventure would take me even to the great famous New York. When I arrived at the hotel, the next morning at breakfast I recognised a colleague I had met in my first contract. We talked a bit and shared our opinions about what waits for us on the new monster Aquarius. I remember we waited quite a long time for the transport to the vessel, but as soon as the bus arrived, I sat all the way forward, behind the driver to take the first photos of the streets of New York. At that moment, I already felt new huge, positive vibrations and the energy of excitement of some new kind! When I first saw those streets of New York, I felt like I was in a movie.

Here we are, we have arrived for boarding, it is incredible how huge that ship is! And again came that mysterious feeling and all sorts of questions the moment I entered the Aquarius. What adventures await me here, I wondered.

As with the first contract, on the first day on the ship you get to know the surroundings, get a uniform, a little more paperwork, a few hours of rest, and we go to a new working area.

It was a pretty big buffet at the Aries, but here at Aquarius, it's huge! It took me a couple of days to learn the layout of that whole floor which was reserved only for the open buffet.

I have to mention, that if you were expecting a story of my new adventures from the Aquarius with as much content as in the first big adventure, unfortunately, this one is a bit shorter since I only did the contract for four months. But don't worry, there are many other adventures after that!

The destinations that followed for only a week were **San Juan (Puerto Rico), St. Thomas (US Virgin Islands), Philipsburg (St. Maarten), Castries (St. Lucia), Bridgetown (Barbados),** and **Basseterre (St. Kitts).**

Of those six ports, the first three I was unable to get out due to schedule while the remaining three explored as much as I could. Who would have thought that after a cold, harsh winter from Croatia, I would be in a hot but refreshing climate, in short sleeves, after only a week?

## Castries—St. Lucia

With a colleague who is also from Croatia (and whom I met from the first contract) and a couple of other crew members, we took a taxi around at least half of the island, made a small tour, and I honestly don't know what comment I would leave here on what I saw. St. Lucia is generally known for its very beautiful beaches and that's all wonderful even though we haven't seen them in person, but it was more for a reason that is unfortunately present in a lot of our cases and that is lack of time to explore more areas. That environment and nature full of palm trees are beautiful and that is the true charm of the Caribbean places. What shocked us was when we saw what kind of built houses more than half of the poor population lived on that island.

Not only this island but the whole Caribbean area is like that. They undoubtedly have some of the most beautiful beaches in the world, but when you see the conditions in which these people live, it would never occur to you to complain that you are missing something at home. When a man sees such scenes, they remain etched in his subconscious for the rest of his life, and he learns to appreciate even that little what he has at home because even that makes him richer than most in the Caribbean. At least on the moral side.

## Bridgetown—Barbados

At the time if I was well informed, Barbados is considered to have one of the three most beautiful beaches in the world. Whether true or not, I agree with that statement. Fabulous what a beach, what a sea, what a climate, what an ambience…

I went out here alone as I had not yet made new friendships. How and why I will explain later.

Yes, there was a lack of good company, but again, sometimes you need to learn how to enjoy nature by yourself. I walked down one long beach for which I have no idea how big it was while the sun was scorching, but it didn't feel so much because of that pleasant Caribbean breeze. When I got to the end of one side, I said, it was time to sit down for a bit and have a drink. Of course, my curiosity was still present when we talked about the traditional beer tastings from each place. Their most famous beer *Banks* sat down nicely and gave me half an hour of relaxing enjoyment overlooking the beach. I would stay and order one more, but this watch seems to have too strong batteries. It's time to go back to 'rowing'.

Few interesting facts about this place:

- Rum's birthplace is Barbados starting to be produced from the seventeenth century.
- The Inhabitants nickname is 'Bajans'.
- The first name of this island was 'Los Barbados'.
- The grapefruit's origin comes from Barbados.
- In 1666 Bridgetown, the capital of Barbados was burned down.
- Back in the day being 'Barbado'ed' was a punishment for people who were against the crown. They were sent off to Barbados as a slaves during 1640–1650.

## Basseterre—St. Kitts

When I went out to this port, right near the tourist centre, the first thing I did was to take a picture with that little naughty monkey you can see in one of the pictures. I took a walk around the souvenir shops, and after a while, I said to myself—even here it's hot! (what a miracle) let's try what they pour here. 'Carib Lager' is also a delicious beer that provided a touch of relaxation. As I sit and enjoy with lager, in the distance beautiful nature filled with green mountains when suddenly appears my colleague, with whom we went out to St. Lucia. Times as in most cases on slices, and what else to do in such situation but stay, drink another one, talk a bit and get back on the ship.

Not even a full two weeks had passed since my boarding, already we were changing a ship's itinerary. So these six ports we visited in less than two weeks, I was able to see half of them which was also the only opportunity.

Castries, St. Lucia

Bridgetown, Barbados

Two monkeys at Basseterre, St. Kitts.

The next destinations are **Port Canaveral in Florida (USA), one private island** from the Cruise Line company, **Nassau (Bahamas),** and of course **New York**, which as embarkation day we did not change the whole contract. We visited these destinations until the beginning of May.

After less than two weeks, I started exploring that Aquarius as much as I could in my spare time. The ship is huge and it is simply impossible to pass everything and see in a couple of days, at least not with my limited free time. While I was still studying that buffet area at work, what I managed to see was the huge main restaurant, let's call it 'Queensz', the Brazilian Obrigado Churrascaria' located above Queens, and two other restaurants that were included in the price of cruising, 'Mimosa' and 'Orchid'.

I managed to see even some lobby at the main reception and quickly take a walk on the 8th floor on the open deck from one side, which was filled with all sorts of cocktail bars and pubs. The famous 'Wave dance' (waterpark) was somehow the closest to me because it is on the same floor and next to the Buffet area where I worked. I remember even seeing Muhammad Ali's boxer shorts somewhere.

And that was practically what I was able to see from the guest area. As I said, this vessel is oversized, and I honestly believe that 60% of guests (maybe even more) don't explore the whole ship they have for a whole week at a time. What I stated about the Aries, absolutely all of this and twice as much contains this Aquarius.

But my most common radius of movement was in the crew zone, which consisted of a crew mess, an area with movies, a gym, and a very little crew bar that was very different from the previous one, in other words totally uninteresting and unattractive but twice as well arranged. It's simply not the right one, how we would say.

I can freely mention something about the crew after such a short time spent on the Aquarius, for which I do not have to spend a lot of words this time, unfortunately.

If the crew capacity of this ship is around 1600, without any doubt and reflection I can write that at least 70–80% (maybe more) of the crew were Filipinos and Indians.

This is going to sound pretty bad now, and I don't want to be misunderstood but this is just another one of the realities happening on the ship. This ratio, which I pointed out above, was detrimental to all the remaining minorities on board.

Very but very few Balkan crew have been on this occasion, which now explains the situation better than before why I went out alone in the Caribbean. No matter from which department, anyone who was not Filipino or Indian did not have any real chances of greater promotion or at least some proper teamwork by the majority.

Simply, when the majority of one or a couple of nations prevails, it is logical that they will push theirs to a better place than someone who is not 'of their blood'. It is part of a harsh, but this time too harsh reality in such circumstances. Again, hand on heart, we need to be completely honest until the end here and must be admitted that such a scenario would probably be present in any other nations if they were to lead in proportion, so I do not consider now that these two mentioned nations are the only ones. As we would always say to each other jokingly—*mafia, brother, mafia.*

What I admit to Filipinos is that they are great hairdressers. They will cut your hair for an hour but the difference is quite visible between them and those of our average hairdressers (no offence, I don't mean anything bad, and I don't claim that our hairdressers are bad because they are very good).

This was, in a way, the most depressing part of my contract. Both to me and to every individual who did not fit into the 'elite' society.

But again, there were the good sides to this ship. One of the bigger advantages the Aquarius has beaten Aries is food for the crew. Seriously, I'm not kidding this time. The Crew mess was much bigger and the reason for the good food was precise because all the crew members came here for breakfast, lunch, and dinner. From the dishwasher to the captain. This time there were better soups and meats. The gym was also better equipped while I shared the cabin this time with only one crew member—an Indian who was a very good and respectful roommate.

What I need to mention on this occasion is how the power of God was still present with me. One afternoon when I finished lunch and passed by the area with movies, my eye caught a couple of movies. *The Encounter* is the movie that strengthened my faith but also opened my eyes even wider about some important things. In the afternoon, my roommate was always free at the same time as me and spent time in the cabin, but that day I was left alone and took the opportunity to watch the movie with maximum concentration and the wonderful peace that was given to me. I definitely recommend this film to everyone because it really makes you think deeply.

What drew my thoughts to the fact that there are no Balkan people and that half of Asia predominates on board is that Elizabeth joined me just two weeks after my boarding. Somehow God brought us together again, and I was grateful to Him for that because that contract was a sign that we get to know each other better and start to open common views in the near future.

Something I absolutely never imagined in my wildest ideas is this situation that not only stunned me but everyone else on board. When we arrived in frosty **New York** one Sunday, we had something to see. Thick ice on the surface of the water and the temperature I don't even know how much below zero which resulted in a few moments later for our cruiser to turn white. Those were scenes for taking a picture, as you can see below, a pool and deck chairs in the snow while after already two days hot environment in Florida and short sleeves.

I have to mention as far as winter in New York is concerned that I have never experienced anything like that (at least not so far). I went out in New York for a short time to sit down somewhere, drink something warm, and talk to my family, but during that walk, my blood froze in my veins. I don't know what the minus was but it was terribly cold which I think was the cause of the city towards the open sea. I squeezed so hard while walking that I felt some pain in my shoulder. But the best part of that day was when I went back to my little warm cabin and slept for about an hour. It was a glimmer of paradise. I also visited on a couple of occasions the famous Central Park, which was hard to see the whole park with my limited time.

## Port Canaveral, Florida, USA

What to say about this port? Short and clear—hot and in shopping mode. For more, I do not know unfortunately although I believe we were able to visit the famous beaches of Florida.

Florida is truly desirable and searching for a shade under the hot sun. Everyone took advantage of the large shopping mall in that port in terms of clothing and footwear while I 'stocked up' in my favourite way. From the very beginning and how the contract went, my thoughts were more and more in Brazil, which hosted one of the biggest soccer events—the 2014 World Cup. To take good care to stay motivated and excited day by day, I bought a ball with the Brazilian logo and colours to remind myself every day of that incredible anticipation and euphoria that was fulfilled in June. That ball always stood in the corner of my bed as my biggest inspiration, which was quite impossible for a single day to pass without my eyes flying over the ball.

What pleasantly surprised me when we sat down to have a drink and cool that desert in our lungs in such a climate, was when I saw one of the famous Croatian beers in the fridge which was beer Karlovačko. I travel the world and taste all kinds of beers, but nowhere I can say that I drank one 'homemade' in America.

## A private island from CL2 company

I believe that every major cruise company has its own private islands and so does CL2.

The island looks more artificial than natural as it can be seen that each palm tree is planted in a perfect corridor. But that does not mean that there is no beauty, fun, and relaxing atmosphere on the island because there is a lot of it. From sandy beaches full of deck chairs, volleyball courts, water parks, snorkelling, riding a Jet Ski and other means, and I don't know what other types of entertainment and activities this island offered.

Personally, I went scuba diving a couple of times, and I enjoyed it. At least until I realise I was surrounded by hundreds of little jellyfish that were almost invisible. It was impossible to get around them and not touch them so when I got back on the ship I had light burns all over my body for a couple of days. But nothing terrible.

## Nassau—Bahamas

When you just read 'The Bahamas' and start thinking about an amazing destination that many dreams of visiting, let me tell you a realistic picture first of all from my side.

At first yes, I can't say that Nassau is not an interesting destination.

We had a very good time and saw as much as we could, but while you travel like us, to the same destinations for about three months every week, it is logical that you get a little bored (poor me, I'm bored of the Bahamas).

We didn't spend our free time on the beaches and swimming as you might have guessed as soon as I mentioned the Bahamas, but we visited the fascinating Atlantis and wandered around to end up in a good old 'Señor Frog's' and relax with refreshing cocktails (they were really excellent) and Mexican food with a view of the beautiful and crystal clear water, palm trees and parked cruisers in the distance.

Something wonderful that will remain in my memory is on a couple of occasions, when we sailed near the Bahamas, where we were joined by a large number of dolphins. It was something like scenes from the movie *Titanic* when dolphins swam and jumped next to the ship. The same once even turtles appeared, and I have to mention that seeing these scenes is something wonderful and special.

At the beginning of May, we started with a route from only one destination but very special to us. Three days (with two overnights) weekly we spent on the island of Bermuda. This port totally blew us away!

First, about Bermuda, I only heard and watched movies about the Bermuda Triangle, second, I didn't even know that there was a Bermuda island, third, as for the exact cruise route to that island... hehe... I will just say, not all those Bermuda Triangle stories are meaningless.

From reliable sources by officers from the ship who spent years on these routes, no one is joking about this triangle. All sailors strictly avoid sailing on either side of that triangle because the stakes are simply too high to be brought into mysterious situations that no one knows the ending of.

Unusual scenes on a cruise ship

Nassau, Bahamas

Atlantis, Nassau, Bahamas

Feeling like a king

Visiting Atlantis

Aquarium

Amazing water

## New York—Bermuda

Bermuda…

Where to start with a description of this island?

I'm just afraid not to forget to mention something because to talk about this destination, there are a lot of good topics.

In Cozumel, Mexico, the water was a beautiful turquoise colour just like all over the Caribbean. The Bahamas also have the beauty of water, even in the third contract I have words of praise for Greek Corfu and the Portuguese archipelago of Madeira as far as the sea is concerned… but what can I tell you about the colour of the ocean near Bermuda?

How can I give you as clear a picture of this famous detail as possible without mentioning the same words that I have used before in other destinations and thus actually get the impression that everything is the same—because it is not!

These pictures where I'm trying to point out the beauty of the place cannot completely reveal everything. People say that a good picture can tell a thousand words, but in an environment like this, I tell you even that is not enough! If you could jump into every picture for a moment and live that moment, 10 seconds would be enough for you to fully understand what a sense of enjoyment and satisfaction I am trying to put on paper.

I remember it like it was yesterday, the first time we anchored on the island of Bermuda, we all wanted to jump off the ship just to get out as soon as possible and explore this beautiful island. To increase the anticipation to an even higher level of excitement, this was taken care of primarily by the safety exercise—The boat drill, which we were obliged to do once a week. As Elizabeth and I waited patiently for the last minutes of that boat drill (and I believe the others as well), our minds were already flying all over the island. Even then, from the ship, I fell in love with those fascinating colours of the ocean that were surrounded by the island.

Freedom! We ran outside as if they had let us off the chains. We wanted to use every minute of our free time to explore the island.

We first set off through a small landscaped park where we visited the first beach which is open during the day for everyone but closed at night for parties only for crew members while the guests had to pay the entrance fee. Since we didn't have much time left after that, we walked around the park a bit more and toured a couple of nearby places, nothing too far from the ship for the first time.

What was an advantage at this port is that we stayed for three days (with two overnights) which meant that during the day the ship was quite empty and there was not too much work while in the evening—hurricane, tornado, and Armageddon—no panic, for that part I mean on guests, not the weather. ☺

The climate was phenomenal! During the day the heat is accompanied by ocean refreshing breezes while in the early evening when the sun sets, a wonderful temperature like perfectly created for walks along the island, with beautiful ocean views. I just mentioned walks before sunset because I remember when I saw that scene from the Buffet area, I wanted to return immediately to the island with Elizabeth and at least briefly sit somewhere or take a walk and enjoy that climate.

That day I also bought the first souvenirs that have good meaning.

Literally half of the cup that says: *'Bermuda was so expensive I could only afford half a cup'*. Funny but true meaning. Bermuda is expensive, which is logical since it is an island that is quite far from the first point of the mainland. And another souvenir, a magnet with a red triangle and the text: *'I survived the Bermuda triangle'*. Regarding the triangle, I mentioned earlier how dangerous that could be.

On the third day, we decided to go to the capital Hamilton and visit the zoo. Yes, I know it sounds strange and maybe shocking that we decided to visit the zoo when we don't have time to waste, but the big advantage was that for the rest of the contract we sailed only to Bermuda and thus created a lot of opportunities to explore the island as much as possible.

But let's start from the beginning.

From our port, Hamilton can be reached in two ways: by bus or by a shorter route—by ferry.

We opted for the bus because we wanted to explore the whole island. The first scenes from the bus were captured with a slightly creepy mode of the cemetery we passed by. That cemetery was similar to those from the movie *Pirates of the Caribbean*, which was stretching across hills and valleys, with crosses and monuments very close to each other. I do even not dare to think, how there looks like after midnight in full moonlight. We also heard some stories about pirates who came to Bermuda in the past, but that requires a little more detailed 'digging'. Slightly more beautiful and relaxing scenes follow filled with small charming coves, sandy beaches filled with palm trees while next to them rich array of luxurious villas with landscaped parks. As we got closer and closer to Hamilton, we saw more and more those bays filled with all kinds of boats. Only that bus ride to Hamilton brightened and completed our day with beautiful pictures of Bermuda.

Here we are in the capital of Bermuda. The city is interesting but also very tidy and clean which pleasantly surprised us. The people are very kind and friendly.

We didn't stay too long, just long enough to see the city centre and after that, we headed towards our planned destination, which was not too far from the centre.

What we didn't expect is that the zoo is actually not just a zoo, but also an aquarium and a museum. Very rich content from each part and something special to explore. First, we went through the Aquarium which showed us a huge number of different species and shapes of fish, crabs, and the rest of the sea world. We had a good laugh here because some fish looked like old-timers, but for the giant lobsters and creepy snake-shaped eels, we didn't have such an opinion. I don't want to sound like someone who doesn't like animals, but omg some fish are really ugly, like in a horror version. Thank God there are also beautiful sea creatures that give you inner peace when you watch them. After the amazing aquarium of the sea world, we arrived at the open zoo.

Galapagos turtles that can weigh up to 200 kg and live over 120 years were an interesting experience. But I realised why they could live so long. According to my theory, looking at the speed of their movements and eating, probably dear God himself feels sorry for them, so He gave them a twice as long period of life. ☺ However, due to their 'fast speed', these turtles are by no means qualified for the roles of the famous 'Ninja Turtles'.

Parrots, peacocks, bats, owls, kangaroos, various rodents and lizards, monkeys, and snakes. For an island miles away from the mainland, there are quite many animals from all continents. And lastly, a museum that contains the history and anatomy of animals from Bermuda and beyond. Besides, it has the entire history of Bermuda from those first settlers and the way of life in those times. And that was it for the first week of Bermuda. We enjoyed the wildlife of that island and now we are waiting for other opportunities to explore other mysteries.

Welcome to Bermuda!

Here we are in the second week. This time I found out that there is an official prison on the island of Bermuda very close to the port. Yes, prison. You read that right. Whoever manages to escape from that prison (if ever was but I doubt it) still stays on the island with a question mark overhead on how to get to the mainland.

Near the port, there is an open soccer field on which one, members of the crew of different companies usually met and play soccer. I also wanted to go a couple of times to play because I hardly ever refuse soccer, but this time I refused with a heavy heart couple of times because I knew that I had to use even this little time I have for Bermuda because who knows if I will ever have other opportunities again. Right next to this pitch, is a small nice bay where the man can take a relaxing time and enjoy in the shade. That really is a cure for nerves.

Do you remember that beach I mentioned before, where there are night parties for crew members? After work, we went to check on what it actually looked like. A typical Caribbean rhythm and outrageously expensive drink prices. When we were already there, I thought, o come on, it will not be the end of the world if I buy two cocktails, but dear readers, listen to those next scenes I experienced now.

By the people who worked as bartenders, they didn't exactly look like people of normal morals and characteristics. In other words, I doubt that they know how to work well, the same as for counting. I ordered two cocktails for about $ 20 each. Since I had no money change, I paid with a $ 100 bill. The guy returned me the rest of the money in $ 10 and $ 20 bills, but I counted it right away and it was missing around $ 20. When I mentioned that to the 'cocktail master', he pretended to be confused and at that same moment, took the money from my hand, only so he could 'personally' count it—check it one more time.

The detail that this genius thought I wouldn't notice was that when he was giving me the rest of the money, I noticed that he was holding some money in his other hand, which led me to check my change right away. When he realised that I had noticed how much was still missing, he added quickly those missing 20 dollars. And of course, when he knew that the second time he was giving me back enough of the money, he wanted to make a scene, trying to make me look illiterate and himself a victim in front of everyone present, of this 'terrible crime'.

But how else to react to such a situation than to just smile at this kind of people, letting him know that I have discovered his game, I left calmly. While he also realised that is behaviour only embarrasses him and that no one plums

169

him, he fell silent like a baby when you put a pacifier in her mouth, after crying. Elizabeth told me that that was not the first time that happened, that this kind of people trying to take advantage and in such a way because they think that everyone is drunk.

On this occasion, I want to emphasise how careful you should be with money when travelling and shopping in souvenir shops, nightclubs, restaurants or public transport such as taxis and buses because the longer and more you travel the greater the chances are to run into insidious and arrogant dorks like for example, in my case here.

If you can't peacefully solve the problem, I by no means recommend some physical confrontations because remember that you are in their territory, and you can never know which kind of sickly crazy and reckless heads there are and what they are capable of doing. So calmly try to contact the police if it is absolutely necessary, and I don't believe there will be a problem.

The next day we decided to visit another museum, the one next to our port. The advantage of working on a ship is that as a crew member you get the right to free museums, beaches, clubs, etc. The history of Bermuda is very interesting and extensive. Next to that museum is a pool where you can swim and take pictures with dolphins. After that, we took a walk around the old part of town and caught beautiful pictures of the open ocean of those turquoise colours.

A week later, we visited the 'Gibbs Hill Lighthouse'—a lighthouse from which you can see a good part of the island. The parks that surround this lighthouse and the road to it are, as usual, everything on this island—neatly clean and beautiful. Unfortunately, we couldn't enter the lighthouse that day, but the beauty of this island was not lacking. When we reached that top, in this sun and heat, we sat for a moment under the palm tree in the shade, and my dear Lord, I can feel still today that refreshing breeze under that palm tree which relaxes you so much and spreads incredible peace throughout your soul. I wanted to take a nap there i.e. when I think about it I don't remember a better place for that type of relaxation. But by no means Goran, there is no time for such things…

After this piece of paradise, upon returning to the ship a little more beauty along the way of this island such as specific beaches, various plants, and everything else a bit.

Say no more!

Open nature

One of the beaches; taking a picture with Poseidon

At the top of Bermuda

At the top off Bermuda

Simply beautiful!

As the weather flew by, we were already in the middle of May which meant a good start to the warm and pleasant weather on land as well. So we were able to feel this New York in the transition from spring to summer, which was definitely good after the brutal and harsh winter from a few months earlier. I don't know what makes us go to Madame Tussauds, a museum of life-size wax celebrity figures in human history. There are all kinds of 'people'. From Jackie Chan, Nicolas Cage, Jennifer Aniston, Oprah, Angelina and Brad, Denzel Washington, Morgan Freeman, Bill Clinton, and other American presidents throughout their history and even Fidel Castro and always dear to all Pope John Paul II.

Marilyn Monroe, Louis Armstrong, Johnny Cash, Jimi Hendrix, Brazilian legend Pele, Jamaican icon Bob Marley, The Beatles, the phenomenal Jon Bon Jovi, Tina Turner, and one of my life motivations—Muhammad Ali. There were many others but why so much description now. If you ever visit noisy New York and have extra time, visit that museum if you want to get to know a part of American history and the wider region in more detail. It was nothing special for me to see those wax figures but again we had a glimmer of fun when we measured ourselves with everyone who was taller and who was smaller (at least those who stood). I have to point out a couple of interesting facts about such a big city:

- The population of New York City is over 8 million.
- It is known that in New York City is spoken more than 800 languages.
- The Statue of Liberty was given to the United States as a gift by the French in 1886 for its centennial Independent celebration, which was shipped in 214 caskets into 350 pieces, assembled on Ellis Island.
- New York City holds the largest gold storage in the world storing gold bars value around 90 billion dollars located in the Federal Reserve Bank more than 24 m underground.
- The 3rd largest library in the world is in this metropolitan city, which contains over 50 million books.
- The biggest Chinese and Jewish population outside of their countries live in New York City.
- The first capital of the United States of America was New York City.
- The genius brain from Albert Einstein together with his eyeballs remains in the City that Never Sleeps

But let's get back to a few more adventures from Bermuda.

Literally, in the last days of May, we headed to Crystal Cave. One of the natural beauties that are underground, quite huge. When we got to the end of these caves, it was advisable to return as soon as possible because the next group was on hold. Elizabeth and I were left last and at one point on our way back they turned off the lights in the middle of walking on a bridge. It wasn't funny for a moment, but in a few seconds, they turned on the lights again, letting us know we had to speed up our exit. Later we had a good laugh at that scene.

At the beginning of June, the last time we went to the nearest beach in Bermuda, we relaxed under a palm tree, and how could it be that we didn't try this part of the open ocean as well?

I tried to swim a bit but it wasn't very feasible. The waves came every few seconds which made it difficult to swim so I said OK, I felt the ocean of Bermuda and that was enough for me.

After a few hours later, we said goodbye to one of the most beautiful islands we have seen and sent him off with that sad look at the moment of leaving with the ship.

That feeling when the image of the island diminishes more and more in the moment of leaving makes you wonder if you will ever be able to return to this beauty of nature. I really hope we will, but that time as a tourist. To rent a bike and explore the island in a much more relaxed and enjoyable rhythm than just running in all directions to see a little bit. Thank you, Bermuda for unforgettable memories.

Of course, I needed to share with you also some interesting facts from this incredible place:

- Over 300 wrecks were found since 1600s around the Island which makes it the shipwreck Capital of the World well known due to heavy storms.
- It was believed by the sailors that demons inhabited the island.

The Spanish and Portuguese sailors were frightened by both, the treacherous reefs and bizarre noises after the sunsets. Comparing these noises as if infants were crying, to be believed that sea monsters and demons possessed Bermuda. However the real reason of those sounds were actually from seabirds (Cahows) in the breeding period.

- More than 20 – John Lennon's songs were written in Bermuda.
  To John Lennon, Bermuda was truly an inspiration and source of energy for writing his songs. (I'm not surprised at all that such a place inspired him)
- At one point, only three people were living on the island.
  The first people who step on the island were those from Sea Venture's wreckage, marking the beginning of human colonisation. Nevertheless, they stayed just long enough until rebuilding their ship and left soon as possible, leaving behind only three persons. But this changed with the arrival of a ship named 'Plough' in the 1612 intending to live there.
- Onions are part of New Year's celebration
  Bermuda was known as best onion quality exporters in the world. The legend is still alive and on every New Year's Eve the Bermudians let fall a huge onion fully decorated with Christmas lights at St. George's Town Square.
- William Shakespeare was also inspired by this island
  *The Tempest* was intended to be set in the Mediterranean but ended up on the remote island due to the big news about The Sea Venture shipwreck.
- This beautiful island is a paradise for golf players
- English is the first spoken language by Bermudians, and Portuguese is the second
- Bermuda is in fact an archipelago, with around 120 little islets.
- There is no sweet water on Bermuda so Bermudians collect water from the rain through their limestone roofs
- In order to avoid traffic congestion, visitors can use only public transport and no rented cars
- The sand in Bermuda is pink, a tone given by the crushed fragments of shells and invertebrates making fascinating beaches
- Bermuda has two delicious national cocktails, made with the famous Gosling's Black Seal rum, the Rum swizzle and the Dark & Stormy

As the week wore on, my Sign Off arrived. What hurt me less this time was that departure from this ship. As I mentioned at the beginning of the second contract, there was no fun team here like on the first one. The circle of people I spent having fun with was Indonesians. Crazy but also modest and capable workers.

After spending only four months at Aquarius, I decided to do half the contract just for the reason of coming home and not missing the biggest soccer spectacle.

Yes, I am so obsessed with soccer that I can find ways and come back from America. As the main reason for terminating that contract, I told them that I had to go home urgently because of my father who was preparing for spinal surgery. This was not a lie because my father really had serious problems and consequences of the spine due to a driver's career for over 30 years, which I was able to prove to them in writing. Thank goodness he didn't have to have surgery in the end.

Elizabeth also terminated her contract for medical reasons a few days later and returned to her family in Peru. Maybe it was even better that we both terminated the contract and took a break because this contract was truly exhausting. As Elizabeth said sarcastically on one occasion, this Aquarius really breaks you.

'It breaks your body, it breaks your mind, it breaks your soul'.

Which was not far from the truth.

Croatia opened the first match and the World Cup with the host Brazil, and now should I miss such a start? There is no such force! From just listening to the songs and various introductory videos in the 2014 World Cup that I watched and listened to during this contract, I was already held back by the incredible euphoria and that wonderful feeling of excitement of that soccer event. What I especially remember about the end of my second contract is the way I surprised my family. Namely, I returned home a week earlier than expected. As I approached the door of my house, I called them on Skype and gathered them in my room in front of the computer where they usually conducted conversations with me. When I got them on the line, we started talking and at that moment I came into the hallway, and they heard my voice on both sides before they saw me. They were so confused. Completely lost in those moments. What invaluable reactions. When they came to their senses from all that shock and surprise, I just asked them with a big smile: *'Did you really think I would miss the World Cup?'*

Not only because of my indescribable desire for soccer but also because of my physical hard work, I needed more than a break. This 'vacation' lasted even until the beginning of October 2015.

Statue of Liberty, New York

Crystal caves, Bermuda

Crystal caves, Bermuda

A bit more of Paradise

# 1.6 Kansas and Sporting KC

Unfortunately, the Croatian national soccer team did not achieve the desired success of the 2014 World Cup. It's OK, the next World Cup will be unforgettable.

After soccer, hanging out with family and friends, Elizabeth and I decided to travel to Kansas City, USA for two months.

## 1.6.1 The American experience

Why now suddenly Kansas?

Namely, on a couple of occasions, Elizabeth met at the Aries and talked to one guest who liked to cruise very often. As this older gentleman valued and appreciate her as a person, he offered her a little help—to come to Kansas with him and his girlfriend and to stay until he tries to sort out the paperwork so she could start living and working in the USA. Between all that, Eli mentioned to him about me and my incredible desire for soccer. It surprised him, even more, knowing that something had to be done and help us both. At the time when Eli began to tell me what kind of opportunity was being offered to us, literally, I had just arrived on the ship and immediately cast doubt on such an opportunity.

I wanted to be careful with people I didn't know well enough, and I admit that I was afraid, and to be completely honest, I didn't even listen to Elizabeth completely about what the opportunity actually was. Because of my 'stubborn fear', we let it all go and resumed ship life. Maybe it was a big mistake.

On the next contract, Elizabeth exchanged a few emails with him where he invited us both to his place. This time, as the plan to terminate the contract went, I listened to what was actually to be offered. When I became aware that I could get a try-out at Sporting KC in the professional MLS American soccer league, I didn't think about anything else. Let's go!

After the 2014 World Cup, in early September, each of us got ready at home and met together at the Kansas airport. I will never forget the scene from the window during the landing when I saw a city full of lights in the night-time and wondered what my destiny would show me here.

In the first few days spent in Kansas, I was disappointed. The try-outs I was coming to turned out to be a couple of months earlier so means that I come too late. What a disappointment!

On the other hand, I tried to look at it all positively. Since we took the tickets for two months, we are here now, and we have to use that experience anyway just in the right direction.

And it was like that. We also felt what it's like to live on American soil. We had a lot of fun in those two months, but that doesn't mean we just lay on the couch watching TV and spending time shopping. Since our friend had a fairly large house, we decided to help him with household chores and also sometimes with cleaning the houses that he rented which was his job as well. He was a very correct and OK person, and I can say that he did not remain indebted to us for providing our help around the house.

The neighbourhood where he lives is just like the movies. Overland Park is a magical place. Very tidy environment and nice neighbours on all sides. We also went for a couple of days to his other house, the house on the lake. Green nature there gives you real peace. Like I mention, feeling like in the movie. One evening he decided to take us out on the town for dinner at a Brazilian restaurant which Cuisine is familiar to us from before. Truly I don't remember ever eating so many different meats and vegetables.

Since I came for soccer as the first reason, I had to feel the soccer world in Kansas as well! Through our friend, we went to attend two matches of Sporting KC. They have a beautiful stadium and their team was great that season.

When I saw that lawn, those striped blue jerseys, and realised the emotions of the fans, I simply told myself that I have to be back here and at right time! I just felt a too strong connection to get that try-out! Soccer in the MLS league is growing from year to year. There was a clear difference in these matches between the European and American rhythms. MLS is not yet at the level of European leagues, but it is not as bad as it is presented. While watching those two games, I wanted to jump on the field full of excitement and play!

Indeed, if at that moment I was approached by the back then (and still present) Sporting coach Peter Vermes and offered to enter the game in front of some 18,000 people, without any doubt or fear, I would jump into the field like a rabbit after a carrot!

Because of the combination of all these positive emotions, I concluded that the team I will cheer for, in the MLS league will be Sporting KC. Even today, I like to look at the table, occasional games to see how they stand. Unfortunately at the moment, they don't stand too good. One of the games we attended was Sporting KC against the New York Red Bulls. I insisted on tickets for that game because I had a great desire to see one of the soccer legends Thierry Henry who was back then playing for the Red Bulls. But what bad luck! He was not there that game due to injury. Unbelievable! Such an opportunity and that feeling when you know you are so close and yet so far away.

The Sporting players that I somehow remember best that season are Dwyer, Zusi, and Sinovic. Dom Dwyer, who looked quite physically powerful and whose wife is Sydney Leroux, is also a professional soccer player. Graham Zusi, one of the strongest links in Sporting's team, is a true leader who has an incredible sense of scoring. And Seth Sinovic, who I somehow remember mostly because of the last name. The left-back, who played quite solid but effectively. I fell in love with that Sporting KC so much that I almost bought their jersey in one store, but just back then they didn't have an M size except S, which was really too tight. I have not only watched soccer but also played. At one point I even found myself in some Mexican team at some tournament. When it comes to soccer you have to try all the possible options that are offered to you because every experience enriches you.

During our stay in Kansas, we also visited a couple of smaller churches where we also went to the Mass. A lot of things surprised us in Kansas. People are very approachable and always willing to talk. What was quite satisfying to me was the climate. It was exactly as it should be by the calendar. I enjoyed it every time I went for a run around the place. Our friend had an incredibly smart dog, a golden Labrador that made us laugh to tears. From patiently waiting to throw him a cookie, to picking up and delivering mail, all the way to the hilarious jumping into the pool.

A couple of days before leaving Kansas, I decided to go play indoor soccer on artificial grass a few more times.

3 November 2014, will remain for me as one of the best soccer days.

I joined a team that played in the league and an important game was scheduled for that day. A tense game led to 2:2 results, and it was one of those games in which you can't know what will happen until the end. Of our two goals, I scored one and assisted for the other one. I enjoyed those moments until one unfortunate duel.

When I took the ball, I didn't notice that an opponent was approaching me from behind on my right side. His approach to me looked more like when you release a raging bull on some poor guy in a red jumpsuit. He ran into me very tough and strong which was the cause of my painful neck a few seconds later.

That picture looked pretty bad, to me and others. It took me a few minutes to get up and when I managed to do so with the help of a teammate, I already noticed Elizabeth running towards me with a bag of ice. As she holds the ice on the back of my neck I slowly began to catch my normal breath.

When you watch the rest of the game and just feel like you are needed by the team at that very moment, I didn't last long to just sit down and watch. Another reason why I wanted to continue is that I couldn't leave Kansas without making the most of playing on this beautiful field. After maybe about 10 minutes I got up, circle my head a bit to see if my neck was OK and entered the rest of the last few minutes.

The match ended in a 3: 2 victory for us. In the last seconds, I scored the winning goal!

Out of three goals for our team, I assisted for one and score two goals. How proud I was and filled with that happy energy that I had completely forgotten about that pain in my neck. The boys were sad that I was leaving soon from Kansas, so was I, of course.


## 1.6.2 Back to my own—preparation

Five days after this fiery match, Elizabeth and I were waiting for return flights to our countries. When the time came for us to separate, Eli started to cry because we both knew and were aware that from then on, it would be even harder for us.

I went to Kansas for soccer professional try-outs that I didn't get, but I got something else instead—a picture of our relationship that became clearer to me during those two months spent together at our friend's house. We got to know each other in other important factors that affected the ability to maintain a healthy and mature relationship. Something I could never have known at the place where we met. When I wiped her tears at the airport, I felt and said, *'One day I will marry you'*. I wanted to make it clear to her that if you work hard and believe, nothing is impossible.

When I got home I started planning big things.

We talked quite a bit with our friend from Kansas about our real possibilities of obtaining a work permit and a US visa. He was a person who had pretty good connections everywhere but again not good enough for such things. We wanted it very badly because we had practically already everything in our hands. He would help us with accommodation, around things, cars, and even jobs, and by that, I don't mean cleaning and renovating houses but very nice and well-paid jobs. During her stay in Kansas, Elizabeth was offered the opportunity to work at one of the best restaurants in town, but the brake was, of course, the visa.

We threw ourselves into a real detailed digging of how to get those visas. How many pages have I read about all the possible laws and procedures that I could feel my brain spinning a couple of times in my head!

I have always wanted to go abroad, especially to America. Kansas was really something. Of course, I do not underestimate the value of my own home because a home has always been and will be just one. All of these life opportunities and experiences were calling me. As I mentioned at the far beginning, the economic situation in my country is not good and because of that situation, people emigrate more and more every day.

After a few months of digging up information on how to get a U.S. visa, our friend's lawyer made it clear to us that we would need to wait up to even a year to get a visa, which has to be paid massively and all just to get a permit for only about a year. That didn't sound like the best option. It is how it is while another way to get permanent residence is to get married to a US citizen which of course we avoided at any cost.

Doesn't matter, I could not lose hope for a better tomorrow so we decided that I will train and prepare by the beginning of June 2015 for new try-outs in Sporting Kansas while Eli travelled for a couple of months to Miami where she got a job as a nanny with a lady from her country.

It was not easy to maintain that relationship at such a long distance for so long. But on that occasion, we actually built even stronger trust in each other. On the other hand, I had enough time to be focused only on training and my own progress.

After another beautiful Christmas with my family, preparations for New Year's Eve 2015 followed, but this time I decided on something I had never done before.

I decided to spend the last minutes of the old 2014 and the first seconds of the new 2015 where I actually felt best. In my own peace and silence, away from people, with God himself.

I took the car and drive to my hometown of Varaždin to a very special church for me. To avoid the harsh questions and surprises from my family, I just told them I was going to town with friends for New Year's Eve. The friend who was doing my best company at that moment was God himself. Although the church was locked at that time of night, I parked in front with a nice view of it and minutes before midnight started praying and opening my soul to dear God. Why did I do that? What led me to such an act? And right in the middle of New Year's Eve? Many would say, o come on, OK if you like to pray but you can do it some other time, why need to be exactly on New Year's Eve?

I understood and was very well aware that a very challenging year awaited me. I felt that no one but dear God could help me at least a little and turn a few things to my side. I sought God's help so much that nothing else mattered to me, neither time nor place. By this act, I believe that I have given my free time and will to the One who may have been waiting for me the most, and thus show Him that He is more important to me than a one New Year's Eve.

You have to be strong sometimes and show how much God is really worth to you no matter the circumstances because I'm sure he sees it and will remember. Most people think that if you celebrate New Year's Eve in the best ambience, that means that the year itself will be great, well… it doesn't work that way.

The moment I greeted that New Year 2015 in some tears of joy, something inside shouted loudly to me that God was watching over me. To guide me and show me the way.

A new capacity of positive energy was born in me at that moment and it was worth much, much more to me than wasting such minutes on noisy fireworks with litres of alcohol. Don't get me wrong, I'm not saying that now everyone has to shut themselves in and stop moving around the others. What I insist on is that each of us should sometimes surrender to God and try to hear what He has to tell us, and I believe there is a lot of it for listening.

One of my moments was exactly the one I chose myself. This was quite similar to that scene from Russia when I mentioned sitting alone next to a cruiser and immersed in my thoughts. I promise you if you do it a couple of times, great things in life await you. I am a living example. I began to feel that blissful peace in my soul already a few days before Christmas when I saw phenomenal colours in the sky above my house. That sunset was something special.

\*\*\*

Since I was planning to work out in detail training that should make me better and ready for those upcoming try-outs, I honestly didn't even know where to start.

Until I came across a person in those days who completely changed my soccer life. Simply since then, my view of every training session and game and the soccer world, in general, has never been the same again. It was only back then that my eyes opened wide, and I became aware of a lot of things I had been missing before.

Dylan Tooby, a Canadian who has opened new pages of possibilities for us (me and everyone who strives to progress in soccer) both in sports and in life.

His way of thinking, teaching and motivating people is amazing!

It's enough just to listen to him for a few minutes, and he will awake in you those crucial steps you will want to take right away. To make it easier to reach as many people as possible, he teaches us through the famous YouTube channel where he holds over 400,000 followers—subscribers. From day to day he posts very valuable videos in which something new and useful can always be learned. Topics that are generally available are healthy sports nutrition down to the smallest detail, psychological mentality and ways to learn and develop self-confidence and motivation, how to deal with the most painful failures, and also self-discipline when you achieve great success. Different training methods unquestionably with or without the ball, tactics, and up to the most important part—individual training that includes absolutely everything. He is a very active and successful person which speaks quite enough that a couple of years ago he received an invitation from the national team of Canada in Futsal.

In addition to all this success, he is a fairly simple and approachable person, but due to the thousands of interests he receives from all over the world every day, it is logical that he does not have that much time to spend with everyone. Personally, I had the opportunity to talk to him a couple of times about training and questions on which he gave me very productive answers. I still follow him on YouTube today because learning new things never stops.

After learning about Dylan's videos, I felt an endless motivation that continues to this day.

Simply the person who guides me step by step to individual goals is truly a blessing to me. I will always be grateful to him until death for awakening in me that dose of passion I have always had for this wonderful sport and making it even stronger.

I believe I am not the only one who thinks so. Massive training schedules and the creation of the development of even stronger inner self-confidence began.

Even though I was left on my own, I always kept Dylan's advice in my mind.

I trained a lot on my own even before I ran into Dylan, back there with 14, 15 years old, only those training didn't have any meaning and so much effectiveness before. This time it was clear that this was the beginning of some big change in me and my soccer.

Soccer has been on my mind 24/7. I trained twice a day, while in the evening I relaxed with my favourite FIFA—soccer video game.

A friend I practically grew up with, almost never turned down my invitation to 'FIFA time' nor did I when he called. We've always come up with new and more fun challenges throughout each year. I was so excited that I even wrote different clubs on pieces of paper that we pulled from the balls, something very similar to the Champions League draw ceremony.

When it comes to soccer, my excitement always grows invaluably no matter what viewpoint. There were all kinds of clubs, from those completely lower leagues to today's giants, which was the result of quite countless comedies. But one derby will always remain an 'eternal tradition' among us. Manchester United against Real Madrid.

Since 2003, when the discovered pearl from Madeira joined the ranks of United, in full development, Cristiano Ronaldo has become the main icon of the club from season to season. Since I was constantly following his games, I somehow fell in love with that club so that's how it started. While for my friend, Real Madrid became a favourite club in the time of Brazilian Ronaldo, the unforgettable Raul, the legend and today's coach Zidane and other famous names at the time. But as the years went by, some changes took place in those clubs, which is normal. But I admit that since our best Croatian national team player (for me and in the general history of Croatian soccer), small but again so big Luka Modrić, joined Real Madrid then I have also fallen in love with that club.

As the month of June was approaching, it became harder to control my emotions. Emotions of excitement whispered to me how much I could get if I succeeded as a professional while on the other hand emotions of fear that constantly pinched me in the subconscious knowing it what was waiting for me if I failed, great disappointment and the mystery of dealing with it. To shake off all that discomfort from me, I always happily remembered that Sporting Kansas stadium and how fulfilled I would be if I had the opportunity to play in a professional league.

The dream of every soccer player is, of course, to get paid for what he likes to do the most. The pinnacle of soccer and the dream of all dreams indeed is to play in Europe in big giants like Real Madrid, Barcelona, Bayern Munich, Manchester United, Liverpool, Chelsea, Juventus, and many many others but since I fell in love and realised my passion for soccer I thought 'more modestly '.I don't need clubs of that size. My dream would come true if I succeeded even in the second, or third; so-called lower leagues and even in much less popular clubs, as long as I would be paid for what I love the most. I don't need million-dollar contracts, and I don't know which kind of other crazy numbers. For me, the salary I receive now as a bartender (who is still on the way to improving knowledge of the profession) would be quite enough, but more on that later.

I believe human dreams are divided into a couple of levels, so considering soccer dreams in my case, the dream of all dreams would be to experience the English or Spanish league while some middle dream would be to play an MLS league, which actually might fill me even more with happiness than European soccer. Many times I have heard that inner voice telling me that I would fit well into the American league of course with the condition and opportunities of quality and regular training. I don't know if it's because of the English I love to speak so much or that ambience I felt in Kansas, whether I have a feeling that there's not as much pressure in that MLS league as in Europe or so it's something else entirely.

A week before the try-outs, there was a friendly match of the Croatian national team in Varaždin, which I had the opportunity to watch live. It's amazing how it feels when you observe your role models and feel that professional energy when you're so close to them.

### 1.6.3 Wake up

11 June 2015 finally arrived. And again that day falls on Thursday, the day of my birth. I don't know if I felt excitement or fear anymore. When you are aware that an opportunity of life awaits you in which only your performance decides, I think it is normal to be nervous. Believe it or not, it was for such reasons that I went on a ship, hoping to meet someone who could help me at least a little bit in soccer. Sounds crazy but again possible. I barely saved for a fly ticket these half a year, but again, you need to be ready for such an opportunity.

Already at the airport in Zagreb, my day started incredibly. While waiting for boarding, I noticed the same seconds of former national team player Niko Kranjčar and his father Zlatko.

I asked Niko for a picture and thanked him a couple of times. A moment later as we were going by bus to the plane, I noticed them again and didn't dare even hope if we might fly in the same direction. Until the moment Niko sat a couple of seats in front of me on the plane. Truly amazing, I didn't believe it.

Since I was taking the next flight from Paris, I assumed that the Kranjčar family was flying there. Anyway, we didn't even take off, I was already looking for ways in my head to have a conversation with Niko. My thoughts jumped with excitement like corn seeds when you make popcorn. I just felt that it was an opportunity that I must not miss and a clear sign that there must be some reason why we fly on the same day, on the same plane just when I go to my biggest soccer try-outs. Then suddenly a light turns on over my head.

I asked the flight attendant for a piece of paper and a pen, so I quickly described my situation in the shortest possible lines and modestly asked for some advice.

When I asked the flight attendant again to forward my letter to him, she asked me with a wide smile if I wanted to meet him in person and talk to him, which made me even more nervous so I just continue to insist on the letter. As she approached Niko with each step, I was sweating more and more. When Niko received my letter and got up from his seat after a moment to check who had sent it to him, I froze and just lowered my head behind the seat.

In the next scene, Niko Kranjčar approaches me and asks me if he can sit next to me for a moment as the seat was empty next to me. At that moment, if someone was sitting, I would throw him out, even throughout that small window, just to have a few minutes of conversation with such a soccer genius. This time I explained a bit more broadly what it is about, that I am leaving with the desire to break into professional soccer and that I would appreciate a few words of advice. He seemed very calm and correct to me, and after that short conversation, among other things, he advised with words something I will not forget:

*'Don't put pressure on yourself, just be yourself and do your best'.*

The only thing I regretted at that moment was that it wasn't a long flight. We would have talked a lot if we had a couple of good hours, which would have taught me even more, but either so, I was still grateful to heaven for such a moment.

In Kansas, my dear Elizabeth was waiting for me again, who let everything go and came to support me. Here we are, again in a city where great hope has sprung up for both of us.

This time we didn't want to bother our friend with accommodation since his house was already full, so his transportation to the hotel and Sporting camp was more than enough. We stayed in a hotel that was about 20 minutes away from the camp, which was quite acceptable. The next day I tried to rest as much as possible which in those moments was pretty unfeasible given the emotions that were constantly jumping. I didn't do any training that day just a bit of stretching and mental preparation for the next big day.

## 1.6.4 The two most important days

**13 June 2015—The first round of the Sporting KC professional soccer try-outs**

What can I say dear readers except that I could not have even breakfast in peace?

From minute to minute I tried to ignore and remove any doubt and leave the focus on everything I have to do my best. I kept telling myself in my head that no matter how many times I do something bad, I must not give up and continue to do my best. For the last month at the age of 25, I have been chasing my dream hoping that although I fail, it will not be the only opportunity.

When our friend left us in that camp, I joined my group while Eli as my guardian angel was somewhere on the side-lines. On that day, 200 young players appeared, of whom we all had in common to live that soccer dream, even if that meant only for the next few hours.

Of the 200 of us, the Sporting Kansas professional staff selected the best 45 players for the next round but also the last of these professional try-outs. When I realised what types of players appeared that first day, I asked myself for a moment the question 'what am I doing here, when I see this competition, it felt like they will eat me!'

The truth is, most of them looked physically very ready but I immediately shake off any doubts and remembered why I came here. My **why** is much more important than anyone out there! In the same second, I remembered Niko's words but also all those hard training.

We were all divided into a couple of teams of about 10 players and so played short games on different fields, where at each one a professional staff accompanied us.

After a couple of quiet solid games, I managed to make one assist. I thought it was a great start for me, but it can and must be even better. The last game was played in front of Peter Vermes, in case you forgot, the head coach of Sporting Kansas.

I remember like it was yesterday, I was playing my right-wing position, and he was just standing by my side. In one duel with some Mexican, it ended quite painfully for me which paid attention to Mr Vermes warning that player to calm down and letting him know that Mr Vermes did not want anyone to get seriously injured.

When I heard that he showed respect on that side as well, that he cares about the players even though he doesn't know them and doesn't train them, I was somehow relieved and given the strength to continue. Given the huge competition, it is understandable that everyone wants to impose themselves and fight for themselves. But that day I have to admit, they beat my legs quite well. The last scene I remember on that field next to Mr Vermes, was when I led the ball towards the attacking third and beat the opponent with the 'Ronaldo chop' trick, and passed the ball to a teammate.

When that game ended, I somehow felt disappointed knowing that although in addition to a perfectly well-played game, I could have contributed even more. But how it was it was, I tried to be positive and optimistic about the results during that day. I would get a list for the second round of try-outs by email in the evening hours. I was indescribably exhausted as to the consequences of that fighting day.

When that impatient email finally arrived, I was so scared to read that list hoping to find my name on it, that I just didn't have the courage so I just forwarded the cell phone to Elizabeth. In those minutes as she searched for my name on the list, I held my fingers tightly intertwined with the rosary and prayed from the deepest part of my heart for God's hand in that situation.

After a silence that has been too long for me, Elizabeth exclaims my name with all excitement and is already in tears of joy! Amazing feeling! I passed to the second round! Out of 200 tough players, they chose me in the top 45 for the final round. It's not enough just to say how I was back then filled with so much happiness but also peace of mind. I was finally able to lie down with a wide smile to rest and recharge my batteries for the next big day.

## 14 June 2015—The second round of the Sporting KC professional soccer try-outs

In the second round, 45 players were divided into three teams. Each team played two games, but this time much more minutes. I played in the starting XI for the whole first game, but this time the professional staff of this great club put me in the position of right-back, which did not suit me at all, but again I could not complain about the opportunity that was given to me. That day was not like this one from the previous day. That position of right-back further exhausted me. I wasn't in too much contact with the ball and when I was, I thought and play as a team player and got rid of the ball quickly, which didn't really beneficial to my performance too much.

Since I was aware of that very well, I knew I had to attack and show off on the offensive side. My teammate who played wing on my side actually did me more harm than good. Not a single good opportunity opened up for me, even if I tried with some interception or cross from the side. None, zero, there is no strength, the heat dries out the lungs, the sun burns and it is almost impossible to concentrate in such conditions, especially not after the first day of these try-outs. After that game, they left me on the bench to rest, and in the second half, again run for proving. I wasn't happy about that decision but I had to be realistic, I really needed a break in those moments.

I described to you very well in detail how hard it was to work on the vessel, for a minimum of 10 hours a day to a maximum of some 14–15 hours while for sleep 5–6, and sometimes fewer hours. It was a really strenuous exhausting rhythm but never, never did I feel nearly as exhausted as those few minutes on the bench waiting for a new chance. Literally, I was on the edge of strength. Seconds separated me from collapsing there from fatigue and giving up… but I couldn't, I shouldn't have. I just put too much into all this.

Again, I called on God's grace to give me just a little strength to endure those few more minutes. I could feel my brain burning from all the effort I went through, from the physical to the mental part. When I felt on the very edge of the last atom of strength, suddenly what I was calling for so much appeared, it was God's power, and I could feel it. I will never forget that moment and it is one of the moments when I felt 'someone' lifting me up.

When it came time for my remaining minutes, I went in and ran in all directions, doing my best, but unfortunately despite so many selfish teammates, I didn't have a chance to jump out. I entered the part of the game when it started to get complicated by certain players who intended to impose themselves on their 'personal' performances. As it all came to an end, although knowing how it would end for me, I was still trying to do something, but when the last whistle sounded, my head went down and my knees were on the ground.

I dropped from fatigue first to my knees and then to my back and tried to catch my breath and calm my breathing. After this second and final round, Sporting KC selected only a couple of these 45 players and thus offered them short professional contracts in which they later still had to prove themselves. All in all, unfortunately, that's where my Kansas adventure ends.

When the players started to disperse, Elizabeth came up to me and comforted me and after a while, I got up with tears in my eyes and glanced at one further field where the first Sporting team was training. As I was leaving, I took the last look at that team with the question in mind, *'Will that day ever come for me?'*

When we arrived at the hotel and entered the room, the same second I put down my bag and could no longer bear to hold all that accumulated sadness and disappointment in my heart.

I cried in disbelief that I had missed such a great opportunity. Being so close, and getting to it so hard, and then on a couple of occasions incredibly quickly everything turns around just like that. The next morning we each went our separate ways. Elizabeth was returning to Peru while I was going back to Croatia. We didn't talk too much, so we left our situation without the strength to settle things in a natural way, so after a couple of days, we try to decide what to do next.

## 1.6.5 Conclusion: A look into the future

What followed after all this was a struggle with myself.

I was very depressed because of that failure and there was no way I could find at least a little strength for anything positive. I was totally lost. The thing was back then, that I experienced a great disappointment of this type for the first time, which meant I had to learn to deal with the brutal reality of this world. I talked to Dylan and tried to accept his advice and somehow regenerate myself, but it took more than a month.

I remember sitting at home on the balcony overlooking the place where I grew up with that passion in my heart, trying to figure out and solve this inevitable question of how to move on now. I didn't even have the desire to

194

celebrate my birthday in those days but again I admit that hanging out with the family helped to relax my thoughts a bit.

I couldn't stop looking for details where exactly I had done the wrong things, which in the end was such a result. The first big mistake I made about these professional try-outs was that I arrived just a day and a half before the try-outs which by no means gave me enough time to rest especially considering the time difference of some seven hours. All that lack of sleep and the mental burden I was taking too much of what now I see as a life lesson.

Another mistake that has definitely weakened me is the diet. Lack of fruits, vegetables, so many important carbohydrates and proteins that were more than needed by my body. I didn't drink nearly as much water as I needed to. And the last mistake I look at is that I was too tense mentally that day. I pushed my body too hard not giving it the best possible fuel.

So looking at myself in that state I was still able to get through the first round, while the second one, unfortunately, arrived too quickly. Not to mention other circumstances such as 'teamwork' in the field. That second day, things just weren't on my side and the only thing I could do from all of this was analyse and learn from those crucial mistakes.

What I don't like too much about myself as a person is that I find it hard to face patience.

I came back from Kansas where I, in both ways won and lost, and because of that big disappointment, I expected to recover as soon as possible which was by no means realistic. As much as I struggled from day to day, trying not to think about yesterday, nothing went by force. It took that time of God for everything to sit down in some natural flow. That stress, that nerve-wracking game wants to force us as humans to believe that everything will be resolved in an instant, and we know very well that it never ends that (our) way. Those true roots of faith come from the moment we let it all come in God's time.

There must always be a reason why it takes longer for some things and shorter for other ones. And what is the easiest way to surrender to God in difficult situations?—In a very simple way! Get out of the house, take a walk in nature because once again I am writing to you dear readers, once you get to know the colours of nature the answers will come on their own accord. I believe that even the good consolation of loved ones does not calm down, as Mother Nature does in her own unique way.

195

In the last stages of that recovery, I also began to ask myself if I was even capable of succeeding as a professional soccer player.

As much as I listened to the negative thoughts around me, I came to the conclusion that no one has the right to tell me anything about it. I know well what I was going through and no one can convince me of any other theories. Neither do I have the right to tell someone that he is not capable of something he loves to. People will always look at the first picture in a negative direction no matter how much good has happened from those situations, and I can't understand at all this way of thinking.

Here, for example, when I began to doubt my abilities, at the end of it all, a clear picture of myself came to me. If I showed up to those try-outs and failed in the first round, I think that at that moment I would deal with that and start to think about how I'm really not for soccer. I would let everything go.

But the first round I left behind, I proved to myself and others that I was worth something. Being better than the other 155 very good and quality players is no small thing, at least not for me. Now, I see it as a clear sign that it is possible, I just need to believe and work hard, diligently and smartly, and not give up.

After those sentences in my mind, I felt some relief. My father always taught me that I have to be realistic in life, so when it was the hardest for me this time as well, I assessed my situation in the most realistic way. I may have missed a very valuable opportunity but that's why I need to be wise and brave, and move on with my head held high.

Yes, I was physically and mentally exhausted at the end of those last atoms of strength and lost that day, but deep in my heart, mind, and soul, I did not let go of that passion! That love that I have always shared and that made me the way I am—relentless! (in a good way)

I must never forget the words written on my back. Those three small but so steely words that no one can oppose. *Impossible is Nothing!*

I have to keep believing, and I know that sooner or later a new opportunity will come that I will welcome even better.

Elizabeth and I decided. We will return to the ship once more. To do one more contract, save money as much as possible, and then seek forward to the best-developed countries. I had to accept that because staying in Croatia for me would be entering a new depression. After everything I've been through, I knew I could face newer and even more difficult challenges.

Since we contacted our CL2 company for an easier and faster return to ship life, we asked of course to sign-on on the same ship. We wished for everything, just not the Aquarius and similar ships, when suddenly we were told that new adventures await us on 11 <u>October 2015,</u> on the ship Liberty Wave. A ship that is very similar to the one from the first contract, the unforgettable Aries.

What made me happy was that I had the opportunity to help my parents in our traditional grape harvest and attend at least one birthday, of my brother Velimir, who is four years older, just like Elizabeth.

This time I boarded in Venice, Italy, which is about five hours away by car from my home. But as new adventures filled with all sorts of scenes awaited me, I see it started funny from the first day and not just boarding. The company sent me a plane ticket, watch out now—from Zagreb, via Vienna to Venice. I just spent more time flying, transferring, and waiting at the airports than travelling by bus to Venice. But if they already pay, then let it be a 'luxury' for me. ☺

The night before I left, I spent time with my family again with a new box of questionnaires over my head about what awaits me on the Liberty Wave. That was a return to the best experience of my life.

Games of Sporting Kansas

At the stadium

With Niko Kranjčar at the airport

Tryouts (I'm the first from the left)

# 1.7 Back to the sea – Cruise Line the Liberty Wave – the ship that offered me the best opportunities

This time, Saturday morning when I was waiting for the 'carriage' in the hotel with the rest of the future crew, I was not as excited and terrified as the first time I faced the *Aries* but would somehow call it that kind of mature excitement one step higher. Having been through this twice already, I had no reason to get excited about something new unexpected as far as the ship and crew were concerned. But when I found out where the Liberty Wave was going to sail everywhere, I was excited, for sure!

You always look very positively with great impatience at places you have never been before but you know you will visit them now. The ship Liberty Wave sailed the Mediterranean during a cruise in Europe while crossing the Atlantic to America, through our well-known ports of the Caribbean Sea. Three days after my boarding in Venice, Elizabeth joined me. She had a sign-on in Kusadasi (Turkey) which they later cancel visiting that port for security reasons.

The date of disembarkation and completion of the contract is on 11 June 2016, again in Venice. Wow, this looks pretty long when you just look at boarding in 2015 and the date of disembarking—next year.

But we needed it, not only because of the financial situation but for many other reasons, so the next eight months or 245 days of ship life will sit as an excellent and probably the best contract of all so far, which was very unexpected.

*Ship's Itinerary (11 October—29 October)—Mediterranean*
*Ports: Venice (Italy)—Disembarkation/Embarkation day (Saturday)*
  *Dubrovnik (Croatia)*
  *Piraeus (Greece)*
  *Kusadasi (Turkey)*
  *Split (Croatia)*
  *Corfu (Greece)*
  *Santorini (Greece)*
  *Mykonos (Greece)*
  *Katakolon (Greece)*
  *Valletta (Malta)*

*Palma (Spain)*
*Barcelona (Spain)*

You already know from the first two contracts how it goes. That start and adjustment, which is the most difficult thing for beginners, while for us 'old sailors' it is already managed with 'half-strength'. It is the truth, that we had a break from the ship for a little over a year, so it took us a short time to adjust to that 'lively rhythm' of work back again. But as for everything else, as soon as you start working again, all things come back to you in the blink of an eye.

Feels like you never even left that place. We also saved a lot of time by saving all those documents and certificates from passing any pieces of training from before which we did not have to repeat again, while for the main safety test after only two or three days on board, we definitely had to take again. As I mentioned a little while ago, the Liberty Wave is very similar to the Aries, which made it easier for us to be better oriented on the vessel.

After a week and a half already, Elizabeth and I got a chance to go out together in hot Santorini. A very popular combination of white houses and blue windows and roofs makes Greece special and unique in its Mediterranean way. Since Santorini is an island, we 'parked' the vessel not far from the island and took a small tender to the pier. Fascinating is that the city is above water and up to some 300 metres which gave us three options on how to get to it.

The first option, also the fastest, is a cable car trip to the top, for which we had to wait patiently in long lines, which again may not sound so fast after all.

The second option is in the old classic way—on foot. The only way you could walk to the top was also the way used, if you want to get to the top by riding a donkey. But while this may sound appealing and fun to you at first, trust me, it isn't. Pretty scary and sad what those scenes are like. These poor animals look on the edge of strength, carrying 'princesses' up and down the stone path with all this incredible hot climate.

But, logically, such an 'attraction' fills Greek tourism, and they do not care how—in which way, but how much money they get. Since we didn't even think about such an option, we decided to take our steps to the top. What's pretty bad about this option (besides good sweating) is the air you breathe during this effort. The path you climb is full of donkey faeces, plus that summer heat—calculate for yourself and imagine how much it can stink something like that and be really uncomfortable. As a person, I have quite satisfactory endurance limits, but passing this was some higher level of an endurance test.

According to the information taken from the Internet, it takes approximately 600 steps to walk this path, insignificantly uphill or downhill. It took us about 20–25 minutes. There was a third option, and that was to take a boat to the other side of the island and from that side by taxi to the city, which did not suit us because of too much waste of time.

Once we reached the top, we took a walk through the city which fascinated us with that Greek ambience. From every angle a beautiful view of the sea and our (back then from this angle) 'small' cruiser, while on the other side, the famous Greek volcano, which I heard can be organised tour by helicopter. The town is nice, nothing too special, but considering our free time (you already know it well) we didn't stay too long, and with this view, we took a piece of relaxation with a couple of cocktails and after that, this time we took the cable car on the way down. We have more stories from this famous place but about that more later.

Two days later a new opportunity to go out popped up in Katakolon, not far from Olympia where I went this time with the company of two colleagues. One Peruvian and the other from Indonesia. Both crazy and talkative to the point of asking yourself, next to them do you have the right to speak. What can you do, that's how it turned out. When you get a chance to get off the ship, sometimes you're not able to choose a company, but by that, I don't think at all that these two are bad people. Beating a hundred words an hour is another story. Ah… women, what else to say. ☺

Olympia is the birthplace of the Olympics where you don't have much to see but a pile of rocks. But of course, there's a little more behind that pile of rocks, so here are a few sentences about Greek history. According to older Greek beliefs, I assume you have heard how much the Greeks worshipped their gods. Among many, one was ahead of all and that was the god Zeus. Out of immense respect and faith in Zeus, the Olympics were created to show how much he truly meant to them.

In his honour, they organised this great festival of games which is organised even today but of course, no longer in the sense in which the ancient Greek ancestors did it. So, back in 776 BC, the first Olympic Games were opened, which took 1,503 years to revive, after the first opening in the capital of Greece, Athens. What it looked like back then I leave to the most interesting fans of

Greek and Olympic history to look for documentaries about it. But looking at such a large area of pillars, paths, statues, and other stones, I admit that I was also curious about what games of this type used to look like.

Of course, in addition to my company, I didn't have a minute of downtime since I had to take pictures of those two as if they were at a fashion show next to all those stones. In addition to being exhibited outdoors, you can also visit a museum that reveals a little more detail about this place. After this port, we turned towards the exit of the Mediterranean Sea which led to the end of the Europe cruise (at least for the next six months).

Before that exit near Gibraltar, we visited Malta and two Spanish ports.

## Valletta, Malta

In general, this island state below Italy and a little less than 300 km from the African coast has a fairly thick history, primarily due to its strategic position where many wars have been fought throughout human history. One of the more important roles was in the participation of the Second World War. But lest I turn out to be a professor, regardless of history Valletta looks like a solid and very prosperous city, besides, it is a very Catholic country with many churches. What particularly caught my eye were the small green parks.

Very organised, and I guess also organised country. People are nice and very approachable.

## Palma and Barcelona, Spain

I can point out a few words about Palma de Mallorca, while absolutely nothing about Barcelona. There was simply no opportunity to go out to see one of the most famous cathedrals in the world or one of the soccer temples of Camp Nou. I thought, maybe more luck on my return to Europe after half a year. But that's why I had the opportunity to see at least one of the cathedrals with Elizabeth, in Palma. Truly something fascinating. Although we weren't able to see it from the inside, this amazing view from the outside was quite enough. Huge size!

We liked the climate quite a bit, which is very pleasant. I can say that their food is not bad either. I am sorry dear readers that I cannot tell you more when I have neither seen nor passed more than that. So I would rather write this short experience as well than invent whole novels just to meet all your expectations of this book.

A day or two after leaving the Gibraltar Gate, I took a look at the schedule of ports we will visit when I was suddenly shocked when I saw the next and last port before crossing the Atlantic Ocean to the American mainland.

## 1 November 2015. Funchal, Madeira

I couldn't believe with my own eyes that we will anchor in Madeira. Why was I so excited? Well maybe because this is the birthplace of one of the best soccer players in the world, Cristiano Ronaldo! Amazing news for me!

I went crazy the same seconds from worrying about being able to get out on that port! I was willing to beg on my knees to my superiors, and even if I had to come to the captain just to give me some free time at that port. But thank God, He understands my soccer passion so I wasn't forced into such acts. It matched my schedule that I got free just like Elizabeth and was looking forward to the opportunity to go out in this phenomenal port.

I have to mention on this occasion, that there was quite a lot of crew on the Liberty Wave, from Elizabeth's country Peru, so we started hanging out with most of them. One of them—Jorge joined us on this outing. Jorge is an amazing person. A true caricature and creator of unforgettable adventures and memories that have not passed a moment without laughter. He also loved soccer which meant a lot to me to have someone with whom I could share soccer topics. We often played soccer on the ship, on the field as I mentioned in the first contract. If he hadn't mentioned it to me, I wouldn't even know that Cristiano Ronaldo has his own museum on the island, so the first option was to visit the museum of this soccer genius.

Do you remember perhaps when I mentioned my first impression of Bergen (Norway)? When I first saw the place, in the still half-dark dawn with a thousand lights. I mentioned that I had such an experience in my last contract, right now. Madeira looked beautiful and too good in such an ambience.

The Cristiano Ronaldo Museum was not far from the port at all but as soon as we reached it, despair and sadness in our eyes—closed. We wondered, what is it now, is it possible to have so much (un) luck. When after a while we realised it was closed for two very logical reasons, we took a taxi and explored the island a bit in those few hours. The museum was closed primarily because it was Sunday and even if it was not Sunday in terms of the calendar, it was a big Catholic holiday, All Saints' Day. Incredibly what a coincidence that it all matches together.

I no longer remember if I mentioned it before but I will still briefly describe it now. Because of ship life and incredible pace, you totally lose track of time. Instead of by days of the week and dates, you orient yourself by ports and that's quite enough for you. In which month you are, you pay attention here and there, depending on how you are approaching the end of the contract, but considering that ours has just started, I didn't even think about the date of disembarkation. Given that fact, we got completely lost and forgot which day of the week we go out. This example from Madeira shows the best.

This will probably sound insensitive, but while our families lit candles in cemeteries at home, we were in a totally 'different world'. When you are in such an environment, you lose that temporary feeling for the upcoming holidays, which you have always been used to. The moment we became aware that the museum was closed because it was 1 November, we said OK and moved on. I don't think you have much to choose from in our situation. What I am trying to point out is this lack of conscience towards the more important days. A very similar thing was with the first two contracts at Easter time. Because of such circumstances, you don't have any special feeling that would make you think like, *'Oh, holidays are coming, we have to prepare and get ready'.*

Madeira is truly beautiful! An island like this one has so much to offer. One of the beautiful pictures was the gradual banana plantations. It may not sound anything special, but seeing it on those hills was great. The taxi driver took us to Cabo Girão, one of the highest points of Madeira, even amazing about 580 m above sea level. The view is remarkable!

A good part of the island can be seen as the view of the ocean shares one of those images in which it seems to you that the ocean and the sky merge in the distance.

What made Madeira quite surprising to me was the beer. They have an incredibly delicious beer called Coral, which is only produced in that place. Definitely my favourite so far.

On the way back to the vessel we had the opportunity to see the soccer stadium of the Marítimo club. Although I regretted very much that on the other hand, I had to temporarily leave soccer training and forget the failure from Kansas, I knew I had to be strong in heart and mind and believe that my time would come once again. Opportunities like these, touching the soccer world in some way were enough to give me the strength to keep believing.

Knowing that on our way back to Europe we would be stopping again on this beautiful island, I was aware that I had to find a way out again if I was going to have a workday scheduled.

Madeira really surprised me and is definitely on my list as a destination I have to visit again, but as a tourist and to do a 'detailed inspection'.

Santorini, Greece

Olympia – Katakolon, Greece

Valletta, Malta

Palma de Mallorca

Madeira, Portugal

Madeira, Portugal

With Jorge and Elizabeth near stadium on Madeira

After we left this beautiful island behind, a good week of clean ocean followed in which we must not forget, moving the clock back every night which was a blessing but also an opportunity for the crew to organise parties.

But as we sail the wide-open ocean, let me tell you about my work adventures.

Since I was returning to my third contract after a long break, I got the starting position again, but that doesn't mean I had to start from scratch, like the crew mess in which I spent the three worst months of my life, but also incredibly steely after of that in all aspects.

I started at the usual big buffet on the deck 12th where I was doing a pretty good job. But after a short time, there was a tangle of some mixed misunderstandings whose consequences would change the total course of my progress on the ship.

One of the crew members who worked the night shift at the buffet, as soon as he noticed us 'novices' tried to convince us with skilful words how good his position is in terms of work and schedule. His goal was to get off the night shift as soon as possible, and at that moment there was no one to replace him, so he hunted 'fresh and naive' to jump into his shoes.

Of course, for me who went through those things, I knew all too well what awaited me if I were to be caught for that bait. I still don't think the night shift is a bad thing, but for a person like me who went through such an experience and was eager for new different challenges and ambitions, I ignored that role in every way on this third contract. As that person began to insist more and more that I take over his place, I was increasingly letting him know how much I didn't want and didn't need it. One evening he exaggerated every measure by starting to talk to the supervisor of that department—the buffet.

I heard something, how he was trying to persuade a supervisor to put me on the night shift, as new, and him in a restaurant with a promotion. I don't know if I came across it at the wrong time, or there was another topic, but since I paid more and more attention to his behaviour and the reaction of our Maitre'd, whose picture did not show me anything good, I decided to speak with the Maitre'd that very same evening. Our boss looked like on the edge between these two decisions, whether to put me in the night shift or not after who knows how many persuasions by the 'night bird'.

My first attitude towards the Maitre'd regarding that topic was firm, determined but also wrong. I let her know if she was considering shifting me to the night shift, that it was out of the question and that there was nothing that could force me to accept this.

Because of my attitude like that, she took it as an example of disobedience and changed my job anyway because of it but not in the night shift.

For the next few days, I was doing 'the punishment' where else than in the crew mess—the crew canteen. I was very frustrated and dissatisfied with such a decision of my superior, for whose situation she did not consider it reasonably or realistically, but according to the typical 'boss' custom *'I am the main one here, not you'*.

I'm not saying I have such privileges that I can choose a job, but given my previous experience, anyone normal would take that into account. After those few working and very desperate days in the crew mess, I was approached by back then the temporary restaurant manager, a very nice and exemplary Indian who was my Maitre'd in the first week—two in the same job where I had worked so far. Unaware of my situation, he was completely surprised and curious so he asked me why I was in the crew mess. We didn't meet much during those weeks when we worked together at the buffet, but again it was enough time to remember me very well for my work habits and desire for constant progress. When I explained to him in a few words, what he said next completely revived me.

*'You will not work in the crew mess at all. You start tomorrow in officer mess and after a few months, you go to a restaurant with a promotion!'*

It really was like that! For the next three months, my job was in the officer mess. A room with six tables intended exclusively for higher positions onboard such as the captain, the staff captain, the safety officer, the environmental officer, the navigation officers, ship's doctor, nurses, higher positions of other departments, and many others similar to them.

I worked there on my own, which I really liked, but not always, I admit. During the whole day of sailing (sea day), the officer mess was very full, for which I needed help, but on other days, it was not too crowded. It's great that you work alone because that's the way you force yourself to find your way faster, and you catch the strings because you work as a professional waiter. The days in officer mess were my best during my third contract.

The schedule was acceptable, I always had the opportunity to go out in the ports, tips started coming, I started to be a favourite among the officers, which meant a lot to me because I was in some way protected if I had any unpleasant and hostile experiences with other crew members (which did not happen after all) but also one of the best things was the possibility of taking food from the kitchen intended for restaurants one deck above. Of course for privileged people, it is also a privileged food while no one drank alcohol so it meant I could afford and treat myself every day (not to overdo it) with very good food. I hope I don't have to remind you what kind of food is served in the crew mess, and for that very good reason, that main advantage in the officer mess meant a lot.

Since I am still on the subject of food, there were days when, even after serving lunch, I used to sit down and in peace having lunch and watching soccer on TV, which I fortunately had. I laughed to myself when, after nesting myself so nicely in a chair with my copious lunch in front of a rather large TV, I suddenly noticed a camera on the ceiling that was facing me directly. But I never received any warning from anyone for such an act. It meant a lot to my soul that I could also follow the English soccer League. It was also the season when the very likeable club Leicester City surprised everyone and won such a tough Premier League.

Before we anchored in Houston, USA, which was our main port for boarding and disembarking guests for the next five months, we stopped at two more ports, St. Thomas and Miami. Miami looks great at sunset, the combination of natural colours and colourful city lights shows a special relaxing image.

## ABOUT GUESTS (from all three contracts)

I almost forgot to write something about the guests in all three contracts. Hm, what about that? What best picture to show you and what words to choose regarding this particular topic. Maybe I should start with the expression '100 people—100 wonders'. Or with a typical list based on appearance, character, nationality, and other moral meanings? Ok, I will try to describe how much my heart and mind contribute to me.

As for nationality and where they come from, it is truly an endless topic. I met people from every continent except Antarctica, meaning literally from all the other six. (The penguins did not want to come on a cruise.)

Most often people from all over North America. There's not a single crew member who hasn't met Americans from Washington, California, Arizona, Texas, Kansas, Nebraska, Missouri, Iowa, Minnesota, Michigan, Ohio, Mississippi, Vermont, New Hampshire, New York, Pennsylvania, Connecticut,

New Jersey, Virginia, South and North Carolina all the way to Florida until Mexico. They make up the largest percentage of guests because I guess it's their most common form of vacation. The same is for Canadians. I would put Europeans behind them. The Spanish, the British, and the Germans seem to me to be the greatest participants in cruises from this continent. There are, of course, others from all over Europe, but not as many as these three nations.

Asia? Well, dear brother… when will there be more anyone than the Chinese. Anywhere, Chinese everywhere. It is not my intention to sound or think anything bad and with that underestimate that nation, but if I got every time a penny for situations where they try to communicate in English without knowing the basic words like coffee, tea, sugar, toilet, up, down, front, hot water, exit and similar words that are very simple, I could afford with that money a decent car, no joke. No one expects a doctor of English grammar but my dear friends, if you have travelled to America even from far distant like China, how did you manage to do so without at least one or two words of English?

Then there are the Indians and the Arabs, not too many of them, but still. The Japanese are my favourite. When they finish eating, they even clean up after. The tables looked so clean like no one was ever eating there. I mean, my bow to them, that country is very disciplined and if I will ever choose Asia as a holiday destination there are only two locations on that list—Japan and Bali (Indonesia). Of course, the reason is not just because of people, but because those are beautiful countries.

Guests from South America? There are many of them, the whole Latino population. Guests from Australia and Africa also often come to cruise. I tell you, there are people from all over the world that come to cruise.

What are all those guests like in terms of culture and character?

All kinds. Within nine months (but also from the first two contracts) I came across so many different people that even if I start to tell you about absolutely all guests, I guarantee you, you would not believe me. How even could, when half of the guests are with no common sense. I would call each cruise ship, an encyclopaedia from A to Z when we talk about the type of people. So here we go, I decided to play with words a bit and challenge myself to describe the guests in alphabetical order:

A – arrogant (I am the most important, others do not matter), allergic, angry, afraid, annoying (really sometimes way too much), argumentative

B – bizarre, boring, bossy, brainy, brainless with 'brilliant' ideas, boastful manners (we don't eat at the buffet because we are VIP guests)

C – censure (freedom of expression), charismatic, charming, cheerful, childish, clumsy (a very common case), curious (omg let me not start about this)

D – demanding (dear Lord, give me strength), determined, dull (with questions and comments are the best)

E – elegant, emotional (comes to dinner in the suit, cries for dipping his tie in soup), easy-going, energetic (make the space on the dance floor), enthusiastic

F – fantasy ideas (can we have dinner in this restaurant but order food from another), fearless, foolish (those two examples are many times combine), forgetful (they forget something you told them 2 sec ago), friendly, funny (best part of doing a contract)

G – good (not everyone is bad, most guests are good), generous, greedy, grumpy

H – happy, hilarious, honest, hungry (ou boy)

I – idealistic, interesting, imaginative, immature (we understand you are on vacation but still…), impatient (when it comes to food, they are unbearable), impulsive

J – joyful (so happy to cruise), jealous (why he got 1 inch bigger steak than me)

K – kind

L – lucky, loud

M – mysterious, (once guest asked me if he could have a wooden box from the buffet, where we kept all sorts of tea bags), mean, messy (ou dear Lord)

N – naive, no common sense (no comments), naughty, noisy

O – obsessive, outgoing, outspoken (totally)

P – patient (very rare case), polite, pleasant, picky, persistent (she will not leave before she gets her cookies), problematic (they make a problem that doesn't exist), patriotic, playful

Q – quick-tempered

R – rigorous, rude

S – spontaneous, simple, scared (in some situations), selfish, sensitive (no comments), serious (because like on the cruise you have the reason to be), shy, silly, stubborn (I could write another whole page just about this), sneaky, sweet, stupid with questions (ou yea), spoiled (omg how many), suspicious

T – talkative (I could finish my entire shift listening to an old lady about her life), thoughtful, tired (after this cruise I need a vacation), tough (one of the inevitable obstacles for us, crewmembers)

U – unhappy (but why?), unusual (often the case), upset, ungrateful (I mean, really?)

V – very everything above

W – wise, wild, worried (leaving with a tender boat on shore and countless times asking crew will they come back with a tender for them—how annoying you are with such a stupid question, we should leave you behind)

X – I really don't know any word to describe guests with this letter, maybe x-man ☺

Y – youngish

Z – zany


Ok, I can understand, you know… when after a lot of waiting you finally go somewhere on vacation, to completely relax, not think about work, unfinished things at home, worries and everything that burdens us, to finally escape from all this to your piece of paradise and feed your nerves with 'milk and honey'.

That's all stands and it has to be that way. But my dear people, where in all this should it mean that you are totally disconnected from those simplest functions that your brain performs on a daily normal basis? Where it is written that when you go on vacation you can ask so many meaningless questions, do absolutely what you want without thinking, and completely ignore common sense. Vacation is for a man to relax from everyday life with fulfilled obligations but that doesn't mean turning off the brain like I turn off a cell phone. It is neither healthy nor useful, and you are only harming yourself.

After the following sentences, you read you will think that I am a big great liar without limits, that I invented everything just with the intention of making the book look more interesting and better in some particular direction. I didn't start writing this book with the idea to come up with some topics to create a masterpiece or I don't know what, but to describe my real experiences with the people this life has given me and whether you want to believe it or not, it's really not up to me, but only on you. On the other hand, you will laugh perhaps like never before, as I laughed again as soon as I remembered all these comic situations.

With the help of friends who made up my 'ship family', I made a list of the most common possible questions from guests that we could remember, and with that to add another comic page to this book. I also want to thank them for their help!

A little warning—some questions are really abnormal and meaningless to the point of pain, so you can imagine how it was for us, which we had to, with an always ear-to-ear smile, kindly answer these same guests. Eh, when I better think about it, all the questions are meaningless, but that's not the saddest thing, it's the fact that these guests ask such questions with the most serious intention. God, throw a brick and be precise.


*When sailing, the ship sways slightly at times, which is normal, but not for some guests when they attack with questions such as: *"Can you talk to the captain to drive the ship better?'*

Our answer: *'This is a common occurrence, ma'am, I'm sure it will pass in a moment'.*

What we actually think: *'We'd better send you to sail the ship!'*

* or similar: *'Why doesn't the captain just turn off the engines and wait for the waves to pass?'*


* *'Where do you live, under the sea?' or 'Do you travel home every night and the next morning back on the ship?' or 'Is the crew sleeping on the ship or?'*

Our answer: *'Sir, we have our cabins where we sleep'.*

What we actually think: *'Yes, we travel by helicopter every time. It's a little bit expensive for the company, but what else can you do?'*


* *'On which floor is deck 12?'*

Our answer: *'On the 12th floor, ma'am'.*

What we actually think: *'Good woman's head, are you aware of your question?'*


* *'Has this ship ever sunk?'*

Our answer: no comment.

What we actually think: *'Sure, we pull one out every Monday, vacuum a bit and we're ready to go'.*

\* *'Do you help to sail the ship as well?'* (Question to the waiter in the restaurant)

Our answer: *'Sir, I'm just a waiter'*.

What we actually think: *'Of course, we also connect cables in the engine room and inflate lifeboats'*.

\* *'How deep is the ocean below us right now?'*

Our answer: *'I'm sorry, I wouldn't know'*.

What we actually think: *'Well, it's deeper than your brain for sure'*.

\*On the day of embarkation when the ship is at the port for half a day: *'Why do we have this ugly view of the parking lot from our balcony?'*

Our answer: *'Ma'am, we haven't sailed yet'*.

What we actually think: *'We are sorry. To avoid looking at that parking lot during the whole cruise, it is better to draw the curtains'*.

\* *'Do you see fish in the sea from your room?'*

Our answer: *'Ma'am, we don't have a window in our room'*.

What we actually think: *'Of course, we also hang pictures on the walls, we just have to be careful not to drive the screws too deep so that water doesn't penetrate'*.

\*When sailing from America to Russia: *'Does time stand still when we travel through time zones?'*

Our answer: no comment.

What we actually think: *'Yes, just for you'*.

\*Once you board as a guest, it is almost impossible not to notice the information and Ship's Itinerary on every corner, but for some neither that it's not enough: *'Where are we tomorrow and how strong the wind will blow?'* or a question of type *'Will be sunny in two days?'* and *'Will it rain when we come back?'*

Our answer: *'I'm sorry, I wouldn't know'*.

What we actually think: *'Do I look like a meteorologist to you?'*

*'Why is the flight from San Juan shorter for the Americans than for us British?'

Our answer: 'Because of the distance, sir'.

What we actually think: 'Why did you miss geography classes as a child?'


*When visiting castles in England: 'Why were they so fond of building ruins in England?' or better yet 'Do you know anything about the undiscovered ruins?'

Our answer: no comment.

What we actually think: 'Please from the deepest part of your mind, think again about what you just asked me!'


*'How can we have electricity so far from the mainland?'

Our answer: 'Because the ship produces its own'.

What we actually think: 'Via the cable we've been connected to since Miami'.


*'Do we take a shower with salt water?' or 'Is there saltwater in the toilet?'

Our answer: 'No'.

What we actually think: 'Why on earth are you interested in that?'


*'Do these elevators drive forward or back to the ship?'

Our answer: 'No'.

What we actually think: 'Just for you, they drive you straight to your cabin?'


*'Why my microwave in the room doesn't work?'

Our answer: 'Ma'am, that's safe'.

What we actually think: 'It works, you can also set a password if you want'.


*At photographer: 'How do we know what our pictures are?'—one of my favourite.

Our answer: no comment.

What we actually think: 'Do you need a mirror!'

*'Do you keep chickens on board? How do you have fresh eggs then?' or 'Can I have an omelette without eggs?' or 'What's a ham and cheese sandwich made of?'*

Our answer: no comment.

What we actually think: *'Oh my God, give me strength!'*

*'Is Croatia in Russia?'*

Our answer: *'Sir, Croatia is a state unto itself'.*

What we actually think: *'Of course, it is the capital of Russia'.*

*Once a guest complained and rated the cruise as a total disaster because she had to walk quite a bit at the airport.

*'Why are excursion buses old in the Caribbean?'*

Our answer: *'I wouldn't know anything about it'.*

What we actually think: 'You can be happy not to ride on wooden wheels'.

*'Which currency is used in Alaska?'* (question from an American guest)

Our answer: *'It's US dollars, ma'am'.* ☺

What we actually think: 'As long as I know, Alaska belongs to the USA, or?'

*'Do you have chocolate doughnuts?'* and after we answer no, they ask immediately *'Can you bring two?'*

*'Where is the butter?'* (guest asking the last day of the cruise)

Our answer: *'Right here ma'am'.* (Pointing with a hand half a metre away)

What we actually think: 'You have been here the whole week and now you ask me, the last day for fricking butter?'

*One couple asked that if they take a private excursion that lasts about 10 hours, can we (the waiters) arrange for the ship to depart 2–3 hours later than scheduled at the port.

*Upset guests after arrival from the port: *'The beach we went to contains too much sand! We had to clean everything when we got back to the room'.* or *'No one told us there would be fish in the sea! The children were scared!'*

* *'They should not allow topless sunbathing on the beach. It was very distracting for my husband who just wanted to relax'.*

* *'Why is our one-bedroom apartment smaller than our friends who have a three-bedroom apartment?'*

Our answer: no comment.

What we actually think: *'Maybe because there's less air in your room, that must be the reason'.*

* *'When we were in Spain, there were quite a lot of Spanish people there, and they all spoke Spanish. Nobody told us that there are so many foreigners in Spain'.*

Our answer: no comment.

What we actually think: *'I will pray two 'Our Father' for you'.*

*In some ports, the ship cannot dock with the mainland, so it can be reached ashore by smaller open tender-boats, so one question regarding such an occasion: *'Why there is no air-condition in tender-boats?'*

*When going on an excursion: *'I was bitten by a mosquito during the excursion! The description of the excursion does not state that there are mosquitoes!'*

*Question to the waiter in the restaurant: *'Do you work here?'*

Our answer: *'Yes, ma'am'.*

What we actually think: *'No, I'm wearing this uniform just to impress the girls'.*

*Question to DJ during the party: *'Why do you play the same songs every day?'* or *'You must be very happy when you always listen to the same good songs'.*

Our answer: *'Thank you'.*

What we actually think: *'No, you're the one who's happy because you listen to those same songs for a couple of days while I listen to them every day for half a year'.*

* *'Do these stairs lead up or down?'*

Our answer: no comment.

What we actually think: *'Lead left and right'*.

*The guest calls the reception by phone: *'How do I get out of my room?' I have two doors, one leads to the bathroom and the other has a 'Do Not Disturb sign?* '—this one must be the winner but still, I can't be so sure, competition is huge.

*When crossing the Atlantic: *'Do you know when a whale comes from the ocean so we can see it?'*

Our answer: *'We definitely don't know'*.

What we actually think: *'Now I'm going to text him to come'*.

* *'Can you tell me the number of unemployed on the ship?'*

Our answer: no comment.

What we actually think: *'If I hit you on this empty head with something, then you will know at least for one!'*

* *'Is this island completely surrounded by water?'*

* *'What do you do with ice sculptures after they melt?'*

Our answer: no comment.

What we actually think: we don't think any more after such a question.

***

What to say? What message do you get?

Do you understand me now when I'm writing what kind of guests are onboard? Although OK, not everyone is like that. Most of them are normal, and we really met wonderful guests, except that twenty times per cruise we come across those with little common sense.

I don't know, my dear people, what else to write to you about this topic...

They say the hardest part of the job on a ship is being kind to the people with little common sense which is true, so to stay calm in such situations and not lose patience to which limit you've approached a million times, you just have to see the funny side of it. ☺

I remained in contact with some guests even still today, but my favourite circle of guests is Americans. They are somehow the most approachable, the most open, and in most cases very friendly type of guests. When I just remember how many invitations we received from them, if we ever visit their city or place, to let them know (they leave us a contact) to meet, offer us their own house for accommodation and overnight stays and things like that. I'm telling you, they are very simple. And on the other hand why they are among my favourite guests because of the good tips. What it is it is, Americans have always left good tips. ☺

What is also important to note is the rule that the crew must follow when we talk about relation to the guests, which is—no intimate companionship and any similar things. Now, that sounds very strict because it is, but again the real picture is that you always have individuals who can take advantage of such opportunities but also cover up because some guests come to cruise to have fun and relax, which I mean literally kind of fun without normal limits. If happens that a crew member totally falls in love with a guest or opposite, it remains a secret, but still shows a different picture.

Most often, those who take advantage of this type of pleasure are people in the highest positions, and that is why the mentality of 'no one can do anything to me' reigns, and, logically, they protect each other. Maybe not so much with the guests as with the crew members. We have now come to the part which I am incredibly disgusted with and which I thought to avoid but since this is a book on such a subject I simply have to mention because if I had pointed out only the most beautiful things about the ship everything would sound too good to be true while like this for people who preparing for a ship, I want to fully open up the whole picture of where they are going because better they are aware of such things than end up under some punishment or depression because they found themselves in the wrong place at the wrong time.

People who go on a ship of all positions, leave at home their families, wife, husband, children, and once they come on a ship and feel that different kind of freedom, they change in the blink of an eye (of course not everyone!). I have seen it with my own eyes as they transform from peaceful, naive, and good souls into something they are not and thus immensely harm the trust of their families. The most bizarre thing I heard happened on one occasion on my first contract was when one of the crew members got the news that his wife had given birth at home, and he was so excited without total control that he abused that joy and happiness by sleeping with some girl that very same night.

In my second contract, the girl who shared a cabin with my friend rarely spent time in their cabin but with one supervisor. Soon as that same supervisor got the news that his whole family was coming to cruise on that same ship, his so-called mistress was of course forced to pick up all her belongings from his cabin and hide any possible evidence of adultery. After a week as soon as his family left the ship, everything went back to 'normal'. These are just a few cases out of many, but not to go on, you got the picture I'm talking about.

It's terrible what man becomes onboard—the part I mentioned at the beginning of the first contract when it is very important to be aware of everything you do. Of course, not everyone is like that, some people really present themselves as an important example to follow. For me personally, even though I didn't have a wife or kids at the time and had total freedom of behaviour, I never allowed myself to fall into such habits for a couple of good reasons. I am neither raised that way nor do I feel that kind of need. It is all a type of pleasure that lasts only in those moments until after that, your mentality and characteristics as a person, and at the same time, your whole life changes completely and will never be the same again.

Why would I have such things on my conscience? I firmly believe that you must strive for something valuable in life. That you always have to radiate positive energy and present yourself as an example that someone new will see and follow at some point, and that is very important for the younger generations. Things like adultery and affair that many have done on a ship are for me nothing but the biggest and most selfish act a man can do (Ok, there are more but in such circumstances). This is just one of the so-called devilish temptations because as I mentioned, you have to be aware of what you are getting into and the consequences that await you because the temptations on board are very many and very different.

To stay sober and in some way protected in spirit and body, I always had a rosary with me. You have noticed that I have mentioned a few times so far in the book how important God is to me and how much I trust Him. The rosary is something that has bound me since 'a couple' of years ago and something I became aware of how powerful it is when you spend a few minutes praying for it. Faith is the strongest force in the world! If you want to create and achieve something, some goal, without your personal faith you would never succeed. If you truly believe that you can achieve your goals no matter how many obstacles hit you on this very very brutally difficult path to success, only faith is the strength and fuel that can lead you to the end.

From the day I realised this, I do not stop praying because not only does God protect me from Satan's temptations, but He also gives me small blessings and allows me to progress in very small steps every day. Believe it or not, more than 10 years have passed since that day. I spent 10 years every day either morning or evening with that one prayer. I still don't mean to stop because, as I mentioned, wisdom and strength come from human faith—the strongest force in the world!

I do not consider myself a saint or sinless now because of what I do because I sin like everyone else, but while we are talking about sins similar to the ones I have mentioned, for me they are very serious things that I do not intend to get my hands dirty. If I hadn't had that way of thinking so far and so much faith in God, who knows where I would have ended up and what I would have done, maybe nothing good and exemplary.

I read once, *'When prayers become your habit, miracles become your lifestyle'. Unknown*

After everything I have been through and what I am still going through, I have experienced both small and big miracles, which strengthen my faith every day. I believe that one of the many reasons I came across Elizabeth is that she protected me in some way from such people who might drag me into their world and a life full of lies. From the first day, we started hanging out, it was clear that there were no such intentions as exploitation and selfish pleasures that some share. We both felt the natural flow of creating a love for which only the dear and Almighty God brought us together in an amazing and unexpected way.

Here you go, I hope that I was able to describe to you a broader picture of what kind of people there are on board and at the same time advise how to deal with them. But on the other hand, a vessel without guests would not be fun and give you one of the greatest and most valuable gifts that exist, and that is a life experience in which you learn from people more than you have ever tried to understand or even imagine.

So once again I suggest not only to future sailors and guests who are preparing to cruise but in general to people who travel all over this crazy and beautiful world, to meet as many different people as possible because once you step out of your comfort zone, you realise how much new you can learn, which is a phenomenal feeling and a wonderful ability given to us.

***

*Ship's Itinerary (14 November 2015–16 April 2016)—Caribbean Sea*
*Ports: Houston (Texas, USA)—Disembarkation/Embarkation day (Saturday)*

> *Cozumel (Mexico)*
> *Belize City (Belize)*
> *Roatán (Honduras)*

I started to work in the officer mess from the end of November 2015 until March 2016. It was also my first Christmas without my family, which made me very depressed for a short time. It is by no means easy to have a clear conscience, knowing that your family on the other side of the world spends such special days in the best company, fun, and homemade food, while you are kind of 'alone' in this (in some way). It meant a lot to me and made me happy when they put a little Christmas tree in the officer mess. After all, it was easier and faster to feel that Christmas spirit next to my sweet tree.

Four days before Christmas we went out in the hot, already very well known to us Cozumel. While my family and friends from the other side of the world were making preparations for the holidays on minus degrees, I was sweating from the heat in Mexico. This was one of my most bizarre experiences when you walk before Christmas days in short sleeves and watch at Christmas trees in sunglasses. Unbelievable how a weird feeling, especially for those of us who are used to and quite always grown up in that more winter environment looking forward to Christmas time. This here now is honestly something I never want to experience again. It's the truth that we do not have always the weather we want, the so-called white Christmas, but it's still so much better than this heat in December, at least for me.

On Christmas Eve, I remember after finishing work in the officer mess, when I had cleaned and prepared everything for the next day, I stayed sitting in that room with the lights off, watching in that blissful peace—the Christmas tree with the little colourful lights that gave me just that same feeling I have every time at home when we (my family and me) observe and admire a beautiful tree. I prayed briefly before the last minute until Christmas and went to pick up Elizabeth who was finishing her shift at that time. When we returned, we wished each other a

228

Merry Christmas, and I gave her earrings as a Christmas present which she immediately fell in love with (after a year, she lost them ☹).

A week later, while most of you were running around the shops and filling carts with some kind of fireworks and other artillery, we spent New Year's Eve in Honduras. *Salva Vida*, their popular beer that cooled our throats at all that Caribbean temperature. The New Year's Eve on the cruise was organised in the main lobby of the reception area where a considerable number of people could fit, while the main fireworks could be watched from the 12th and 13th decks outdoors. Since Elizabeth was called to help in the main lobby, we also welcomed the new 2016 there, which will mark a lot.

As I mentioned before, the company on this ship was just as good as on the first contract.

Since it lasted a short time, at first my roommates were Montenegrin, one from Serbia, and I don't remember much whether the third one was an Indian or some another nationality, but later when all of them finished their contracts and left the cabin, I was alone in the cabin even for a few days, which was on the other hand very relaxing and necessary for sleeping. But as everything that is beautiful always lasts (too) short, I was soon joined by two novices from Serbia with whom I was quite OK at the beginning. Here now follows another story about the crew and basic communication with people.

Namely, when these two guys came and started to get excited about everything on board such as the work environment, our crew bar, meeting other crew members (especially the female population) of the different ports that follow, and everything else that comes with it all, they started really exaggerate in some things. Ok, I can understand that. Since they were completely green and naive to any situation on the ship, everything seemed interesting to them, what I didn't like about them at all was their attitude in the cabin. Almost every night they went to the crew bar, as is the case with most of our mentality, to get drunk and have a good time, which I don't mind because it's not my personal thing but that's why constantly bringing the rest of the company into the cabin and partying for a few more hours behind two o'clock in the morning, when the crew bar was always closing, it really bothered me.

Yes, I admit I did it too but in very small quantities. It was enough, when you want to rest a little, that someone wakes you up in the cabin during the day because of the noise they make, so let me not start how frustrated is when that happens after a whole day when you finally lie down to sleep. Although I admit that towards the end of the contract I became so immune to any sounds that on a couple of occasions I think even the cannon couldn't wake me up. Since most of the company was 'ex-Yugoslavia', I had no intention of reporting them, behind their back and complaining to the people who were in charge of the order on board.

I was thinking more and more about what kind of conversation to calm them down in some way, but also to spare them the additional exhaustion and fatigue they created for themselves. I did not want to quarrel, but to touch that 'click' in their head with a calm conversation when they become aware of the situation, but also more mature, to make important decisions that will affect their further progress in the ship's career. One evening I started a conversation:

*'Guys, I understand that it's great for you in the crew bar and even better when you think that no one can forbid you to spend that time like that, but spending almost every night even that little energy that remains after a day's work is not smart at all. I beg you but at the same time, I advise you to reduce your passions and excitement about all this because the whole contract is still ahead of you. Eight months is not a small amount, and as you started, you will not last even half of the contract. I am telling you from experience, listen to me because you will be very exhausted and your free time which is given to you on drips should be used wisely.*

*You can't expect the daily rhythm of going out in the port for a couple of hours, working all day and after work until the early morning getting drunk which gives you only a few hours of sleep, and then the same story all over again. I'm not bothered by your daily adventure, but I'm bothered by the noise you bring because it also affects my resting time. You have to become aware that there is a time and place for everything, you can't do everything at once'.*

When I tried to explain such things to them in that friendly tone in good faith, they just looked at me in amazement and looked at it as something negative. From that moment on, I felt that they began to consider me as an enemy, for which I was not too surprised because that is how our mentality is, most of the time.

When you want to help someone, the smart one will accept the advice while some brainless people are held by an ego full of arrogance. I gave them the limit that if this thing doesn't change I will have to improvise in a different but also the hardest way. I really didn't want to report them for disrespecting discipline and order because we as our people always stick together no matter how they are, but this time I had to make this kind of decision because it was starting to greatly affect my health due to lack of sleep. They both decided to move to another cabin after that, but only one of them really did that, while the other one stayed for a bit longer. I ignored the stories that followed since my decision because I knew I was doing the right thing and after all, I have a longer and more experience onboard than a couple of novices.

Soon the other one who stayed got a transfer from the buffet to the crew mess, which I liked because I knew he would learn to appreciate the little things. Until recently, he considered me an enemy in the cabin, but after a couple of weeks spent in the crew mess, things turned around. I knew that the rhythm in the crew mess would wake him up and thus encourage him to change further habits. What bothered me at first has now stopped. Everything came to its own, and he felt my words that I had told him before, but still, after a while, he moved out of the cabin, which suited me very well because there was always some negativity in the room between us from that day when I told him (and to the other one) and tried to open the eyes about some things.

In the meantime, two new ones moved in. Branko from Bosnia and Vladimir who was either from Macedonia or Kosovo, I don't remember now but he lives in Serbia. With their arrival in the cabin, the atmosphere changed completely. We broke out jokes and nonsense to the point of unconsciousness which reminded me of the good old days from the first contract. Towards the end of my contract, we were joined by one from Turkey who still had a contract or two until retirement. That person was over 60 years old certainly and still in the position of assistant waiter. Although it was initially a topic of ridicule for us, I believe it opened our eyes to the fact that we should never stay in just one place, remain stubborn and be afraid to take on greater responsibilities. Life is terribly too short and that is why the man must progress and constantly learn, that one day he can leave a positive mark and become an inspiration to someone else.

*** 

But while the comic 'Balkan mafia' prevailed in the cabin again, the rest of the company were, as I mentioned before, Peruvians. How funny people they are, from first to the last one. We often went out in the ports and created unforgettable new adventures and memories, which is the point of travelling and socialising.

On one occasion we went out in the great Cozumel and headed to *Paradise Beach* where we enjoyed the great temperature of the sea, sandy beaches, and a pleasant breeze in the shade under palm trees with *Sol* beer in hand. No matter how tired you are, those few hours fill you with some joyful and positive energy to have the strength to finish the day and go out again next time. I often hung out with Peruvians also in the crew bar, where they really had their own territory— the dance floor. The Latino party, which was held frequently, screamed from all those Latino American dances.

Something amazing to see! I think anyone who didn't grow up in South America should see it at least once, what an amazing innate talent and gift this Latino population has for dancing! Of course, I did not dare on the dance floor because they would demolish me from all these movements. What I learned on those occasions is one very important lesson from Latino countries. When you stand (like me) like a log on the side and observe this art of dancing, you begin to be more and more aware of how important dancing is to them. More than life! So it happened on a couple of occasions that one, two Peruvians who were in our company, came to me, to ask me for permission if they could dance with my Elizabeth.

Since Eli couldn't expect me to dance like Latino, I saw in her eyes how badly she wanted to dance, and I didn't want to forbid her that, and also, I had no right to be offended by something like that. It just wouldn't be right. It is very important to understand this culture especially when two totally opposite countries are intertwined in terms of mentality. If I had the attitude of some arrogant and jealous peasant, as is the case in some percentage in the world, I would start a fight there when someone approached me and asked me to dance with my, back then still girlfriend. Since I'm not an aggressive person, in those moments I had to talk to myself and calm that inner ego that wants to rule in all of us, and calm the glass of jealousy because this is not about the desire and intention of someone to steal my girlfriend but about dance culture and a tradition very important to them.

The other day I read about a Peruvian woman who arrived in Croatia a couple of years ago and went to school and started living in Zagreb. After a long reading about her experiences in Croatia, I couldn't help but notice the detail she mentioned, which was that she only missed her Peruvian food and dance. Dance!

She jokingly mentioned that she would like us Croats to get a little better on the dance floor, which she means in other words, that we are too wooden and with an awful little passion for dancing (not everybody of course).

Elizabeth also admitted to me that she went to the crew bar to dance with the company almost every night before we met. Regardless of gender and age, for the Latino population dance is I think number 1. They take it as the most important passion they can share with others and also something they are incredibly proud of. As I mentioned in my case before, if I were a typical man, I would create awkward scenes, but thank God this way I stayed sober and open-minded tried to understand, and at the same time learn this experience.

People are sometimes so full of egoism thinking they know everything and don't really know anything. If you remember Dylan I mentioned before (my coach), he mentioned one saying several times:

*'A foolish man thinks he knows everything, while a wise man knows he knows nothing'.*

*Amanda Hocking*


When you come to a totally different environment and start catching different views than the ones you are used to every day in your area, only then do you begin to be aware of how much more there is to discover, explore, find out, learn, experience and all get to some way, a new blessing.

I remembered another very funny example. In our crew bar, you could sign up as a DJ and play different music. Since I'm a pop music fan, I played that night a little bit of everything. A hill of the great list by many, but that evening remained for me pale and desolate in terms of work as a DJ. Not that the crew bar was empty, but no one was coming to the dance floor. I thought, what the heck is this, doesn't anyone listen to pop hits. It wasn't until I put on songs like *On the Floor* by Jennifer Lopez and Pitbull ft. Ke$ha—*Timber* that a couple of them came to dance, but in the last 10 minutes, before the crew bar closed, a hilarious scene happened. That crazy Peruvian Jorge arrived and persuaded me to let him play some music, I said OK, it can't be worse than it is now.

When in those last 10 minutes suddenly he filled the dance floor with his Latino music, which I couldn't do all evening. And up to that point, I was telling Elizabeth to start dancing to which she had an excuse that her legs hurt, but by the time Jorge started thundering from the speaker's Latin rhythm, she was already on the dance floor. We laughed to tears at those scenes, so I thought 'you Peruvians and the rest of South America no pop music just fire up to your rumba, samba, mamba, salsa, pachanga, bachata, and I don't know which million more dances. Yes, yes. Jorge embarrassed me well as far as DJ work is concerned but here, I gave another example and described in more detail the picture of what dancing means for South America.

I also played soccer with him very often on that ship field. I mentioned in the first contract that we often played with the guys from the Caribbean as well. Most of the players we had for soccer were from the Caribbean. Which kind of all pictures reappeared on stage with that Caribbean humour, Jorge and I literally fell to the floor laughing.

I remember one evening when we were joined by a tall one, brother to brother, he was 2-metre tall for sure. Something told me to try that 'rainbow' trick on him (when you lift the ball over the opponent). You can do that on anyone, but doing that to someone who is 2-metre tall was a real challenge. And look at the miracles, I managed it from the first try, but the action failed soon after because others started laughing at him because of what trick I sold him, which of course was contagious at the time and impossible not to laugh at. I remember that evening as one of the most fun, an evening in which we laughed a lot because of them and their accent—the way they speak English.

***

Beautiful memories remain on one occasion when Elizabeth and I went out to Playa del Carmen, a part of the Mexican coast to which we had to take a boat from Cozumel. What can I say, but more or less the same—great pleasure to see and feel.

We walked the streets of that city and came across an incredibly fascinating little chapel that I want to visit at least once more in my adventurous life. I liked it so much that I even thought of trying to organise a wedding one day in that very nice chapel, which didn't happen in the end, but at least now I have an excuse to visit it again. ☺

After a lot of walking, it is known what follows—the pleasure of trying Mexican food and this time, cocktails.

At the end of February, a step forward in my ship career took place.

I got a promotion for an assistant waiter and a transfer to a restaurant called 'Atlantic'. But that was not all. When you think it can't get better, when it does, it can!

I also received written information that I was nominated for the shortlist for the Employee of the Month (in February). Every month, around 20 best employees are selected, and from those, the best four are also selected. I had that honour! Incredibly, of the more than 1,000 of the crew, I was among the top four. Also, I received smaller prizes that came in that package such as a free dinner in one of the speciality restaurants, staying in a guest room for one night with champagne and strawberries topped with chocolate, an additional bonus on salary, an Internet package, and I don't know what else. It is a wonderful feeling when after hard work you feel appreciated, which comes back to you double.

I must also mention my supervisor who was in the crew mess and officer mess at the time, an older gentleman from Turkey, one of the few who has that particular sense of humour that always cheered us up.

An interesting fact is one person who 'followed' Elizabeth and me on all three contracts. From my first contract at Aries, the next one through Aquarius to this third one the Liberty Wave, we constantly had an old acquaintance from Nicaragua. Fate wanted us to meet on even three different ships. Totally funny person but also very friendly. His job was in a senior position at the Casino, but soon during our contract, he left the CL2 company and the last thing he told me a couple of years ago was that he worked for a while in Las Vegas and then returned to his home country where I guess he still lives and works. For us, he always radiated positive energy and vibes of good mood which means a lot in such a place.

During this third contract, we visited three times the Peruvian restaurant *Machu Picchu* in Roatán, an archipelago that belongs to Honduras. Elizabeth insisted that we and a couple of Peruvians go to that restaurant, which led me to conclude that she missed Peruvian food, but also I was very curious to taste one of the best cuisines in the world. My impressions? Do I need to retell anything further, when we visited that restaurant three times? The truth is it wasn't 100% Peruvian food since we were in Honduras but they weren't far from it either. In my opinion, very tasty and rich food, while Peruvians complained a little about the food that was not properly prepared.

It was great food for me, so I can't even imagine what the original real Peruvian food tastes like, but I'll have the opportunity to try it sometime later.

Since Elizabeth and I have been together since my first contract and have gone through some situations, we continued together no matter what. I firmly felt that this was leading to some more serious path. When we visited that restaurant for the third time, drinking the famous Peruvian cocktail Pisco sour, I looked at that big picture of Machu Picchu on the wall, and then at that moment a light turn on in my head, and I said to myself:

*'From now on, I'm working on a plan to get Elizabeth there and ask her one important question!'*

Only 147 days have passed since then until the moment when my plan and wish became a reality. But for now, I apologise, but we're still on ship topics so you'll have to flip through a few more pages to reach the Peru part. ☺

After my relocation and promotion, it wasn't hard for me to fit into a huge restaurant with quite a bit of pressure. Why?—well because I went through most of those situations in the officer mess by myself. The restaurant was divided into stations, so each head and the assistant waiter was taken care of a couple of tables, for easier and faster action in the service.

My first head waiter was some guy from the Caribbean. I can't remember the name but he was pretty OK, and I liked him as a person. I never had a problem with him, and we always worked at some good pace. He always took orders from the guests and took care of the drinks which the head waiters do while I ran with the food and served it. We were a good team and because of that, we were often rewarded with good tips. For us assistant waiters who ran to the kitchen to pick up the food, we also enjoyed the endless scenes filled with all sorts of parodies.

When the executive chef came along and took a look at their chefs and the food they prepare, it can sometimes look like cartoon scenes. I admit it's the part of life I miss, those few minutes spent in the kitchen waiting for food while on the other side of the counter, endless comedy to heaven.

But even that came to an end sooner than I could have expected. At the end of March, one of my colleagues was working in one of the speciality restaurants 'Burgundy Steakhouse'. Her contract was about to finish at the end of the month which means somebody else needed to replace her. One evening we were talking in the Buffet area and out of the blue, she mentioned to me that she would recommend me to her supervisor (who was back then in that restaurant). Until then, I didn't know much about Steakhouse restaurant, I just heard that there is a lot of competition to join the team there because as soon as you start working in a better restaurant, you get an even better salary and with that better tips. In a restaurant where there is a team of six head waiters and three assistant waiters, back then the supervisor was Mr Panuta, an Indonesian who taught me so much in so little time.

\*\*\*

After spending just a month at the 'Atlantic' Restaurant, I got an invitation to Burgundy Steakhouse Restaurant. I was totally surprised. But so that now does not look like I used connection by a colleague who recommended me to Mr Panuta, that month when I started working at 'Atlantic' an important detail happened from which Mr Panuta will remember me in a very positive way. When you work in one of these two big restaurants, you're actually working in two different places—the restaurant and that Buffet area.

The evening was always reserved to work in the restaurant while the morning or afternoon shift was at the buffet. Both for us and for the supervisors. And one afternoon I was working at a buffet where Mr Panuta was sent as well that day. I remember that we were at one of the ports that day, and that afternoon was quite peaceful around the buffet. Most of the guests came out which gave us a little bit of a break, not to work too hard, but that's why they didn't spare us for work later during dinner. Anyway, I noticed that there were dirty cups left in the dishwasher, and I wanted to put them to wash, but since there were a lot of them, it would take me up to 20 minutes of work, for which I wanted to inform my supervisor first.

It is very important during the work that the supervisor is always informed if you need to go somewhere, for example, a toilet or help somewhere because otherwise if your job is in the buffet and the supervisor cannot find you, a problem can arise. And so I went to look for Mr Panuta and let him know if it was okay to take care of the dirty cups because there wasn't too much work in the buffet anyway. With that question, I put a big smile on Mr Panuta's face. I wasn't even aware of what I was actually doing at that time. I was just thinking right, to do something productive and not just walk without the head, while on the supervisor's side that meant a huge plus.

He recognised my good work habits, which he really liked, and I left a great positive impression on him with just one small act. A couple of weeks later, that crucial step happened when a colleague talked about me to a Mr Panuta to work at Steakhouse restaurant, to which I received a positive response because he remembered well what kind of person with work habits I am. On this occasion, I would like to thank my colleague from Serbia once again for giving me the opportunity to progress even more.

The schedule at Steakhouse restaurant wasn't bad at all. Only once a week I have to do BLD (breakfast, lunch, dinner) while the other six days I was always free for either breakfast or lunch. Since this restaurant is much smaller in capacity and there are only three assistant waiters in the team, the three of us helped each head waiter, whoever called us we went to him. The whole team was very good, we always had that spark of humour in such an environment especially from one head waiter from the Philippines. Gemi was the main trigger to relax the nerves. I stayed at that restaurant until the end of the contract and as for the team, only a couple of them changed.

On 16 April, we had our last embarkation day in Houston. The third day after that we arrived in Miami, the port from which we sailed again across the ocean to Europe, but before these new adventures, let me tell you which memories gave me Miami.

This time, only went out 'the Balkan mafia' in this 'Little Cuba' city, as some call it. Branko, two guys from Serbia, and me. We first walked along the coast, then along the famous Miami beach—a beach that really leaves you speechless. Since we didn't stay too long on the beach, we decided to go somewhere to sit down for a drink and freshen up a bit before we got back to the vessel. We sat in a bar where a girl from Serbia worked. After reading for a while the cocktail list, Branko and I decided to take the *Miami Vice* cocktail. Here comes a situation that has taught us one more lesson in life.

The list of cocktails did not include prices, which is a very deceptive trap for tourists. At first, we thought, come on, it doesn't matter, we won't bankrupt for one cocktail, all of them cost more-less the same… yea right, you wish. When she brought each of us half a litre of cocktail, in which there was more ice than liquid, questions began to shoot over our heads how much do these cocktails actually cost?

When we were getting ready to get back on the ship, they brought us a bill, and omg! One cocktail costs around $ 80! We were shocked, we were saying to each other: *'Bro, what is this now? Is there anything else coming with the cocktail? Did we get drunk from this ice and the sun hit us? Maybe we can't see these numbers well? What is it, what's going on?'*—we wondered and laughed like crazy at the same time.

What else can you do, we paid, learned, and remembered. Although we weren't happy to take out $ 80 for something that's not worth even half the price if you look at the other side of this scene it's funny. Have you heard that one: *'Some things are fun to do just once?'*—it certainly is, since I mention this for the second time. The first time was Warnemünde with Sasha and Edin when we were shopping nonsense for a price I am ashamed of even to repeat. I would attach these experiences to that saying for sure. And never again.

***

After these 'cheap' cocktails, we turned to Europe and thus to the old, well-known custom, moving the clock forward every night until we arrived on the European mainland. What else to say about it than that moving the clock was torturing.

As soon as we turned to Europe I went crazy with happiness because I knew that after the ocean our first port was again that beautiful Madeira. Of course in my workplace, I did my best just to keep making a good impression on Mr Panuta, and for that, he gave me the choice of going out to Madeira or a few days later to Barcelona. I didn't hesitate for long but made it clear to him that I needed to be able to go out in Madeira, even though I admit I wanted both.

Also, one thing I didn't talk too much about in all three contracts is the rocking of the ship, or as we call *raft sea* that happens every time we do the cross—Atlantic or sea days. There is not much to write about it except that people (especially those for the first time) often get seasick because of such an appearance, so I can only advise if you come across such a scenario, do not overeat in the buffet and in restaurants thinking it will be better after because it won't.

I speak from personal experience. In the first contract during such days, I overate, thinking that only need to keep immunity well, which turned out to be a bad option.

As soon as I left the crew mess to the Buffet area, after check-in, I ran right to the toilet and vomited everything I had eaten half an hour before. I apologise for this ugly picture but I just want to warn future sailors. When you feel bad about the *raft sea* drink some soda water, not too much and a couple of dry crackers and a green apple should help. At least that's what they told us, it helped me.

Paradise beach, Cozumel, Mexico; my working area – officer mess in Christmas time

Cute Chapel in Playa de Carmen; Relaxing time

At Machu Picchu Restaurant, Roatán, Honduras

New Year's Eve

Miami beach

*Ship's Itinerary (29 April—11 June 2016)—Mediterranean*
*Ports: Funchal, Madeira (Portugal)*
       *Barcelona (Spain)*
       *Palma (Spain)*
       *Valletta (Malta)*
       *Venice (Italy)—Disembarkation/Embarkation day (Saturday)*
       *Split (Croatia)*
       *Corfu (Greece)*
       *Katakolon (Greece)*
       *Santorini (Greece)*
       *Mykonos (Greece)*
       *Piraeus (Greece)*
       *Dubrovnik (Croatia)*

This time it was neither Sunday nor a holiday, but an ordinary Friday so Elizabeth and I jumped out of the ship as soon as possible to take advantage of as much time as possible in such a beautiful place. But you know where I really wanted to go from the beginning! The CR7 Museum was waiting for us with its doors open this time. For me, this experience was truly a touch of a small part of a soccer dream, but also a huge motivation. Amazing how much this museum is filled with some individual but also team awards and trophies of only one man, with the fact that I visited that museum in 2016 so I guess since then they have been forced to expand the museum or move it to a larger place because this fantastic soccer icon still is filling up the showcases.

I also met a nice salesman in the museum who was quite sympathetic to the Croatians, especially Luka Modrić, Ronaldo's teammate at the time at Real Madrid. I love soccer, and I have a list of favourite soccer players who have been and remain a great inspiration to me but since I started to follow Cristiano in 2004 until today, no one has awakened that soccer passion in me as much as he has. Simply only his work habit and a boundless firm desire for progress every day is a picture without words and motivation without end. Cristiano passed 35 and is still 'killing' on the field, and looks like a 20-year-old. In short and clearly stated—a phenomenon.

After touring this (to me) piece of paradise, we took a short walk around the city and sat down to eat something. Their food is amazing! I mentioned last time that we enjoyed the famous *Coral* beer but it's not a lower-level food either. Very cordial and approachable people and indescribably proud of their soccer heroes. After spending a few hours in Madeira you can feel how much people love and appreciate Cristiano Ronaldo. An island that was hard for us to leave, and another destination that we definitely put on the list to visit at least one more time and explore new experiences to the smallest detail.

After great food and the Ronaldo Museum, we headed to Barcelona. As I mentioned before, I didn't have a chance to go out this second time in Barcelona while Elizabeth had that freedom so she went with Branko and a couple of them in the company to the Camp Nou stadium and the rest of the city.

After Barcelona, the ports that are already known to you follow, but this time we are adding the Greek ports Piraeus.

As soon as we started wandering around the Mediterranean, time somehow passed faster and faster. Two weeks before our signing off and the last disembarkation as crew members, Mr Panuta's contract finished. The gentleman from Indonesia, who taught me so much not only about work but also about life, really left me a deeper mark.

When I think about how many times I've had incidents at a restaurant, like breaking a plate or a glass, spilling a cocktail on a guest, serving the wrong dish... when I look at the whole picture of myself in the first week or two at that Steakhouse restaurant, I wonder what kept that man so much patient so he didn't kick me out of that restaurant and find someone else, which I believe most other supervisors would have done. But not Mr Panuta! He always gave me the opportunity and with enough patience and will, gave me time to grasp all the strings and learn more than with any other supervisor. And not only that but if you do your best he will return you that favour already in some way. Before his departure on 28 May, I will never forget the last words he addressed to me.

The reason he was so patient and trusted me is that I felt in many conversations with him that he saw some kind of passion for success in me, just as if I needed better guidance. There was a moment when we were left alone in the restaurant, and he called me on the side and started wisely advising me on how to succeed in life. How I have to be very hungry for success, that I will be tested many times in my life and be forced to sacrifice some things if I want to achieve something.

*'You have to achieve something in life!'*—he told me in that fervour and with the best of intentions. He truly was one of those pushing you forward, both in business and in life. I have great respect for him. That evening I asked for a

picture with him, to have as a souvenir, and asked him so curiously when he would return to the ship to which he replied:

*'I'm done with a ship, I will not return'.*

A month after he left the Liberty Wave, Elizabeth and I were sitting with friends (who also worked with us) in Zagreb, having a drink and suddenly we got the news that Mr Panuta had passed away. What a shock! None of us could believe it and especially me! Even today, a wave of sadness strikes me when I think of that day. This can't be true I thought, why him?

Unfortunately, what he told me about returning to the ship, he kept his promise in the worst-case scenario. Either way, Mr Panuta will always be in my good memory.

After his sign-off, we had two weeks left before ours. Amazing how much time began to fly, especially when I became more and more aware that we will not return to work on the ship, which on the other hand saddened me because I knew it would follow once again but this time an even stronger farewell from all our friends who were like family.

One Tuesday, Branko and I got a chance to go out in the Greek Piraeus. That was the last time Branko and I went out together alone. Why am I mentioning this now? Because sometimes it is important to go out with only one but also a very good friend, without much company and to experience adventures with only that one person (as I did in my first contract with a couple of good friends). Branko and I have become good friends since he arrived on the ship, but since he moved into my cabin, only then did a stronger friendship develop. We often went out in hot Cozumel where we also shared unforgettable days filled with laughter. Not to forget also, how many times after work I ran to the cabin when Branko had an hour, two free just to play some soccer on the popular PlayStation.

Such is destiny on a ship, life fills your days with people you thought you would never meet, and build a strong friendship with them. If I knew all my friends from every contract before ship life, I don't believe that all of us would bond as tightly as on the ship. Because only that ship, let's call it, 'locks' you in that circle of people with whom you spend more time in half a year than maybe with your own family at home.

I mentioned the contract lasts for about nine months. Now you can try to imagine spending somewhere with a couple of hundred people that long. If we were to look at each particular department, that means each department has its own daily schedule. Our free time (in the cabin, crew bar, crew mess, going out at the port) and working hours are always at the same hour. The bottom line is that you literally only don't spend time with someone when you sleep those five to eight, maybe nine hours.

The other 15 hours you are constantly in contact and company with people. You can calculate if it's 15 hours a day, how much of that turns out to be nine months. It was out of curiosity that I checked this information from the last contract and on my 245 days spent onboard it would mean that I spent about 3,675 hours in the company of other people. Wow! Now definitely based on this information you can more easily understand what it's like when you spend so many hours with friends who become one of your best and how used you are to them, to the point of how hard it is when you leave, knowing you'll never see them again (at least most of them).

Elizabeth and I have stayed in touch with many friends from whom we hear occasionally and with some, we have even met after our ship career.

All those names I had mentioned in the book, all those I didn't, but also many, many of those names I forgot, but not in my memory... they are all friends who have influenced our lives, even if they had the slightest impact, but they are all part of a great adventure filled with things that a man in such a 'short' time simply cannot experience on land.

And so Branko and I went out to Piraeus and decided to visit the Acropolis in Athens. Two horses like us didn't even notice we were passing Olympiacos soccer stadium and even twice! Later when we returned to the cabin after a while Branko figured out for the stadium. I said, well brother, you really remembered on time.

As we passed through the city, we already saw a temple on a hill over 2,400 years old from afar. When we finally got to the Acropolis, another ingenious stupidity followed.

They charged 25.00 euros per head for the entrance to the Acropolis. We look at each other and philosophise, whether those few stones are worth so much money. We decided to go after all. A classic thought—'O come on, I'm not here every day', as usually ruled.

When we toured and saw everything there was to see, I can't say! The truth is that Acropolis might have looked fascinating thousands of years ago. Another of the wonders of the world for which you are constantly questioning how and in what way ordinary people pulled these huge stones and built something like that without any machine and modern technology.

When we went down the hill, we did not go out through the same door where we each left 25.00 euros but somewhere on the side. We realised that this Acropolis has more entrances which means we nicely threw 50 euros in someone's pocket for something that is maybe for free. What a beauty. It still hurts me those $ 80 for a funny cocktail in Miami when here comes a new round. Once again dear readers, learn from my mistakes and explore as much as possible every detail of the journey which in our circumstances was difficult and unpredictable.

After that, the next outing was with Elizabeth in the magical Santorini again, which was only the second time during the whole contract. Sitting like that on top of the city with a beautiful view, I thought I would love to have more time to explore this place, but since it is not easily feasible in our situation we decided to just sit somewhere and eat something. As usual.

This time the food we tasted in one of the restaurants did not meet ours at all but I believe it would not suit anyone's criteria either. Here is another lesson I mentioned earlier, in the first contract, but forgot to apply it in this situation. The first mistake we made was choosing a restaurant that is in the heart of the city, where thousands of tourists pass by. The reason why there, was that we wanted to save time since it was close to us. The other mistake was that we ordered some sort of steak that was supposedly beef, only I doubt it was really beef.

The meat was a disaster, of strange taste, very tough so even after the first bite, we had no intention of continuing with the meat. We even assumed that they might have given us some poor donkey. Come on OK if it's just meat, but the side dishes are also no better. Rice and French fries looked like a street of horror. Just a little salad was OK.

We came to the third mistake I made and that is payment. By no means should I leave 50 euros for something that was not even edible! I was thinking of paying only for two salads and beer, but as we hurried to explore the city a bit, Eli calmed me down and told me to let go and pay, that I would just spend precious time arguing with the waiter, so I said OK, I let go but also learned from these situations. That's how it is for you when you are green in certain situations that hit you in the head, after each such one you record it well in your memory, and you definitely mature after such things.

A week before the 'by-by scene', I arranged with my family to meet in Split as it was a great opportunity for them to see for the first time live a huge cruiser that anchored me hundreds of different experiences and life adventures. Not only did I have that opportunity, but it was also the first official time they had met Elizabeth. When the moment came when they met her, after a few minutes my father asked her if she had learned any Croatian words, to which she replied that she did, and which words, it is really not appropriate to write here, I can only say that they are not most polite.

Among the different nationalities on board the first thing, they learn from each other is to swear ugly words which is a comic reality. Almost all nationalities know how to swear in our language just as our people know how to swear in Spanish, English, and other different languages. Why such a choice of words is always the easiest and fastest to remember in the beginning, I do not know.

As soon as Eli 'answered' my father so naively, I blushed like cancer of embarrassment, but at the same moment we all burst out laughing, what else are you going to do in such a moment. After officially meeting my girlfriend at the time, we took a walk around the city and sat down to lunch which this time was much better but also cheaper.

I cannot say that I do not love our Adriatic because I think that there is no man who does not love the Croatian coast whose mother of nature has blessed in every unique way. From north to south every bit is beautiful, and we really aren't aware of what a treasure we own. So believe it or not, whenever we plan a vacation I doubt whether to travel somewhere in the outside world or on the Croatian coast. But somehow this habit of the same thinking always directs me to the outside world which I think is a great consequence of the ship, while I leave many pearls of the Adriatic in the somewhat later years when I will have my own children. In any case, the whole world has natural beauties and charms that we ordinary people like to call 'heaven on earth'.

When I toured with my parents and older brother half the ship, they were simply thrilled to see it. For my part, I was very happy to be able to give them at least such pleasure. I have a great desire to take them on a cruise one day so that they can feel what a special experience it is. As time flies, they had to leave the ship while I went to the Steakhouse restaurant. The days are getting smaller and smaller until complete disembarkation. There are eight days left from that day! Again, I am haunted by various bouts of emotion. Joy and sorrow mix like two wild rivers leading into one. What and how many times it all went through my head in those days, you wouldn't believe me.

It was only in the last few weeks that I became more and more aware that the possibility of returning to work on a ship was very thin, and I tried to use it every day and fill it to the maximum. I mentioned on a couple of occasions that everything that is beautiful is short-lived. This is going to sound both weird and crazy but I tell you that this saying is very appropriate to me also regarding this contract. Nine months is a long time, and I have already written you a page before about it, but when you live a new adventure every day, that period flies by and once it comes to an end, you just stop and ask yourself:

*'It's already over? Omg how fast it went!'*—I am sure that you have found yourself many times in such a moment, when for something that sounds like a hundred years in the beginning, once it passes, you wonder when it passed.

So here we are on our last cruise. The last seven days on the Liberty Wave.

The possibility of going to the ports was only on the first and last, Corfu and Katakolon. In Corfu we really had skinny free time, so we just took one of those tour buses that take you through the city for about half an hour. Anyway, with a 12% battery, tired and exhausted in all ways, we rode on an open bus where the Greek climate with a phenomenal breeze makes you sleepy even more. Corfu has really crystal clear water which looks beautiful and exotic.

In Katakolon for the last time, the Balkan team came out. My roommates Branko and Vladimir, Elizabeth, and I decided to visit Olympia, which has been known to you and me since before. It didn't matter to me where we were going anymore, but just to have a good time last time, which was the case.

Since Elizabeth and I were finishing the contract together, this time we decided that she would visit my part of Croatia, where I grew up, for the first time. We wanted to take some time to rest and soccer, which was followed by a large number of people because of the European Championship that year, and after that, we travelled together from Croatia to Peru so she can also finally see her family.

The day before disembarkation was filled with sailing. (Sea day)

After the last work done at Steakhouse restaurant that evening, we agreed with the whole team to meet at the crew bar, which is always the case before the disembarkation day. It's one of those evenings I don't think any crew member likes. Why? As I've written many times, it's an evening filled with a storm of emotions where at one point you don't want to leave your friends at all while at another you can't wait to get off the ship just for free time to finally rest like a man and to see your family. One of the biggest jokes between us crew members is that at the end of each contract we say it was our last one or one more, and then we will about to finish with the ship life.

But then after some time spent at home when most of the money saved is spent, easily decides on 'another contract' and like that 5–10 years pass, and you are still on board. But for us, it was not like that this time. That evening, our society was dominated by the Balkan mafia and half of South America. Each of your friends is looking for a joint photo to remember and in the hope that one day we will meet again in this crazy world.

A good number of years have passed since my first contract, but still, every scene (and more than that) that I have described to you in all three contracts has remained etched in my memory as if it happened yesterday. Now, when I look at all the adventures we have experienced, I am indescribably sorry that I did not use them even more, I 'sobered up' just before the end of the contract.

Yes, that's right, the hardest is that last night that won't fade in your memory. That evening, as a souvenir, I took a picture of the cabin, which made us the funniest 'house' in 2016, and a place that will always remind me and my friends of the craziest gatherings.

I can imagine this sounds weird to you now dear readers, but when I think back to how many times I actually enjoyed spending time in that little cramped cabin I lacked nothing at all. Most people complained about so little space but not me, I don't even think I would have enjoyed it so much if we had a cabin the size of a normal room on land. Even in the half-dark cabin, with a small light on the wall or a turned On TV, with a broadcast of some soccer game, when I came for short breaks and took a nap on the couch, that were special moments of pleasure. Even today, if I get up early and use those morning hours in the best possible way—with a good workout of soccer session, later after lunch if I still have free time, I lie down on the couch, turn on the TV with some soccer game (no matter which one, as long is somebody playing) and relax to the limit of falling asleep. That soccer really relaxes and makes me happy in different ways.

After this great last get-together, we escorted that night for the last time as members of the CL2 company, and just waiting for the morning to dawn, and say that hard goodbye to the ship life once and for all.

## 11 June 2016—End of the contract

That next morning on the way out we still hugged some friends wishing each other all the best, and what I mentioned at the end of the first contract, when the last time you take off that NameTag and throw it in the basket, and you hear that sound, you become aware of that it is over. At that moment, the feeling I got that very first day when boarding the Aries flew through my body. No one can ever take away or erase that first feeling when I stepped into this type of life. When everything is completely new to you, without any knowledge, you feel that indescribable joy and excitement! If I could, I would always go back to that day and that moment to go through that experience again.

When we were already quite far from the ship in the back then hot Venice, the city where I boarded this unforgettable contract, I turned to the Liberty Wave and saw the ship for the last time, I escort him with that sad look and even a few tears. I don't know why am I such an emotional person about some things but that last look at the ship was the hardest for me at that time. We spent a couple of good hours in Venice and a little wider sightseeing of this city on the water. This time we did not fly by plane but took a faster way (unlike the first time)— by bus from Venice to my dear city Varaždin.

In the museum CR7

Mykonos, Greece

Acropolis of Athens, Greece

Elizabeth and hot Santorini, Greece

Katakolon, Greece

With brother and parents in Split, Croatia

Best house in 2016

Sign Off day, Venice, Italy

# 1.8 Conclusion and end of ship life

My dear readers, up to this point our ship life is over and everything you were interested in and what I wrote and described the ship and beyond, I deeply hope I have answered you and shown you the picture you have been looking for. Indeed, I have put all those most important details on paper so that for you future sailors, you can now clearly see what you can really expect. No matter how difficult the beginning will be for you, remember my advice and words of support because believe me, you can go far, just don't give up because only like that you will know your true self and what you are capable of.

Also for you, future guests on cruises, you have realised what kind of people there are and what kind of picture we have of them so I will kindly ask you, on behalf of all crew members, if you are travelling on vacation, please have patience with any kind of service because we don't ask you much, just a little bit of common sense and reality.

I wish all future sailors and guests who will spend some time on cruises, from the bottom of my heart, unforgettable adventures, to meet as many people as possible, and discover best friends, to learn amazing experiences that have never been before, and above all that, I wish you a peaceful sea! (as we always like to wish that to our ship's family) ☺

If you decide to continue reading this book you can still expect my new experiences with this world because the adventures here are not over. Even after ship life, I continue to expand my horizons and enrich my knowledge of many things that we are obliged to learn in this very short life. I firmly believe that for some sites you might even be pleasantly surprised but I leave it up to you whether or not you want to find out what else is going on after the ship because I mention it also later and often. Thank you if you read at least this part, and I hope you enjoyed it.

*Life on a Cruise Ship shortly described ...*

- *Days of the week don't exist, you are orientated by the ports*
- *A crewmember's easy day is to work less than 10 hours.*
- *There are no days off, only hours off.*
- *Your last name could be confused with a country by the guests.*

- *When you reach a new port, regardless of how tired you are, instead of going to sleep, you always choose to go out.*
- *No matter how you feel, you always wear a smile.*
- *Crew food sometimes is a mystery.*
- *You learn the skill of looking sober when you are drunk.*
- *Every boat drill is like a punishment when you are breakfast off (off duty).*
- *It can happen that you don't feel sunshine for a couple of days, even though you are in the Caribbean.*
- *We are lost when we talk about dates.*
- *Every day is fulfilled with a new adventure.*
- *Hours back means party all night.*
- *Getting drunk in a Crew bar is cheaper than on the land.*
- *To be without a nametag onboard is like being naked.*
- *After working on the ship, you can't stand an alarm.*
- *The Captain is like a movie star.*
- *There is a reason to party every day.*
- *You love the adrenalin of going back on the ship from ports at the very last minute.*
- *Waiting for your turn for the bathroom in your cabin.*
- *Spending a full day with the same people and still after work, enjoying their company the rest of the night.*
- *Laundry room is your next stop after Crew bar.*
- *Being alone in the cabin is like winning the lottery.*
- *No matter how far your home is, feels like you were born on board.*
- *Signing Off from the first contract means going home broke.*
- *When you are onboard, you can't wait to go home. And at home, you can't wait to go back.*

### My colleagues' opinions, views, and experiences about Ship's life

Before I start a new chapter in my life, you have the opportunity to hear the opinions, views, and experiences of a couple of crew members with whom I have shared this way of life.

\*(Entered year of age, are the years with which they started the first contract and not the current age)

Questions:

1. *What made you decide to go to work on the ship?*
2. *What was your very first feeling when you found out you were going to work on a ship?*
3. *First impression when you saw the ship?*
4. *Favourite ports?*
5. *The craziest experience?*
6. *The things from the ship you miss the most?*
7. *The most polite guests? The worst guests?*
8. *Do you ever wish to come back? If so, for how long?*
9. *What was the reason for your departure from the ship, and how did you feel when you left the ship—actually went out through the gate for the last time?*
10. *Would you recommend the ship life to anyone? If so, for how long?*

1.  *First wish for travel. Then because of the bad situation in Peru and the desire for a better job.*

2.  *I still wasn't sure if I should do it because I didn't want to leave my mother.*

3.  *There were five of us from Peru when we boarded that day. For me, that day was a dream come true because we were boarding in Seattle (Washington, USA) and I have always wanted to visit the USA.*

4.  *Bermuda, Costa Maya and Cozumel (Mexico)*

5.  *In Los Angeles (USA), when we went out five of us and were late for the ship, i.e., work, even two hours because we took the wrong bus on the way back. We were free for breakfast so we wanted to use that to go out. It was only our second week on board. Since we were one group that was supposed to start for lunch, due to such a delay we later all ended up in the restaurant manager's office. We all passed without warning which was great luck.*

6.  *The second-craziest and worst experience was in Costa Maya when we got drunk on Corona and Tequila. To this day, I don't know how we went through security without them noticing something suspicious. There was a 'Choco-night' on the buffet that evening, which means a lot of work. Worst experience ever, we all just wanted a few minutes of sleep in those moments. After work, two more beers at the crew bar and finally going to sleep hahaha.*

7.  *What I miss the most is waking up every day in a different port, in a different country. There is also a lack of friends who made every contract memorable.*

8.  *Canadians, some Americans while the worst Russians.*

9.  *Of course, but on the condition that I am younger, but since that is no longer possible, then only as a guest.*

10. *I wanted to go back to at least one more contract but we decided to start life on land anyway.*

*I would recommend it to young people but not to the restaurant department. It is up to them as much as they want and can for a long time.*

### Sasha, 22, restaurant dep., Serbia

1. *I left because I wanted to travel and this was an ideal opportunity!*
2. *I felt excited. I went into something unknown, and I am a person who loves challenges.*
3. *When I saw the ship, I honestly didn't feel anything special because I knew how big those ships are.*
4. *Favourite ports in America are Cozumel and Huatulco (Mexico) and Miami (USA). While in Europe Stockholm (Sweden), Helsinki (Finland), and Warnemünde Rostock (Germany).*
5. *The craziest experience? I don't really know, bro. There were so many that I couldn't single out any, and you were in almost all of them.*
6. *Honestly, I only miss the people I worked with from the ship. Our whole team, the best team ever.*
7. *I don't really remember the guests.*
8. *I was thinking of going back but to a different position. I gave up in the end though.*
9. *I left the ship because I was 'fed up' with everything and everyone. I felt relieved when I finally left the ship.*
10. *I would recommend it to everyone because no matter what, it is a very good experience, and you travel half the world.*

### Ines, 29, Casino, Shorex, Croatia

1. *Recession, relationship, and company breakdown, all at the same time.*
2. *Shock, excitement, fear.*
3. *Enthusiasm, happiness, falling in love with a new adventure.*
4. *Mexico, New York, and Bermuda.*
5. *Meeting a person who has changed gender by surgery from a man to a woman.*
6. *An adventure of meeting new people, cultures, and countries, a closeness to different people that is hard to have in normal life because we are all on a ship far from our lives, and we only have each other. Friendships and feelings that are not forgotten. Most friendships still last and even from the first contract that was more than six years ago.*
7. *The most polite guests are from Texas while New Yorkers are the worst.*

8. *I want to come back but it's hard to say until you come back. After four years at home, you get used to the freedom of movement, food choices, and security that life at home provides, especially after an illness. I don't know how long I would go back and what it would look like now in my new life but I would love to try it once in a while if things get that way in life.*

9. *The reason for leaving was illness. I felt like someone had ripped my life off. My whole world burst like a balloon. I lost my job, the life I loved, my career, my boyfriend, my friends... in just one day. As I walked through the gangway I felt immense sadness and fear of the future. Not only because of the disease but also because my whole life has disappeared in an instant, and what awaits me. I was also afraid of how I would function in the real world after three years of ship life.*

10. *I would not recommend the ship to anyone just those who are curious, adventurous, and who have thick skin. Anyone who is too sensitive or does not have a stronger guard will be exploited in one way or another. Everyone goes through some kind of exploitation he could not have imagined before. The reason is that people are here temporarily and far from their surroundings, so they have a feeling that none of the people they are exposed to at home will know. Also because of the diversity of cultures we have different expectations of good and bad things. We all end up shocked because everyone at least once experiences a deep disappointment that they didn't believe was possible to experience because people don't do it in their midst. Over time, you learn about certain cultural differences and generally know what to expect from whom.*

### Leylla, 25, restaurant dep., Peru

1. *One of my cousins who worked on the cruiser inspired me. I wanted to see the world, save money, and have an exciting life surfing in the sun.*

2. *I was very nervous, and I couldn't believe I was going to work so far away from my family. I was also nervous about my orientation problem. I would probably get lost on the way to the ship but luckily, I travelled with a couple of future colleagues to the same ship.*

3. *When I saw the ship, I thought wow, this is really huge!*

266

4.  *My first three contracts had a few, already to me, boring ports—Miami and the Bahamas. But I admit that I fell in love with the Bahamas and the beaches which are a great pleasure.*

5.  *When I was discovering the city of Corfu by bike. I got to the centre, bought a pizza that I had been waiting for too long, and I had to return within half an hour where of course I was 40 minutes late.*

6.  *Breakfast! When everything is ready right after you wake up.* ☺

7.  *The British are more conservative and will not complain at all. Latino guests are friendly and have high expectations from someone who is from the same country. The Chinese always want only hot water while guests from India disturb everyone in the restaurant with many demands. I think the worst guests are from Italy when I carried three main dishes for just one person. Wow.*

8.  *I love that experience, travelling to many countries, rocking a boat, knowing many different nationalities of which I met my today's boyfriend. After five years of many experiences at sea, now is the time to anchor. I'm not saying no to going on a ship again because you never know if life will get you back there.*

9.  *When I returned due to a health problem, after recovering I expected to do at least one more contract but then came the opportunity to live in Canada.*

10. *Of course, after working in a restaurant everything else comes as a game. My sister is currently working on Princess as a photographer.*

### *Veljko, 21, restaurant dep., Serbia*

1.  *Money and travel.*

2.  *Strange feeling, I didn't believe I was going to travel by ship for 9 months.*

3.  *When I saw the ship for the first time, in my case Aries, it was as if I had seen a spaceship.*

4.  *There are quite a few, but let it be Warnemünde Rostock (Germany) and Stockholm (Sweden).*

5.  *The craziest experience? Well, I don't know, when I went out to Costa Maya (Mexico) with a friend from Macedonia. We enjoyed the beach,*

*spent all the money so we had to beg people on the beach to give us some money for a taxi so we could get back on the ship.*

6. *Mostly a team! The people I hung out with.*

7. *The most polite guests? There are a lot of them, and I am still in contact with them. They even looked for a ship I was on just to see me. The worst guests? Mostly you meet them right away, from day one. They are out of the mood and looking for a reason to complain.*

8. *There's always that feeling that I'd go back to the ship for at least one more contract.*

9. *When you have had enough of everything, tired and longing for your country and family. But only at the beginning, you feel good because soon after a while you start to miss everything from the ship. It's hard to explain.*

10. *Of course, I would recommend it to everyone even though it is quite difficult and not for everyone.*

### Lizzet, 26, restaurant dep., Shorex, Peru

1. *Travelling to different countries.*
2. *Happiness.*
3. *Excitement.*
4. *Halifax (Nova Scotia, Canada), Portland, Victoria, New York (USA)*
5. *Working on a ship is already crazy enough.*
6. *Usual jobs.*
7. *Very friendly guests from the Caribbean while the worst Brits and people from New York.*
8. *Yes, two more years.*
9. *I haven't left yet.*
10. *I would definitely recommend the ship's life.*

### Maria Luz, 22, restaurant dep., Peru

1. *Because I wanted to travel the world and that seemed like a good choice. Travel and still be paid.*

2.   *Super. At first, I couldn't believe it because I had never worked in my life before and had just finished school. Even my parents didn't believe me at first what kind of job I got.*

3.   *I was amazed! Incredibly!*

4.   *All! But I prefer ports in Europe because I love history and that was my main focus.*

5.   *Since everything was new to me, there were a lot of crazy experiences on board.*

6.   *What I miss the most is going to dinner and then to parties. Then going to different beaches every day, playing different sports, having a gym close by...*

7.   *No offence but in my opinion, there are two different classes. Americans are the worst and Europeans are the most polite guests.*

8.   *I would love to come back but as a guest.*

9.   *I left the ship because I was planning to go on vacation with my boyfriend, who was also working on the ship, which was especially difficult to plan for both of us to have a vacation at the same time so I left for such reasons. They gave me a year to decide if I wanted to go back but I decided to stay ashore because I would like to start a family one day and something like that on a ship is not quite possible with the contracts being quite long. I left the Aries in 2018 which was also my first ship to board.*

10.  *Would I recommend it? I personally have never been forced to stay or leave. I didn't have a responsibility in life that I had to stay even though I didn't like it, for money or other specific reasons. I had a lot of adventures and fun and because of that I never looked at the ship as a serious business. Of course, you need to follow some rules but nothing has ever stopped me from doing what I wanted. But again it all depends on what type of job you do and what you really like to do.*

### Ana, 25, restaurant dep., Croatia

1.   *I opted for the ship because, on social media, I saw some acquaintances working on it. I wanted a new experience but also to get over the first serious relationship I came out of.*

2. *I was super excited because I didn't know what to expect. I had a positive nervousness that turned into motivation.*

3. *When I first got off the bus and saw the ship, I was in delirium! Only the weight and size of the ship are astounding!*

4. *Favourite port of Miami (USA) and the whole of Scandinavia. Two different worlds. From a large and developed city to breath-taking fjords.*

5. *It's hard for me to describe one experience. From crazy nights, laughter in the work shift, great friends who motivated me and made me laugh from hour to hour. Even fatigue became a joke to me.*

6. *What I miss the most from the boat is definitely the laughter and individual friendships. A bar also where almost everything is $ 1.00 hahaha...*

7. *It's hard for me to name the most polite guests but the most uncomfortable are the Americans.*

8. *I would like to go back to maybe one contract but only on the condition that I have more free time. Since it is an impossible mission in such an environment, my answer is no.*

9. *My reason for leaving was that I love the freedom of movement a little too much to sacrifice it for a compromise of 'free life on board'. I don't like routine, and I think you never live on a ship with full lungs. When I left the ship, I was full of emotion. Looking over my shoulder at that great floating city where I created some of the most beautiful and memorable moments is not easy to remain indifferent! I think most people wonder if they made a mistake in the decision but I followed my heart, and I knew I belonged somewhere else.*

10. *I would definitely not recommend the ship to anyone as it is not for everyone. In the pictures, everything may seem fabulous, but behind all the smiles there is a lot of work, fatigue, pressure, and even tears. I would recommend it to those who know the limits or have good motivation (such as financial or moving personal boundaries) and to those who are ready for an adventure full of ups and downs.*

### Andrija, 37, photographer, Croatia

1.  The reason for my going on the vessel was simple since I am an adventurer by nature, I like to travel. It seemed to me to be the best choice to travel and see the world and on the other hand, to still be paid.

2.  The feeling was fantastic! Especially since I left a month before the scheduled deadline, as there was a lack of photographers on my ship.

3.  So this is my home... wow I have the biggest house in the world! ☺

4.  I love all ports, but really all of them! Each had something special.

5.  Ugh that was a lot, the whole trip, I would call it all a crazy experience that marked my life in a special way and guided me in a special direction. Without a ship, life would not be the same!

6.  I miss everything! People, friends, acquaintances, crew party... simply everything!

7.  The most polite guests? There were a lot of them, different nations. The worst were the guests who stole. Those who wanted everything for free on the last cruises and somehow we still have to pay them when they are photographed as if they were Hollywood stars, to say the least. Personally, I didn't like the ones who understood the concept of hygiene so much that they didn't take a shower, and then such stinking people came to do portraits.

8.  I always want to come back. The work was hard but I felt fulfilled. I could do that job for a very long time, especially since I progressed very quickly. I took the position of assistant manager after two months as a complete rookie and as my manager, Thomas said, you have a good future in the company.

9.  Reason for leaving? Unfortunately, on vacation I found out that I was not continuing my next contract on a new ship with my old manager who wanted to take me with him, but that I had to stay working on the old ship with a new manager who had been in business for 12 years and didn't know even how to walk, not to mention being a photo manager. He was terribly jealous of my success and knowledge and thus saw in me a direct competitor, we did not understand each other at all. That's why I didn't come back because I believe I would have thrown him off the ship.

10. *After my experience on the ship, I recommended the boat, the trip, and the world tour that you were paid to everyone (even to those who are less smart). Everyone should do this before they decide to settle down and start a family. And for as long as he likes and as long as he feels fulfilled. If I had the opportunity to leave at least 10 years ago, I believe I would have stayed on the ship for a very, very long time. My recommendation to anyone who has an adventurous spirit and is not afraid of the world, go on the vessel, see the world because the world will not reach you. Don't let old age ask you where your youth was. Go through, live, enjoy… "they say you live only once, I don't think so, you live every day, and you only die once." – Unknown.*

*Take advantage of every second, the ship is an unforgettable wonderful experience that everyone should try at least once in their life, even for a short time!*

### Alejandro, 22, restaurant dep., Peru

1. *For three reasons. Number one I was interested in the idea of working on a ship. Under two because I wanted to become independent and have my own money. Under three because I love to travel and discover new countries and cultures.*
2. *I was excited and sad at the same time but for my parents, it was worse. I was happy though because I knew it was time to start a new experience.*
3. *Huge ship! Not even in my dreams did I think that one day I would board a ship like this.*
4. *Mykonos and Santorini (Greece)*
5. *When guests thought I was German or Croat.*
6. *Friends! I have met special people in my life that I will never forget, from different countries. I will always carry them in my mind and heart.*
7. *There are different types of them. Europeans are calmer than Americans. I once served an elderly couple from North America who made a letter saying they wanted to adopt me. Joke aside, it was the most beautiful thing anyone had done for me.*
8. *I thought if, then for at least another two years. I feel like I haven't yet filled myself with such an experience!*

9.  *I had to finish college. I was very sad but I just had to leave the ship because of it. It was 2016.*

10.  *Not everyone. Only people who work hard and don't complain. I would only recommend it for a couple of years.*


### Jorge, 18, restaurant dep., Peru

1.  *Money*

2.  *Freedom and stability but at the same time unknown fear.*

3.  *This sh\*\* is really big!*

4.  *Anchorage (Canada)—nature; Vancouver (Canada)—city; Roatan (Honduras)—ocean, Callao (Peru)—people.*

5.  *Bungee jumping in Acapulco (Mexico) and flirting in Aruba (Caribbean).*

6.  *Travel, money, friends…*

7.  *North America very friendly, Germans the most disciplined and South America the worst.*

8.  *I will, this year.*

9.  *My father got sick, and I had to go back, but I didn't worry too much about leaving because I knew I was going to come back.*

10.  *Yes, at least for six months. Because it teaches you about temperament and patience.*


### Branko, 26, restaurant dep., Montenegrin (lives in Bosnia)

1.  *A journey.*

2.  *Extra feeling.*

3.  *Since I grew up next to a shipyard, I was OK.*

4.  *New York and Seattle (USA) and Cozumel (Mexico).*

5.  *When you get drunk at the crew bar for a Balkan party.*

6.  *I don't miss anything because I'm still working on the ship.*

7.  *The worst from Asia, the most polite from Europe.*

8.  *and*

9.  *I'm coming back obviously hahaha…*

10.  *I would recommend the ship for sure. Once, for a man to mature and see the world.*

*Nill, 27, Entertainment, Brazil*

1.  *I've always wanted to travel the world, make money, and create a career out of entertaining people.*
2.  *The excitement of achieving a personal goal!*
3.  *Amazed, overwhelmed, surprised! Everything is new and there is a lot to see.*
4.  *Barcelona (Spain) and Mykonos (Greece).*
5.  *Party until the morning and anchor in Spain for as long as two months.*
6.  *People and nice surroundings in the crew bar.*
7.  *The best guests from Australia, the worst from Italy.*
8.  *and*
9.  *I'm still working on the ship.*
10. *Absolutely! An amazing experience that only the people who work there know how it is. I would recommend it for at least one year.*

*Ivona, 22, restaurant dep., Croatia*

1.  *There were actually a couple of influences on me that prompted me for that kind of work. At the age of 12, I first heard about this type of work, which immediately aroused my curiosity, but again I did not think that it could one day become possible for me. Six years later, after high school, the idea came to me again, and I would very likely decide to do it but my father was strictly against it even though I was 18 and dependent on him so I could still not live that desire. After three and a half years later, Croatia experienced a major crisis. The recession that made me unemployed for over a year, I have to say heavy and broken heart, I finally went on a ship. At that moment, I concluded that absolutely nothing could keep me in Croatia, and I believed that such a new chapter in my life could help me progress, which later turned out to be the case.*
2.  *I remember it like it was yesterday. I was in my room when a person from the agency (for which I applied) called me and informed me that I had been accepted and that they would find out the boarding date in the next few weeks. I literally felt like this was my first day for the rest of my life. It was a mixture of happiness, excitement, an explosion of fear, and butterflies in my stomach.*

274

3.  *When I first saw Aries, it looked magical to me. I would even say that those same feelings were present six months ago when I received that call.*

4.  *Bermuda, St. Martin (Caribbean), and Stockholm (Sweden).*

5.  *Wow! There are a really huge number of them! Let's say Bermuda when we went to the beach for a party after 10 hours of work. We spent the whole night partying, dancing, drinking, having an incredible amount of fun, returning to the boat early in the morning with a friend from Serbia, one hour before the start of the morning shift at 7:00. The supervisor sent us to the bathroom to freshen up. There was laughter! Finishing the shift without any problem, we left the boat again all afternoon, returning to the evening shift, secretly sipping during the shift, once again finishing the shift without any difficulties and problems, running into the cabin, a little bit more of drinking, getting off the ship on the beach again and repeating all of the above and so on for a month. After that I disembarked, i.e., I finished the contract. I told myself even then that I knew it was going to be the best time of my life.*

6.  *I would say discipline and food. Once I got back to reality and life on land, I realised that these two things were of extremely high quality on board when I compared them to life on land.*

7.  *The most polite and very friendly guests, not only on board but also around the world I would say they are from Northern Europe while the worst guests are definitely from Asia, mostly Chinese and Arabs, without manners and respect.*

8.  *Ever since I found my peace with my partner where I am right now, no, I wouldn't go back to the ship, and I don't miss it at all. I am happy for what I have achieved and when I would go back to 2011 I would do the same thing again but given that we both got off the boat, from that moment on I don't feel the same desire for the ship as before.*

9.  *I found my 'other half'. We met on a ship and since then my world has been totally different. My priorities have completely changed, and we both agreed that ship life as a couple no longer suits us. I even felt relief because honestly, it was like I was stuck on that ship and that kind of life. There were times when I was even scared that I would never be able to leave the ship and thus live my whole life in an unreal dimension. I*

*did not regret for a second that I left the ship because as I mentioned, my priorities changed.*

10. *I wouldn't recommend the ship to anyone because obviously, not everyone has the same feelings and perceptions about it and the capacity to deal with it all. But I would definitely recommend it to anyone who can compare it to the person I was 10 years ago. I speak and will always say that this is an amazing opportunity to get to know life and more importantly, get to know yourself in a version you could never have even thought existed. It's not just a job, it's a lifestyle. You begin to get to know better a world that is nothing like what you thought before. Only then you do actually realise how little you knew before, and that no school or book can teach you, what ship life can!*

### Martha, restaurant dep., Peru

1. *New experience, even better to learn English and earn even more money.*
2. *I was very excited to visit different countries and travel by ship.*
3. *Excited to be there.*
4. *All of Europe, especially Greece.*
5. *Visit the Holy Land, do things I've never been to in my own country, like swimming with dolphins, visiting a water park and going on a huge water slide.*
6. *Travel to different countries, meet different cultures, and make new friends from different parts of the world.*
7. *Very friendly guests Americans and some Latino population, while the worst guests from Italy, some Latinos, and India.*
8. *Maybe, I'm not sure. If I would, then for six months, no more.*
9. *I left the ship due to family problems but also due to fatigue and exhaustion from working on it. I was a bit sad because I knew I had friends I would probably never see again but also because of the good and bad experiences the ship gave me.*
10. *Yes! But I think it's a job just for a couple of years.*

**Selene, 20, restaurant dep., Peru**

1. *My family needed better financial support and that's why I decided to work on the ship.*
2. *I was very excited when I found out I was going on a ship because it was something new, and I knew it would help my family a lot.*
3. *I was scared and excited! I felt a combination of different feelings and great curiosity but mostly fear.*
4. *I love Europe so most of the European ports are among my favourites and that is Italy and Greece.*
5. *I think every time I went out to a new port it was a crazy experience. I never could have known what the adrenaline would be like when you run back to the ship just so you wouldn't be late, it's more than enough.*
6. *I'm still on board right now so I just miss my home.*
7. *I would say Americans are the best, most of them are very nice. The worst guests are definitely Arabs and Indians who I don't like too much.*
8. *and*
9. *Once I leave ship life I think I will not return again.*
10. *I do not recommend it to everyone. If someone really needs a job then definitely but to be honest, this is not a life I would choose so I don't believe it is suitable for everyone. This type of life is not bad, I just think not all people are made for this.*

**Daniel, 33, Youth program, Brazil**

1. *Travelling and saving money.*
2. *Thrill.*
3. *A lot of information.*
4. *Mediterranean ports.*
5. *Attend the Olympic Games in Rio de Janeiro when the ship anchored there.*
6. *People.*
7. *The most polite Canadians while the worst Americans.*
8. *It depends on the position.*
9. *The last time I left was in 2019. I left because I felt my chapter here was over. I felt I had to live a real-life, without a 'curfew' and a lot of rules.*

10.     *Yes, about two years.*

### Stephanie, 32, restaurant dep., Brazil

1.      *Money and places I will visit.*
2.      *A mix of happiness and worry.*
3.      *A little scary.*
4.      *Santorini (Greece) and Barcelona (Spain).*
5.      *Dealing with different people.*
6.      *I miss friends from other countries, which I can't visit very easily.*
7.      *The Americans are very friendly while for the worst I think they are from China.*
8.      *Not anymore.*
9.      *I felt relieved because it was a difficult experience but also a bit sad because I didn't know if I would ever see friends again.*
10.     *It depends on the person. If someone needs 'quick money' this should be a good opportunity but maybe only for one contract.*

### Brigida, 30, restaurant dep., Peru

1.      *I decided to work on a ship because I love to travel, and even at that time I was 30 years old and full of energy for such things.*
2.      *I was very excited to be working on the ship. It was my first experience of this type, and the information itself sounds great that I will be paid for the job I will be travelling on.*
3.      *Very excited when I arrived with the other Peruvians. But I still remember that hard day and the pain in my legs and arms. All-day training and work until 10:00 p.m., I was very tired that day.*
4.      *My favourites are New York (USA), Cozumel (Mexico), Livorno (Italy), Warnemünde Rostock (Germany) and Mykonos (Greece).*
5.      *Ugh I have a lot of them, at least one in each contract but once I was preparing a restaurant for breakfast, and saw a guest walking around the kitchen looking for something. I immediately went to him and explained that he was in a restricted area. I was trying to escort him out of the kitchen when suddenly he asked me, with a laugh, if I knew who he is. Of course, I didn't know to which he replied that he is the captain.*

278

*I asked him to show the documents, which turned out to be the captain, only in civilian clothes. I blushed the same second from shame, but he didn't resent anything and praised me for doing my job well. When I told this to my friends we all burst out laughing.*

6. *Friends. I met a lot of good friends that I miss a lot. They, but also a classic cheesecake hahaha.*

7. *Very friendly and talkative guests from America and Italy. The worst, I think the Chinese, for that reason because they order everything at the same time and are very messy but again very grateful.*

8. *In fact, yes! I want to come back because I have the experience, at least on two contracts but I would have to think hard because it would be difficult since I have a child now.*

9. *I got pregnant and left the ship after just one day since I did the pregnancy test so everything went pretty fast. I was very sad because the father of my child stayed there and when I got off the boat I looked back and started crying because I didn't want to leave him. I was also sad because I knew this was the last time I worked on a ship.*

10. *I recommend it to people who are interested in working on a ship. But the truth is that anyone who goes on a ship has to be emotionally very strong regardless of age because there is always something that can and will surprise you. I do not recommend more than five years otherwise you will become as crazy as I am.*

### Aleksandar, 26, restaurant dep., Bosnia

1. *Youth, travel, money.*
2. *Excited and nervous.*
3. *A huge ship that made me nervous.*
4. *Cozumel (Mexico) and St. Petersburg (Russia)*
5. *There is nothing that is the craziest.*
6. *Travel and NY steak.*
7. *The most polite Germans and Chileans while the worst Indians.*
8. *I do not want.*
9. *I wasn't aware it was the last one because it was decided from the mainland. Going out through the gate has always been a remarkable feeling.*

*10.    Yes but not in the same dep. A contract or two depends on the person.*

***

As for my answers to these questions, given that most of them are throughout the book, here I can only answer which are my favourite ports and craziest experience...

Of all the places we visited it is not easy to pick a couple of them as favourites, I only realise this now when I personally answer, so I believe my former colleagues and friends also had a pretty tricky question. However, I will answer this question a little differently. My four favourite places, which I have visited so far from all countries, and four favourite places that I still try and wish to visit with all my heart.

The four favourite places I have visited so far are Machu Picchu (Peru), Bermuda, Cozumel (Mexico), and Madeira (Portugal).

The four favourite places I still want to visit are Hawaii (USA), the Caribbean, Bali (Indonesia), and Africa. As for travelling, my biggest dream and target is Hawaii. That beautiful archipelago is located so far away in the heart of the Pacific that looks like a piece of paradise. If such a wish comes true, I intend to stay there for at least three weeks. That we have a blissful time to discover almost every island, those green nature, magical waterfalls, and you can guess, those fantastic beaches, where watching the sunset is something special. I would love to even learn a little bit of the language which sounds very interesting to me. (Aloha)

Then the Caribbean, a part of the world that I can never neglect. Although I did not mention a certain place, that's the point because there is no special place. I would also like to have enough time there, to discover island by island (although there is a lot of them) and their unique beauties, to taste their cuisine and culture, and of course, those magical beaches.

Next eager destination—Bali. Indonesia seems to me like another interesting adventure full of very kind people from which a man can learn a lot if he wants to. I mentioned that I met Indonesians while working on a ship, as a particularly quiet kind of people. Their level of humbleness and hard work is at a level that many should reflect. Of course, it is not only the people in question but also the beauties of that country.

Under another desired trip, Africa is also on the list. Of course not the whole just a few places in the north (or rather Afro—Asia) such as Jerusalem and Petra, and South Africa like Cape Town and Johannesburg, honestly I don't even know which one exactly. I would also like to go through that safari one day, which if I do, I hope I won't train running in front of the lions, even though it would be a hell of a useful workout. ☺

Now you know that, so who knows, if I achieve those 'couple' of desired destinations, I might get new topics and inspiration for writing a new book. God willing!

As for the craziest experience during ship life… uh… what to say to this without me already writing. Let's classify it as the craziest—the worst and the craziest—the best.

The craziest—the worst is definitely the movie *Lost in LA*. I wrote about that and why exactly this city I don't consider with nice memories.

The craziest—the best… omg… going out to Huatulco (Mexico) with friends and having an unforgettable time; when we stole an entire tray of chocolate bananas from the buffet, which I smuggled all the way to my cabin; when I ran after the trolly on the floors I left in the elevator that went on, I don't even know how many floors. I just run up and down looking for my trolly. Going to sleep (for an hour) during working hours when crazy El Colombiano was the Maitre'd hahaha… although there are many other crazy adventures, these four are enough.

Here is one a classic joke about ship life:

*Last night as I lay sleeping,*
*I died or so it seemed.*
*Then I went to heaven,*
*but only in my dream.*
*Up there St. Peter met me,*
*standing at the pearly gates.*
*He said: 'I must check your record,*
*please stand here and wait'.*
*He turned and said: 'Your record*
*is covered with terrible flaws.*
*On earth, I see you rallied*
*for every losing cause.*

*I see that you drank alcohol,*
*smoked, and used drugs too.*
*Fact is, you've done everything*
*a good person should never do.*
*We can't have people like you up here,*
*Your life is full of sin'.*
*Then he read the last of my record,*
*took my hand and said: 'Come in'.*
*He led me up to the big boss and said:*
*'Take him in, and treat him well.*
*He used to work on cruise ships,*
*He's done his time in hell'.*
*– Unknown*

\*\*\*

… and finally, something from the heart…

*Life on the ocean…*

*Doesn't matter who you are or where you come from, as long as you are nearby me on this wide ocean,*
*in my thoughts you will exist, without disappearing and full of emotion.*
*My brother and sister, you always will be until the end,*
*missing a sea family is very hard I will not pretend.*
*Remember when you go your destiny is with the ship's family and don't you forget,*
*always carry those blue things because the sun isn't down yet.*

*Take a step, for the last time very proudly, and don't cry, just try,*
*knowing that you've left a trail for something that will never die.*

*The wave of joy and excitement feel one more time,*
*let a new adventure happily fly to the port and become your prime.*

*Where to drop anchor while the soul is thirsty still,*
*and shouts for more, from that unsinkable hill.*

*As the days go by it doesn't matter, as long as your heart lives freely and*
*breathes deeply,*
*    can you see those magical colours on the sky filled and wild completely!*

*Once more time on this gate turn around,*
*and make sure you heard that last sound.*

*My wings will find the mainland one day,*
*but to this love, the colour will never become grey.*

*For wherever I go where there is no sea,*
*every sailor knows this can't be a way to be free.*

*So don't worry my dear mother, that I'm far away,*
*God is my protection and in this nature He wants me to stay.*

*Ship's life left in me a picture very sweet and strong,*
*even today wanna drag me in every minute, I know I can't be wrong,*
*for something I was living for and I was born.*

*Goran Žganec*

*And to close this ship chapter, I would like to take this opportunity to thank
the special people who made this opportunity of a lifetime possible for me from
the very beginning. The only source from which all those desires originated,
which once seemed impossible to realise. People without whom I would not be
able to get and live such a huge and valuable experience! These people are my
parents!*

*Without them and their financial help, I wouldn't have thought of such a
thing as feasible. Thank you dear parents from the bottom of my heart for your
love that you have given me but also for that you continue to give! Thank you for
every selfless act and sacrifice you suffered just to help me reach such a great
goal, even though you were way too well aware that it would be very difficult to*

283

*live with the thoughts and care of your son being miles away from home! Your love is recognised by your deeds! With all my heart, thank you very much!*

*Goran Žganec*

# 2. Life on Land

## 2.1 After the ship

As I mentioned at the beginning after the ship nothing will remain the same which was confirmed later. The whole experience we gained during those few years will certainly never fade and will always benefit us in everyday situations. The first thing that followed, after the ship, was a well-deserved rest. Homemade food, company, and enjoyment with soccer.

The European Championship turned out to be a real drama for us Croats! Unfortunately, Croatia, with a very good team, lost against Portugal after passing the group stage. Unbelievable, how many things didn't go well for us that day. The great Cristiano Ronaldo, for whom I was afraid that he scores, could not do anything for the whole game, against our guys who really did a great job, but unfortunately only that one fatal moment happened, when CR7 appeared in front of our goal and kick the ball to Subašić who save but the ball went straight on the head of Ricardo Quaresma, a player I once admired for the skills he possesses.

What is interesting and common to Cristiano and Ricardo is that Quaresma taught Cristiano some skills when his career began to grow rapidly. And now, like he returned the favour in some way, but I'm wondering, why, why against us now?

After this Croatian tragedy, Portugal reached the finals and won the Euro in France. If we had just passed that game, we were all convinced that we Croats would follow the path of Portugal, all the way to the finals. It was hard to watch our boys in tears and one of our heroes Luka Modrić, whom back then the Real Madrid teammate tried to comfort, and who it was, of course, no one else than the great Cristiano.

This euro was not on our side, but who would dare to think that only two years later, something fantastic will happen in Russia at the World Cup.

After the ship and all that hard pace, once you get back to your comfort zone, you totally relax and don't think about anything else, which means that we often take a nap during some games from that Euro. Literally, Elizabeth fell asleep holding a glass of wine without spilling a drop.

The days followed in which we finally spent and celebrated both birthdays which is why we also shared a birthday cake. We spent the days just the way we should, with family, socialising, music, and mostly laughing. Shortly after my birthday, we travelled to Peru, a country that will open my eyes in another back then undiscovered direction.

Since Elizabeth met my family and saw my hometown, it was time for me to get to know her family and country as well, and it was understandable that even after so long, she sees and spends some time with her family.

## 2.2 Peru

We decided to spend around two months in Peru, which was more than enough to get to know the specific culture of this mysterious country. Since we were both returning to Croatia after that and planning to create some stability on the mainland, I knew it would take a while until Elizabeth see her family again, that's why we stayed a little longer.

Elizabeth's family is very modest and humble but also very big. She has three sisters and two brothers, one of whom sadly passed away at a very young age. Two younger sisters and two older siblings.

If I were to enter Elizabeth's parents 'family tree, it's already a little more complicated.

But just to show you a picture of how it goes in the Rodriguez Callan family, her father has only two sisters, which is a miracle considering what follows on mother's side.

Elizabeth's grandfather, (from her mother's side) had three wives. He had one son with his first wife. With his second wife four sons and two daughters (of whom Elizabeth's mother is), and with his third wife four more sons and one daughter. So when you add it all up, he had 12 kids with three different women which would mean Elizabeth has a very large family. And there are even newer descendants from those generations, you see just one example, her mother who gave birth to six children and so the generation goes on.

The biggest plus and advantage I want to point out, that I have come to know in this country, is the amazing and impeccable choice of food. Peru is the heart and cradle of almost every possible fruit on earth. Due to the different climate that is present throughout the year in a couple of areas of this country, it allows a large number of fruits and vegetables to thrive regardless of the season. Here we talk about hundreds of types of potatoes, corn, chillies, beans, pumpkins, various root vegetables, and fruits that I have never heard of or seen.

While people in North America and Europe have breakfast, for example, oatmeal filled with various additives and sugars, pastries with butter and jam, etc., in Peru breakfast is filled with fried rice with eggs, avocado with bread, a couple of fruits, and instead of milk or tea, fresh juice of papaya, quinoa compote, maca or any other natural source.

The way they prepare lunch or dinner is truly special and creative. If you are ever able to taste their food you will become obsessed with it how delicious and good it is. Here are a couple of very popular dishes from Peru: *Ceviche, lomo saltado, ají de gallina, papa a la huancaína, cuy (Guinea pig), causa, rocoto relleno, anticuchos de corazón, arroz con pato, pollo a la brasa, chaufa,* and much more. Lime, chilli, and onion are some of the most important ingredients without which most Peruvian food cannot be imagined. From the meat, I got the impression that they mostly eat chicken, fish, and sometimes pork. It is very difficult to explain more about food preparation in that country because it all depends on which part of Peru you are in. Each part of the country has its so-called tradition and way of preparing food.

As I stated the biggest advantage, so there is certainly the biggest disadvantage and that is, as you can guess very weak economic development.

Some parts of Lima are very neat and look very solid while some other young districts look pretty bad. So let me describe to you the picture and impression I experienced in the suburbs.

As I mentioned, a variety of natural resources is very accessible. But what is not so well is the environment. Very polluted air (due to a large number of factories and old vehicles) by which you can understand very easily when you look at the sky. Not to mention crime. There's no way you're walking around in the evening with a cell phone in your hand and a wallet in your pocket without attracting the attention of bad people. People get robbed there very often, which is sad and gives a clearer picture of how much impact the police have.

Bribery and corruption are not lacking in this country either. Agh, when you take a closer look, there is no country today where the roots of these 'poisons' are not released. People in such places keep windows and doors chained with bars to protect themselves from burglary. There is no discussion about someone having, as in my country, a nice front and back yard, a terrace, no problem leaving a car in front of the house, etc. (I mean the city surroundings).

People live in small apartments and houses literally next to each other, which woke me up again in terms of how grateful I have to be and appreciate what I have at home. Lima is a metropolitan city, simply too crowded, which tells you the fact that contains about 11 million population. Yes, you read that right. A huge number for one city. The reason for this is that the vast majority from all over Peru (and more recently from other countries) come to that city with the hope of finding a job.

There is no hot water (at least not in those neighbourhoods) which was the first couple of times shocked for me to take a shower in cold water while for

Peruvians it is something completely normal. Unfortunately, that's how people live there in a country that has everything, and yet it seems like there's nothing just because of human greed, which protects the bad and harms innocent people.

During those two months spent in that district of Lima, we also met with a couple of our friends from the ship who was on vacation at the time.

If you remember before when I mentioned that *Machu Picchu* restaurant, and how I started planning to one day bring Elizabeth to this one of the wonders of the world, I don't think there was a better opportunity than now. But before that could happen, I first had to sort out one thing—ask for her parents' blessing so that we could one day enter into married life.

I considered it a very important detail and an inevitable responsibility. Yes, the communication was not at the highest level, thankfully so I had Elizabeth who was my translator. ☺

Her parents accepted me in a very correct and modest way, and have since started looking at me as a new family member. I can say the same that it was with my parents. They behaved very responsibly and paid attention to Elizabeth, to make her feel as comfortable as possible in my home for which I am very grateful to them. After the Peruvian blessing, Elizabeth, her mother, and I travelled to marvellous Cusco for about a week, where we were already greeted by dear Brigida, a colleague from the ship who lives with her family in this very interesting city.

Back again in my hometown Varaždin, this time with Elizabeth

Lima, Peru

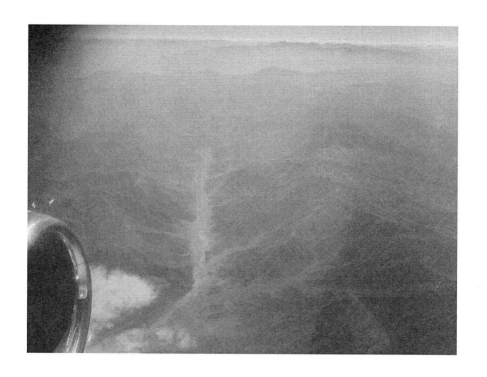

On the way to Cusco, view from the plane of the mountains of Peru

## 2.2.1 Cusco and the history of the Incas

Cusco, a city of amazing history and even more amazing people. The place or better to say, the centre of the great Inca Empire, one of the most impressive civilisations in human history. Their golden age was in the thirteenth century until the fateful 1533 when the Spaniards sniffed out what treasure the Incas possessed and invaded and conquered this city.

The Incas were a truly special civilisation. Apart from the incomprehensible architecture of their buildings even today, they were very intelligent in medicine and also creative in preparing food, some of which are still used today.

The reason why the Spaniards indescribably attacked these humble people is because of the possession of a huge amount of gold and other precious stones. They used gold on almost every corner as much as they had in their possession. There are even some theories that a few Spanish ships loaded with the gold of these Incas sank somewhere in the ocean, which they are still searching until today. But since they were humble people, never forced into many wars, they did not have any creatively stronger weapons to defend, such as rifles and cannons or an army on horseback, which the Spaniards saw as a huge advantage to kill them and wiped them off the face of the earth. I definitely recommend watching a couple of documentaries about the Incas because they stick to a really interesting history.

Already at the airport (in Cusco) as soon as you get off the plane, you are greeted with coca leaves that you take and chew to suppress headaches and nausea in the stomach due to the high air pressure. Cusco is located in the heart of the mountains at some 3,400 metres above sea level while Machu Picchu is a little less about 2,430 metres above sea level.

For most who are not accustomed to living at such an altitude, it can create temporary headaches and difficulty breathing. During the adjustment of the first two, three days, I even wiped the blood from my nose, but all this is nothing terrible for a healthy person.

Now, about the coca leaves. I have to explain well what kind of coca this is so that there would be no misconceptions. Freshly picked coca leaves that are left to dry and later used for medicinal purposes are not the type of coca you most likely thought of at first glance.

This plant actually has many benefits when used for medicinal purposes. It reduces blood pressure and the risk of heart attack and stroke, improves brain function, strengthens immunity, cleanses the body of harmful substances, is great for teeth and skin, and can help even people with asthma. No wonder then that the Incas lived very healthy. But when those same leaves get into the wrong hands that process it all with some kind of chemic, then you get the opposite of good—a poison that creates addiction, so-called cocaine.

That is why it is important to get such a first picture, not to think that Cusco is a city of 'white flour'. After we made ourselves comfortable in Brigida's house, we also drank coca tea, again the same thing. While touring Cusco, I can say that it is a very nice city with very rich food, as everywhere in Peru. As the Spaniards conquered the Incas, all over the city, they built churches and houses in their style, as if they wanted to hide the fact that once upon a time the Incas lived here. I admit, the churches are very beautiful and it all stands, but the truth cannot be hidden so I apologise if I have offended the Spaniards in any way, but it should remain realistic.

Cusco is visited by more than two million tourists a year, which is not so surprising once you understand what kind of city it is. As I mentioned, the Incas were such a creative civilisation that in addition to their mysterious constructions, they also built these sizes in the shape of animals, so the city of Cusco was built back then in the shape of a puma. The body consisted of the most important city palaces and temples, the head was the fortress of Sacsayhuaman, and between legs the main city square Plaza de Armas which is one of the most beautiful I have seen.

The original name of the city in Quechua (Inca language) is actually Qosqo which means the navel of the world. In their time only emperors and nobles lived in that city while the rest of the people outside the city. Of all the temples, the most important to them was the temple of the sun—Coricancha. The entire temple, walls, and floors were lined with gold plates while in the garden there were statues of various animals, including one of the most famous, life-size llamas also made of pure gold.

They also had their own law which has three rules: *Do not lie, do not steal, and do not be lazy.* Already based on their rules you can determine that they were hardworking, diligent, and correct people. It is a great pity, and I believe the biggest minus is that they did not know the letter. Their history and science were transmitted orally which is one of the main reasons why so little is known about their tradition today. The records we have today come from the Spaniards and their view of Inca culture as they wrote after the conquest. Another very interesting detail is that the Incas did not know the wheel, and this gives an even

293

greater mysterious question mark as to how they carried rocks weighing several tens or hundreds of tons, as they built into their temples and palaces.

At the top of a city hill, there is also a statue of Jesus some six feet high facing the city which can be seen even at night. The interesting history of this statue by *Cristo Blanco* comes from people who came in 1945 as refugees and later, before returning to their homeland, donated this statue to the city out of gratitude, which still reminds people that good deeds do not go unnoticed. Truly the view of the city from that hill remains speechless. What gives this view an even broader picture is that you don't have any larger buildings or skyscrapers that would cover parts of the city, so the horizon from that point of view is truly huge.

After that, we visited the famous city market of *San Pedro* for which I would give everything to have it in Europe! How much variety of fruits and vegetables and how rich in all possible existing vitamins and prices that are ridiculously cheap. If you're planning on going to Cusco, definitely don't miss this market.

To sit somewhere and eat something it's not expensive at all. Up to some 15 Sol (Peruvian currency) which would be around four euros, I consider very cheaply, and you can get for that price the whole menu (appetiser, main course, dessert, and drink). I will never forget the taste of Cusco soup full of vegetables, which makes me drool when I think of it.

One of the souvenirs I took for myself is the famous *Chullo* hat which you can recognise in some pictures. The hat has an extended end in which (according to stories from Cusco) people put money. Since there are many locations to visit in such a destination, I suggest future tourists buy the entire ticket, which contains tickets to many interesting places, for better savings.

Perhaps another detail that may surprise you about Cusco is their official flag, which consists of seven different colours, or rather—rainbow colours, which was first introduced in 1973.

In the centre of the city on one wall is a very impressive work that presents the history of the Incas in one painting. Given its size, I was not able to capture everything in one shot, so you can search for it on the Internet under the name 'Mural Cusco' and see for yourself how impressive this image really is.

*Sacsayhuaman* the place I mentioned a little while ago, more precisely the fortress on the hill above Cusco, which I am still not sure if it was actually an Inca military fortress or a place where some ceremonies were held, for example, one of the most important to Incas when they worshipped their greatest god—

the Sun. However, what has most caught the eye of many scientists regarding this place is the way it was built. The Sacsayhuaman is made of huge rocks brought in and from as far as 20km away.

Some of them weigh up to 200 tons and yet are perfectly shaped and fit into each other so precisely that not a single sheet of paper fits between the two. This case is not just in that location but everywhere where the Inca hand appeared. How—is a question for which I do not know if there will ever be an answer. At this place, there is even a neatly arranged circular with stones which is believed to have been the Inca solar calendar or watch.

*Tambomachay* is about 7 km from Cusco and is considered the main Inca bath. This place has a complex system of water canals coming from the mountain. Water was worshipped by the Incas as one of the main sources of life, and they also used this location as a place for relaxing. When I touched that water with my hand I could feel my blood freezing as it was cold, which you can imagine how the Incas bathed in fresh almost ice water from real wild nature at that time. But they say it is very healthy to bathe in cold water sometimes, which is why there is another example of how much Incas lived in a healthy environment.

*Quenko* not far from Sacsayhuaman located in the Inca Holy Valley is a pretty creepy place or so it just seemed to us since we got there already at dusk. Why creepy? Well, for the first reason, because it was a sacred place for the Incas, where they performed ceremonies, or rather more precisely, offered sacrifices to their gods, such as all the natural resources they possessed, animals, and of course humans. On the other hand, because we have heard some stories, how the spirits of the Incas can be felt there even today. Sometimes, at night strange things and sounds are heard from that place so thank you so much for visiting.

*Tipón, Chinchero,* and *Moray* are very fascinating locations. The lands in the mountains that the Incas cultivated and irrigated with a very intelligent system using springs from the mountains. It is interesting how the plantations were gradually one above the other, something like huge stairs. Moray served more as an agricultural laboratory consisting of 13 terraces where each has its own special microclimate. The difference in temperature between the bottom and the top of the hole due to the position of the sun and winds is up to an incredible 15 ° C, which is equal to the temperature difference between the one at altitude and the one at 1,000 metres.

*Pisac* is an Inca fortress built on a sacred mountain in the shape of a sacred condor animal with outstretched wings. The condor is a bird that back then was meant to the Incas as a guardian of the dead. There are two cemeteries in the area of the fort, and one of them is the largest known Inca cemetery with over 1,000 graves. Unfortunately, we didn't get to this place, but that doesn't mean it's not worth mentioning.

*Maras*—salt mines, some 30 kilometres north of Cusco, the largest natural source of salt that the Incas knew how to use. The place looks amazing because, like most Inca places, in the mountains, it is filled with about 3,000 pools from which they got salt and whose process of getting salt still works today.

*Andahuaylillas* is also a quite interesting little place where you can visit various museums that reveal the history of the Incas, how they lived, some details that are discovered and incomprehensible even today, which is believed to be associated with aliens. One of the very unusual details was the shapes of the skull that were elongated. In the centre of this village is the chapel of the Apostle St. Peter, which is full of gold inside. Don't even think to take a picture there because they will not let you out before you deleted it, like to me.

If you travel from Cusco to that place, you will pass by the beautiful *Laguna de Huacarpay*.

A picture of a lake and a mountain as from a fairy tale. Opposite this lagoon is the archaeological site of *Pikillaqta*, the site of another ancient civilisation that existed even before the Incas. The Wari civilisation is just one of those who knows how many civilisations before the Incas.

*Ollantaytambo* is a place we left for last for that reason because if you want to get to the magical Machu Picchu or more precisely, *Aguas Calientes* you can in two ways—by foot, using the Inca route, a trail that still exists even today used by the Incas or by train from this place. I honestly think there is no other solution to one of the wonders of the world. We chose the train because it's faster, and we didn't really have time to waste.

Ollantaytambo is at some 2,800 metres above sea level and is an exceptionally well-preserved Inca site and looks almost the same as 500 years ago. It was also the last refuge of the Inca Empire and the place where they won the only great victory over the Spaniards. The temple of the sun that they built on the top of the hill is the most important holy place for them, which can be reached by a lot of steps. On the opposite side of that temple, there is another huge rocky hill on which the Incas built their storages, in which they kept food.

When you look at what kind of mountain these storages are on, you think only one thing—Why on earth there?

As I tried to figure out what attracted these people so much to building at bizarre heights, one of the guides explained the reason. The Incas always paid attention to every detail when building something, so they chose storage on that mountain because of two reasons: cold temperature and always enough airiness, which kept the food very fresh and long-lasting, and another one because of weather conditions (flood). They designed the whole wind ventilation system. And not only that but when you look closely at that part of the mountain, you will see the sculpted face of the Incas.

When you look at everything the Incas created you can truly understand how fascinated they were by nature. It was as if nature was all their saints as much as they worshipped and held on to it (something that unfortunately people don't do today, and they should very much—in order to protect nature). Each of their cities has a temple of the sun and dedications to an animal. I mentioned about Cusco that they built it in the shape of a puma. Likewise, Machu Picchu hides very interesting details from a couple of perspectives.

*Templo del Sol*—the temple of the sun located on that hill, is built of six huge monoliths for which it seems incredible how they were brought even here so high, and even more amazing how they managed to shape these rocks to fit perfectly into each other.

With today's advanced, top high technology and all sorts of machines, I don't think it would be easy to do that, and how only the Incas did it with their bare hands in their time, I don't think we'll ever find out. I am very attracted and interested in their history, and I can say that if I could choose the only time I would travel through history, I think it would be this one. It is impossible to describe how fascinating the Inca civilisation was.

After quite a walk, we rested and recharged ourselves with the fresh energy of Peruvian cuisine, and took the beds for one night. Early in the morning, we set off for the train station, to catch the train to finally Machu Picchu where the ride took about an hour and a half. The ambience on the train was great! All the way listening to the relaxed Inca melody of *El Condor Pasa* (which definitely you need to check) and scenes of mountains through the window that leave you speechless.

Welcome to Cusco, Peru

Market San Pedro

In front of Coricanche, an Inca temple from the 15th century on which a church was later built

Coricancha, pay attention to detail on the Alpaca with the official colors of Cusco

Elizabeth with her mother on Plaza De Armas;

With the statue of Pachacutec, Inca emperor

Sacsayhuaman, Cusco, Peru

Sacsayhuaman, Cusco, Peru

Inca calendar

Sacsayhuaman, Cusco, Peru

Sacsayhuaman, Cusco, Peru

Source of water in Tambomachay, Cusco, Peru

Tipón, Cusco, Peru

Chinchero, Cusco, Peru

Chinchero, Cusco, Peru; Inca products – natural colors

Inca kitchen; Moray, Cusco, Peru

Salt mines in Maras, Cusco, Peru

Laguna de Huacarpay, Peru

Inca – copy-paste; The way they buried the Incas, Andahuaylillas, Peru

The archaeological site of Pikillaqta and my dehydration; Welcome to Ollantaytambo

On a hike to the top; Ollantaytambo, Peru

Ollantaytambo, Peru

Templo del Sol – temple of the sun; Inca architecture

Ollantaytambo, Peru

Elizabeth

Inca place in Ollantaytambo, Peru

## 2.2.2 Machu Picchu

Finally, here we are! We arrived in the city of ***Aguas Calientes*** which is located not far below the magnificent Machu Picchu, about 9 km. Aguas Calientes has only about 4,500 inhabitants and is a very small and very nice place. It usually contains hotels, hostels, restaurants, bars, souvenir shops, etc. If you arrive by train like us, then on the same day you stay in that town and the first possible return by train can only be the next day.

After the train, you can again choose the option of walking to Machu Picchu or by bus. If you want to walk it takes you about two hours but again it depends on the preparedness of the person. The bus takes about half an hour, whose return ticket costs about 20 euros.

The ticket price for Machu Picchu is around 58 euros. What worried me the most that morning was the weather! Very rainy weather with a lot of fog did not suit me at all because of what I had planned for Eli on that magical mountain. And so as we travelled by bus to that place watching through the window that miserable rain, I was all in my thoughts and worries about how I would perform something that should not show mistakes in any segment, and I know that I have to do it somehow!

When we finally arrived, we first set out to catch the familiar view you see in every picture when this place is advertised, and only then we pass through the entire Inca city, which took us almost three hours. There are a few more places you can visit there, such as the Inca Bridge and the main peak of the Huayna Picchu mountain, but for something like that you should really plan to stay a few days in Aguas Calientes because there is simply not enough time to see everything in one day since this tour is open every day until only 5:00 p.m.

Machu Picchu in translation would mean 'Old Mountain' where it is believed that the last Inca emperor *Pachakutiq* built this city, but according to some theories there is a possibility that the city was built earlier. There are many theories about this place but nothing for sure because as I mentioned, the Incas did not know the letter, and the Spaniards who executed them never even found this lost city. Hiram Bingham III, an American archaeologist was the one who discovered this place in 1911 and believe it or not, quite by accident. He was brought to the city by the Peruvian Alvarez, a resident of this area, more precisely to the very top by his 11-year-old son. An interesting fact is that he was searching for the last refuge of the Incas, the cities of Vilcabamba and Vitcos.

One of the biggest myths is that there is still somewhere a real lost Inca city called *Paititi*, where the Incas allegedly hid their treasure from the Spaniards and a place that was never found. A lot about Machu Picchu, about its construction, purpose, disappearance and later discovery is unknown which only fills the imagination and enhances the mystique that the city already has anyway. Many still believe that not everything that Machu Picchu hides has been discovered yet.

*\*\*\**

When we finally reach the top and experience personally that touch of this wilderness and magical nature, all those pictures and videos we've seen before can't be compared to this when you see it live. Magical, incredible, magnificent, fascinating, phenomenal, marvellous, wonderful, beautiful, and all those other words that I have mentioned many times because of which I am already boring to you and to myself.

Now, here we are, at the top, apart from the excitement of being in a place like this, some amount of impatience erupted in me, mostly because of my long-term plan, which I finally had to present. At first, when we got to that top, it was still raining and the view of the city of Machu Picchu was almost invisible from all that thick fog.

After about half an hour, Elizabeth suggested that we go on a tour of the old town, to which I responded and thought of every possible and impossible excuse, just to stay a little longer, hoping that this fog would disappear as soon as possible. When I felt the moment 'now or never' I went for all or nothing. I asked Elizabeth's mother to start filming while I was giving a speech. It was as if dear God had heard and seen me, the rain stopped, the fog disappeared, the sun appeared, and it was only needed to complete that speech with a very significant question.

I gave Elizabeth a small presentation that took a little longer than expected. With 15 photos (different pictures, which show us in those three years we knew each other) that were part of this performance, I tried to convey as much as possible with the ambience, how much she means to me. After everything I had imagined and planned to say, I knelt and proposed to her.

## 'Elizabeth Diomira Rodriguez Callan, will you marry me?'

I had felt like I was in a pre-heart attack state but it was worth it. After she agreed, with a few tears of joy (at least I hope she was out of joy ☺) and a moment after her mother stopped filming, we got applause from a group of tourists who were one level lower and whom we paid attention to after I knelt, which was obviously what was all about.

I can tell you, dear readers, this was a very special and one of the happiest moments from which you can conclude for yourself as soon as you try to imagine such scenes in such a place. Everything turned out great and with that, the day was totally brightened and thus opened the way for us full of joy and happiness, and a lot of exploring in Machu Picchu.

This place is so fairy-tale-like that I try to conjure up every picture and awaken your imagination, but also a strong desire that one day you will visit Machu Picchu and feel yourself everything we felt. There are about 150 houses in this ancient city and it is believed that about 750 people lived there. Like other Inca sites, their architecture is impressive here as well.

*The main Inca temple* actually seems unfinished, which is probably true because, according to experts, the Incas left this place even before they completed some things, which raises new questions why they would leave this place that the Spaniards did not and no one else discovered.

*Espejos de agua* is two containers, carved into the stone floor in which one was water and from where the sky was reflected (a reflection of the heavens), and thus used for religious purposes such as fortune-telling and similar.

*Intihuatana* is a type of carved stone or more precisely a kind of sundial and a kind of calendar built so that the sun casts certain shadows at certain times of the day or season, and the only two moments when there is no shadow are the summer and winter equinoxes, the first day of summer and the first day of winter. This rock is one of the wonders of the ancient Incas because they counted the time with it and knew when the time was set for ceremonies. Unfortunately in 2000, during the filming of an advertisement, a camera crane fell on that rock and significantly damaged it.

*Templo del Cóndor* is a temple of the condor bird that the Incas worshipped so much that they built it in the shape of that bird with outstretched wings. The Condor temple is believed to have served to sacrifice animals, and some even claim to torture people. The condor was a symbol of cruel justice.

323

*Fountains*—Water was of course very important to the Incas, they knew that it brought life like the sun, and they took good care of it. The irrigation system in Machu Picchu has been brought to perfection and there are several fountains in which they never run out of water.

*The royal tomb* looks a bit unusual and has an oblique gap between two rocks. On the lower part, three steps are carved, which represent three levels of Inca existence: the underworld—the snake, the present—the puma, and the sky—the condor. Numerous mummies and skeletal remains of over 100 people were found in this tomb, of which 80% were women, which would be proof of the claim that Machu Picchu was the temple of the virgins of the sun god.

There are a few more interesting things that hide some mysteries and theories of this place, but I do not want to forget to mention how the whole city of Machu Picchu from a certain angle or bird's eye view recognises it by the shape of one of the sacred animals, the condor. You can also see the face of a puma in the mountain or also the whole body of a puma from a different angle. What we have heard from many guides is that this place, except for its natural beauty, also contains some strong positive energy. I literally mean the hardcore force because a lot of people come here not only for tourism but also for medical reasons.

They say that you have to touch these stones, that this strong positive energy enters you and heals, i.e., exterminates all the bad in you. I don't know how much truth is about that, but many people were healed after coming here, so should we now give the credit because they were mentally relaxed and the body began to 'communicate' with nature, or is it some other natural force in question? I wouldn't say these are fabrications, since I personally felt something similar. A few days before this visit, I had a sore throat that I feared would make my condition worse or I would recover by this very important day.

During my visit to the Inca city, there were simply too many great things that distracted me and thus ruled out any possibility of thinking about my throat. After this visit, when we had already gone down to Aguas Calientes, I remembered my little health problem and immediately realised that my throat was no longer in pain. I don't know what to say to this except that one has always been and always will be for sure—nature is the best doctor!

Remember when I mentioned while working on the ship, how much I enjoyed all those sunrises and sunsets and other natural beauty, and I realised only a few years later that this contact with nature was actually the strongest medicine for me mentally and physically.

Every contact with nature is a slap in the face to a bag full of stress!

I question myself many times these days, how we are actually blessed with so many gifts, one of which is the gift of sight. Isn't it a wonderful gift to be able to see so many amazing beauties in a variety of colours?

What else can I describe to you about this natural diamond other than just words of praise and admiration?

Machu Picchu, a lost mystical city that has been hidden from human view for over 400 years is truly the most impressive and beautiful place I have visited, and let's not forget that I have visited many places so far. All those beautiful destinations I have travelled with a cruiser have their charms, but I have never felt anything like this anywhere. This simply has to be a piece of paradise. Thank you Machu Picchu for this experience but also the energy I felt!

***

When we returned to Aguas Calientes there were still a few hours of daylight left, but that didn't matter to us anymore. We saw Machu Picchu in a beautiful light, discovered a lot of interesting information, had a great time and it was finally time to celebrate our engagement a bit. With food that I don't have to describe how delicious it is and with a very great *Cusqueña* beer. I kept telling you how I sailed the Caribbean, the northern Baltic, and the Mediterranean and tasted all kinds of beers from those parts of the world, so somehow I shouldn't have bypassed Peru either. Although Peruvians are big beer users, this beer with which we toasted our engagement has remained somehow special to us. *Cusqueña* is made only in Cusco, which is why you can recognise it even by the appearance of the packaging, i.e., the bottle with the shapes of the famous Inca blocks—rocks.

Aguas Calientes has a small charming square with a fountain and a statue of the most famous Inca warrior *Pachacuteq*. I was sorry that we didn't stay here for at least another day, but even without that, we don't complain at all because we left with a wide smile and were filled with blissful peace.

Aguas Calientes, Machu Picchu, Peru

Machu Picchu in an incredibly thick fog

Elizabeth …

… & Goran

Machu impressive Picchu – Part 1

Machu impressive Picchu – Part 2

Machu impressive Picchu – Part 3

Machu impressive Picchu – Part 4

Machu impressive Picchu – Part 5

Machu impressive Picchu – Part 6

Machu impressive Picchu – Part 7

This is what an engaged couple looks like at Machu Picchu

Thank you Peru

The fateful YES!

## 2.2.3 Return to Lima

After spending a few more weeks in Peru, I still had a lot to see, but I will only point out a few examples because the most important and interesting ones, I have already invested a good part of my time in these pages, so here are a few more experiences from this country.

A few times when we set off for some better-known part of the city, getting there by car or bus is a real nightmare. Places that are around 20 minutes away turn into an hour and a half. The worst possible traffic I've ever seen, so I can't and don't want to imagine what it's like for those people who commute to work every day. So for future visitors, I definitely recommend that they avoid renting any means of transportation. That's enough about traffic.

I have not mentioned before that in addition to this rich food that Peru owns, the coast of Lima also has very rich seafood. One early morning we headed to one of the markets where you can find half the sea world. Different types of fish, octopuses, squid, lobsters, oysters, and I don't know what else. I remember one scene when we saw a piece of some fish, possibly tuna, which had already been cut in half, but you could get a steak from that piece, dear God, for some even up to 15 people! Huge fish! You look, and you don't believe it! You start to think about what such fish feed on, to grow so much. New-born sharks? It takes a forklift to bring how heavy it is! What's good about that market is that the animals are still alive, so you know they're fresh that they can't be fresher, and I think it's better for sellers because if they fail to sell everything the same day, they can the next one.

It was essentially interesting to play with lobsters, at least to a certain point. We took a couple of types of fish, a couple of squids, and two octopuses I've been craving since Greece. During a visit to one of the Greek ports, Katakolon, we ordered a grilled octopus at a restaurant. It tasted great, so we wish it again as soon as we saw it. The only thing that is not pleasant in such markets is that crazy smell of fish that creeps under your nose like mosquitoes in the summer when they constantly drink your blood, and you hear that sound that makes you slap your head just to drive them away.

Elizabeth's youngest sister was attending culinary school at the time, which she completed a few years later and became a professional cook. Given her profession, she was the one who prepared the seafood. E.g., an interesting fact about the octopus is that before the kitchen it should be well massaged (dead one of course) and thus relax the muscles and nerves if you want it on a plate soft

339

and juicy. There was laughter when we considered two large octopuses to be the main dish when we suddenly took them out of the pot and were surprised at how much they had shrunk, and they eventually turned out to be an appetiser. For one squid when I've been closely following Elizabeth cleaning it, it looks more like some sort of surgery to me. Or rather like a car mechanic disassembling an engine how many parts need to be removed. I thought, *this is a crazy world, I need to finish the course to know how to clean a squid.*

Do you remember Jorge from the ship? A cheerful and crazy Peruvian with whom we had various adventures in Europe and with whom we are still in contact today. At the end of our last contract, he, Elizabeth, and I started planning to attend a couple of matches of the back then European Soccer Championship, which took place in June. I was totally bitten by such an idea and from the bottom of my heart, I wanted to personally experience another European Championship. My first personal experiences of the European Championship were in 2012 when I won two tickets for the match Croatia vs. Italy in Poznan, Poland at a stadium with a capacity of more than 40,000 people.

When I remember that day, that madness and euphoria, you don't forget something like that anymore. It was also the first time I saw live one of my greatest heroes and idols Luka Modrić. It's wonderful to watch him playing on small screens, so you can even imagine how is to watch him play live! Amazing! When you watch such skill and technique live, you can truly feel that you are in the middle of a piece of real soccer art. But to get back to the main topic, Jorge is also a big soccer fan, and he was a person I could definitely count on. When it comes to such big soccer events, Jorge wasn't the person to promise you something, and when the time comes, he let you down.

He was a man of his word and still is. As I started the story, back on the ship we started planning and working out a schedule of which matches to go to and which not to, how to travel, digging up the prices of all the necessary expenses, and all the other essential details. But it seems that I am the one who let down this soccer adventure. During the European Championships that took place in France, there were various riots and terrorist attacks around the country, which is why we eventually gave up travelling there. Jorge was not angry with us for such a decision, and he understood the reality of this world well, but that did not stop him from travelling alone for a couple of games.

Can you imagine, in 2014, when the soccer World Cup was held in Brazil, he decided to travel there from Peru and only with an ordinary motorcycle and a few important things. Jorge is a true adventurer who is ready to go anywhere no matter the circumstances just to achieve what he wants. I can say that with such an opinion, he really lives fulfilled. I was indescribably sorry that we didn't go to that Euro because it was quite exciting and these riots had calmed down.

Surely you have felt such an experience once when you know something you should have done but you were afraid so you didn't, only to later realise how much you made the wrong decision and your time is running out. So it is with human lives and dreams. I believe there are so many talented people who could change this world and make it a better place, but because of the very thought of failure and condemnation from others, people are afraid, and they listen to 'realistic advice' and forget to listen to their own heart and soul, which it is what actually gives them that real advice and answers. Once upon a time, I read that dreams come true because if they were not so, nature would not encourage us to have them (John Updike).

You have to be persistent and patient because if you give your best and even in the end you fail, you will not lose. Already that journey you decide to take will give you an indescribable experience that no one will be able to explain or tell you. It will only be yours, and you will become a better and stronger person because of it but only if you look and draw positively from all of that. The final destination is not what will make you happy but that journey through it. I truly believe in it because if it weren't so, I wouldn't continue to believe in my dream. But about that a little later, I know that I have now totally deviated from the main topics but I just wanted to add to this part because I consider it very important.

Jorge contacted me earlier when we arrived in Peru and invited me to join him at a soccer tournament taking place in Ayacucho which is quite far from Lima, by driving some 560 km. Ayacucho is at some 2,700 meters above sea level which would mean for me who is not used to such pressure in the air, more torture than enjoying soccer. Yet I loved the thought of pushing myself to such a challenge. Peruvians and a couple of other countries from South America with a big difference in air pressure are specific in that when we talk about soccer.

Once a powerful Brazilian national team arrived at a match in Bolivia where they played at a very high altitude which was very hard for the Brazilians, and they struggled a lot in that match. It is not at all easy to make physical efforts at an air pressure to which you are by no means accustomed. We cancelled that trip in the end because anyway it was too far, and we had just arrived.

A week or two before we returned to Croatia, we hung out with Jorge a couple of times. We took a walk along the famous *Costa Verde* in Lima and enjoyed company with him. Since neither he nor I can do without soccer, we had to arrange at least once to play it together, which it was, right on that coast of Lima. And I remember it as one very wonderful experience—soccer along the coast, while the waves are lapping, and we are playing the most beautiful game in the world.

Another event that happened in my journey and catching a soccer dream was the day I was given the opportunity at the Sporting Cristal soccer club. That club is in the first professional Peruvian league and this great opportunity that was given to me was, unfortunately, a fake shot in the arm. During those two months I spent in Lima, we came up with the idea to try to find some soccer chance here as well because after all, I had nothing to lose so I said why not.

But I was very aware at the outset, how profitable that idea would not be. When we went to talk to the club management about the possibility of my try-out, they invited me to a training session from the younger team of that club, I would not know exactly what age but the first one was not for sure. During that training, a couple of scouts also attended, watching the players and looking for their values to perhaps provide them with better professional opportunities. I can say that I was not ready for that day in any way. Literally a whole year before that, I spent on a ship, and I don't have to talk about the training and soccer opportunities there because you know very well how it is if you have read those pages.

After the ship, we had to rest and after a month we left for Peru. During that long period, I played soccer a couple of times and of course, I couldn't expect some great results that day against the guys who are in training almost every day. I was very depressed and disappointed that I did not give any positive result and left at least a little good impression on my game, but what can you do, I am not looking for excuses, my circumstances before, were as they were and the fact that there is simple logic why I failed.

Without training, without hard work, without mental preparation, there is no progress and no results no matter how much I wanted and gave my best that day. I was totally a couple of levels below what I was on 13 June 2015, looking for a way to a dream in Kansas. Equally interesting is the fact that both professional clubs contained the same name—Sporting.

As I said before, you must not look at such experiences that you have lost. You analyse the complete situation and extract all the mistakes you learn from, and because of that you create an even stronger self, and you look for a new opportunity that will be given to you only if you create it yourself. It's very stupid and pointless for me to hear that way of thinking when people talk about how only one or two great opportunities happen to everyone in life, and if you don't take advantage of that, you have nothing further to hope for.

One of the biggest myths that separate a person full of passion from the crucial moments of creating the first steps to goals is to follow others. There will always be an opportunity, but only if you create it yourself! No one will come to your home, knock on your door, and give you everything you have always dreamed of! Remember only if you felt that you had been offered an opportunity you had been waiting for, and you did not use it, remember how that opportunity came about. The steps you took and that caused things to get a little mixed up, and something best came out for you, it came about for your own sake.

Opportunity lost? Not well prepared? Have you disappointed yourself and others who believed in you? I know that feeling very well! What was previously the cause of bringing you to the opportunity you have been waiting for, you must from that moment grow into an even stronger self. The steps and decisions you made then, this time should be stronger and fiercer and believe me, a new opportunity will come again!

I am 31 years old but I still believe I am capable of playing at least some semi-professional league. I know I am. Because I believe. I believe with all my mind, with all my heart, from the deepest part of my soul I believe that dear and almighty God will open that door for me one day, if not in this, in the next life for sure, and it is up to me to wait for that day, more ready than ever.


This was a story from Peru that I hope you liked, especially the Inca site. After all this, with the blessing of Elizabeth's parents, we returned as an engaged couple to Croatia and stayed there for almost half a year to start a new life together in a new country with new challenges from then on.

Costa Verde, Lima, Peru

With Elizabeth and Jorge on Costa Verde, Lima, Peru

## 2.2.4. Madrid

Lima—Madrid—Istanbul—Zagreb was our return flight to Croatia. Madrid, where we spent about 17 hours waiting until the next flight, has remained in our crazy memories.

Ever since Lima, when we got the fly-details and found out that we would spend almost the whole day in Spain, already back then a click happened in my head and the same seconds I realised that it was a great opportunity to visit the beautiful Santiago Bernabèu. And it was like that! As soon as we arrived, we left our luggage safe and took the metro to Real Madrid soccer temple. What surprised me, when buying tickets for a tour stadium is only possible with a credit card. At one point I already started to rage because I didn't have a card, just cash, but Elizabeth saved me this long impatient wish and paid with a card from Peru even though she doesn't like Real Madrid what it is the truth, I have to admit.

After that, we started looking for an entrance to the stadium that wasn't even the best marked, so I walked into one of the offices to inquire. As soon as I entered that room, some 10 m from me the elevator door opened from which Roberto Carlos came out. The Brazilian soccer legend, always of the same appearance and character, did not stay long and in such a good mood and smiling, he returned to the elevator after a few seconds. In those seconds, my brain was totally blocked when I saw Roberto Carlos, and I just couldn't believe it was really him.

Because of my blockage in my head, I didn't have a quick reaction reflex to catch it and kindly ask for a picture, but what can you do, it's one of the few moments you dream about, and once it unexpectedly appears in front of your eyes, you're just not aware because that dose of excitement freezes you all. But well, it's OK. I do not regret at all that I had the opportunity at least such, which also means indescribably much to me.

Once we entered the stadium and saw the size of the field and the stands, I felt incredibly blessed. A touch of a dream that emotions overcame and whispered to me that I might have deserved this after everything I had been through and believed in. I deserve to feel at least a little bit of that soccer magic that I truly live for and for which I would give anything and more!

To see and feel this experience in person, it's one of the many places where soccer history is created. The interior museum looks fantastic! Details of individual players, jerseys, soccer boots, a hundred trophies, medals, pictures of the most important soccer events... all this presented one big picture of the famous Real Madrid.

Keylor Navas, Dani Carvajal, Pepe, Sergio Ramos, Raphaël Varane, Nacho, Cristiano Ronaldo, Toni Kroos, Karim Benzema, James Rodríguez, Gareth Bale, Marcelo, Casilla, Casemiro, Fábio Coentrão, Mateo Kovačić, Lucas Vázquez, Mariano, Luka Modrić, Marco Asensio, Álvaro Morata, Isco, Danilo and Rubén Yáñez were back then the main role of Real Madrid, which I think was the strongest generation that the club had. Most of them remained to this day, while some were taken by fate to other clubs. It almost seemed unreal to me that the locker room I was watching was actually a room where so many amazing players prepare before a soccer show. My eyes shone the most when I saw the jerseys, of my two favourite players Luka Modrić and Cristiano Ronaldo.

This generation of Real Madrid did miracles on the World stage. They won as many as three consecutive titles of the most famous club competition in the Champions League and thus entered the history of soccer success. Cristiano Ronaldo became the first player to score a goal in all three finals and thus once again confirmed his incredible quality and perseverance.

I'm quite sorry that he didn't stay at Real Madrid because it was clear that the club was made for him, but due to a combination of different circumstances and conflicts of interest, he ended up at Juventus, interesting to be the first club I started cheering for from an early age, and whose first soccer jersey I got with the number 10 and the back then big name, Alessandro Del Piero. Juventus has remained a dear club to me to this day, but I admit from the big scandal that happened in 2006, I was quite disappointed, and since then I have decided to become a Manchester United fan who had a phenomenal generation in those years.

A generation in which talent has emerged that the world has never met before. When I say talent, I do not mean exclusively some natural soccer gift, such as what was given to Lionel Messi, but in that sense of talent as an indescribable desire for success, work, work, and just hard work. Cristiano Ronaldo became the most important link of Manchester United under the back then great and for me one of the best coaches of general soccer, Sir Alex Ferguson.

The days when I discovered Cristiano and Manchester United were actually the days when I first truly found myself and that incredibly strong inspiration for soccer. The way Cristiano played back then was literally an explosion of pleasure for both me and the fans around the world. Over the years, he changed his style of play but also strengthened his goal-scoring form, which quite clearly shows the statistics and the difference between what Real Madrid was like with him and now without him.

This visit to Santiago Bernabè Stadium meant a lot to me and fulfilled all my expectations. Of course, I would love to visit this place a few more times, not to mention how much it would mean for me to watch one *El Clásico* or even any other game. Believe it or not, I liked Madrid so much that even for a short period of time I thought about going there to live with Elizabeth. But their (Spanish) economic situation doesn't sound promising to me so that was a loud reason why we didn't go there.

When we got back to the airport and tried to board our next flight to Istanbul, we were shocked when they told us we had to pay a large sum of money due to the excess weight of our luggage. The thing was, we travelled with two different companies that have different baggage rules. The problem was not when we came from South America but when we had to do those two more flights in European territory. Since we didn't agree to pay at all, we had to improvise in a way that seemed very funny. We took a couple of heavier jackets from the luggage and started sorting the other items to somehow equalise the weights of the two pieces of luggage.

After a few minutes, Elizabeth and I looked like we were going to rob a bank. In Madrid where it prevailed up to some good 30 ° C, we were dressed as if it was below 0. No matter how funny it looked back then, we had no other choice. After looking through our fingers, we headed to our terminal, each of us with a pair of jackets on, carrying luggage in one hand, a backpack on our back that almost explode how much was loaded, and in the other hand few more items from the luggage. It makes it a little pointless to me that we were forced to do that because we eventually boarded a plane with the same weight that we arrived in Madrid. Thank God we didn't have any more similar surprises at other airports, and we arrived well in Zagreb.

Santiago Bernabéu Stadium – Part 1

Santiago Bernabéu Stadium – Part 2

Santiago Bernabéu Stadium – Part 3

Santiago Bernabéu Stadium – Part 4

Simply beautiful!

# 2.3 The first wedding

After spending about four months in Croatia, this time Elizabeth got a chance to know the capital Zagreb a bit more, and my beautiful region—Zagorje. Nature in my area is beautiful with all sorts of hills and valleys. That magical place where a man can rest from everything and let the violin of Mother Nature play to his soul. Croatian Zagorje is a region known for its own small hills, or 'behind the hills' which we could consider by a lot of hills with many many vineyards. Not far from my house there is a quiet Arboretum, a park that is great for family walks and recreation. When I remember how many years I spent in that park, I really loved running there because you can feel that fresh purity of the air in it, especially after the rain. Still, when I stop by my homeplace, I jog a few times in that natural peace.

The vineyard that my family inherited from my grandparents is only about three km away. So close but again so far from this noisy and hectic world. I always get images in my head when I think of that piece of paradise, and how my father comments happily and gratefully on this piece of nature filled with gracious peace. Our Zagorje is also filled with many lands and fields that people still cultivate today to get first-class food given to them by nature itself.

Elizabeth met all this and did not hide her enthusiasm at all. How even could she at all? Forests, meadows, parks, creeks... all this is offered by our dear Zagorje.

No matter how peaceful and beautiful it was here, we decided to give ourselves a chance this time together on land, but outside of my country. I believe that I don't have to explain again the reason for leaving because even the birds on the tree know already about this topic.

My home place will always be there for us, and I know that whenever we come back or visit for a few days, we are always welcome. As I mature from year to year, I appreciate this place more and more. Not only because of the most important reason—family but also because of the very nature that I am sure to annoy you with, how many times I mention it already.

But since we are still young and eager to prove ourselves, I still feel I have to expose some things to this world, try to show myself in the best version, evolve in all possible aspects in which I strive to achieve my goals, and fight as long as I have the passion, courage and will to achieve maximum possible range.

One of my personal goals was this book, which I deeply hope will open people's eyes at least a little and lead them to a more mature and better way of thinking.

***

Back in the last contract, I was thinking about which country would suit us where we could have a tidy life. Since the USA failed in the first plan (perhaps even better), our focus was on the top few most developed European countries. In my head, the list was as follows: Sweden, Denmark, Norway, Ireland, and Germany. I wanted Sweden the most, although the other two Scandinavian countries were not a bad choice either, I gave up for three good reasons.

During my first contract, I met a nice Croatian couple, who live in Stockholm, (Sweden) and I heard their side of the story of how difficult, almost impossible it really is to get an apartment there. They have a very quality life, but getting an apartment is the first, and I believe the most difficult obstacle from the very beginning. I doubt that their neighbours are any better off in this regard.

The second reason was the language which when you hear, your tongue breaks out in a couple of ways when you try to say those words. I tried to start learning the language while still on board, in the last contract where we had free access to a computer with the 'Rosetta Stone' program intended for learning different languages. The language is incredibly difficult in my opinion. Kudos to the most persistent who master it.

The third but perhaps the biggest reason we didn't decide to head north is exactly that one. I could still get used to their winter, maybe even to those nights that are actually days and that might drive me crazy after a while, but now that I have Elizabeth from Peru by my side, who grew up in warm regions, I wasn't really sure it would be a good new environment for her. I also admit that I would probably be bothered by that distance from my home. After these conclusions, I gave up northern Europe. Ireland, which was also among them and the next choice after these, a country to which thousands and thousands of Croats travelled for a better life, also somehow changed my mind in the end because of the weather.

The choice fell on Germany. Which sounds the funniest, completely unexpected.

During a visit to Zagreb, we met with former colleagues but also good friends. They were the same people I mentioned earlier in the book. Ivona and Claudia left the ship about a week before we and fate took them to Munich, Germany. Since they were very well aware of how difficult it is to get back on your feet once you leave your ship career behind, they knew we were in a situation like them when they were chasing an opportunity in Germany. After throwing in the trash the options to the north, Ivona suggested we try in Munich. After a few minutes of talking about the possibilities in that country, she convinced me that this could be our future destination. To be completely honest, I never loved the German language and even just because of that I avoided it, but it seems that now it came to me, that big and disciplined country of Germany. Munich also sounded attractive to me because it is only 6, 7 hours away by car to my part of Croatia, so I said OK, let it be Germany.

Since Croatia and Germany are members of the European Union, this was the first important thing that made it much easier to enter Germany, but also the opportunity to work in that country, which thank God, I didn't have to think about a work visa like for America. But for general residence in that country, that was the first obstacle for Elizabeth. If she is married to someone whose country belongs to the EU, then there is no problem, so we focused on the following to do everything right and thus get closer to our goal.

Our wedding had to come one day because if it wasn't, what was the purpose then that special proposal at Machu Picchu and all that before?

After changing the wedding date at least ten times, we finally got away with it. On 12 November 2016, we got married but not in the way I actually wish for. I have never in my life thought or intended to marry only in a civil ceremony, without a church wedding. But as we know to say, life is always full of surprises and so is mine. I had to go on that card this time plus our story and life are totally different from the others. After all, it wasn't that I loved Elizabeth less that way but it just surprised me that I had to choose an option because of such a mix of circumstances. The paperwork took a while, and we lost patience a couple of times due to sloppy and stupid mistakes that could have been easily avoided.

Here we come to one very interesting story for which my father is credited.

Namely, those long years ago when I was born, my father buried two bottles of rakija (a popular strong spirit in Croatia, especially in my region) and two bottles of wine that were just waiting for me to dig up, only the same year when I would enter into marriage. Not even a day or year earlier. This is actually a type of tradition that people applied many years ago, more for fun. An even greater pleasure of excavation was that that rakija was already back then, at the time of burial, more than 20 years old.

Who would have thought that once those bottles saw the light of day again, more than 50 years had passed! Half a century old rakija! Wow. My father did the same when my brother was born four years earlier, but I have to disappoint you even though my brother also got married just a year after me, his rakija is still buried somewhere and undiscovered. The reason he didn't bring his rakija to the surface was the excuse he couldn't find it. My brother simply did not have the patience or too much will to look for his treasure, as I did, for example. Either way, I hope he gets down to business as soon as possible and finds his rakija even if he digs up the whole Grandma's garden. ☺

I'm not much some rakija guy, and I don't consume alcohol often, so I don't know, but what my father, and I agreed on this one is that this rakija has a very rich taste that as soon as it passes through your throat, you feel it cleanses and destroys you and every bacterium in you. Something like this is now kept only for extra special occasions.

Given that we needed money for Germany and a new beginning there, I decided that only our closest family would attend our first wedding which in this case was just mine. Only 11 people at the first wedding, a very modest little gathering just enough to mark our day. Of course, I didn't even think to stay on it, and one day to do all this properly. The church wedding and real party will come three years later.

After this wedding, we travelled on our little honeymoon to the famous shrine of Marija Bistrica, and two nights in a very nice hotel, which we received as a wedding gift. During the summer, Marija Bistrica is full of people not only from all over Croatia but also from all over the world, but since we got married in November, we had a total blissful peace that followed us during every walk. It was a very beautiful and relaxing environment.

Due to our paperwork, which lasted for a while, we spent peacefully and with a little more relaxation Christmas and holidays with my family and the best homemade food and treats.

We can truly say out loud and proud that we have seen off 2016 full of crazy adventures, travels, experiences and closed it off with a major event!

Amazing what a year for Elizabeth, for me, for us! This was definitely my best year for that reason because it was somehow the most meaningful and complete of all the other years, and I don't think there will be any more like that anymore. I am thankful to dear God for blessing us with such a year with so much and amazing. To this day, I want to go back to that year, all the way to the beginning, and live it even better and more fulfilled!

When I just remember all the adventures, tingles pass through me as I write, emotions and fondest memories return in the blink of an eye, the songs I listen to today are the songs that marked my 2016, like a time machine that takes me back to those beautiful images, images that it is impossible for me to erase and remove from my memory. Something tells me that these images will come back to me and be present most strongly at the moment when one day dear God calls me to Himself. Either way, the year 2016 is closed like a closet full of things that don't even allow the door to close normally. Things that peek out and remind us that one day we have to reopen that door and face it whatever that means.

Visiting Trakošćan Castle

Excavating a national treasure

First wedding 12.11.2016; Visiting Marija Bistrica

# 2.4 Beginning in Germany

As soon as we received the final papers, we headed to Munich, Bavaria, with two suitcases in mid-January. I still remember at the bus stop when we said goodbye to my parents, my mother tried to let me know, that if things don't go well for us, we do not hesitate to return home. Ever since we became aware that we were aiming for Munich, I was so sure and full of confidence that nothing would stop us from staying there to work and live no matter how hard it could be.

Simply, it was planned in my head that I would not return as a loser. I was expecting a difficult start but I was willing to create our best way, a mentality that I applied to myself just like those days when I was preparing for the ship.

As soon as we arrived and settled in with a friend, I started to work on getting an apartment in the same building. Do you remember the story of the apartment in Sweden? The same scenario awaited us here. Getting an apartment in Munich, a city that is predominantly among the most expensive cities in Europe, is an almost impossible mission, not to mention the prices on rent and bail. To get an apartment, I have to have a job, i.e., in writing that I can prove where my income comes from, and to get a job I have to convince them that I have an apartment or address of residence.

What to say to this, except you don't know who's crazy here. I had been looking for a job since the first week when we had arrived, and I was firmly aware that I had no right to take any break, not even to think about it. After sending I don't know how many emails and submitted resumes around town, I didn't choose the location of the job but just accepted the first one that proved to be an opportunity. I got a job in a private hotel, a morning shift to serve breakfast which, although it did not promise any big money, I had no right to complain at all, as I was accepted without knowledge of the German language.

My role this time was huge and crucial. Elizabeth could not look for a job because she first needed to get permission to live in Germany with me, and for that to happen I had to have solid evidence that I had enough income and opportunities for her as my wife to be safely cared for. Once I got a job and an apartment (for which there is a special story) Elizabeth was given the right to a German ID card and residence for the next three years, which also meant the opportunity to find a job. From the beginning, all the burden was on me and every day I was more and more aware that if I fail, we have nothing to look for here.

The money we saved went like the wind and especially because of that I knew that if I give up back then, after so much invested, then I will never succeed here. Talking about the apartment and how I got to it I won't bother you, but I can only say that I was even on the verge of tears a couple of times, when I wasn't sure until the last minute whether to get it or not, after a lot of effort and money. It was a very difficult fight with a lot of effort and patience. The most important thing in such situations is not to lose your head, as Ivona says, to whom I give a lot of credit because she and Claudia were very supportive and very helpful to us!

When faced with difficult situations you must not falter, you must not give up and look at everything negatively no matter how it may seem. Fear always came to my mind, and I admit that I was afraid that if I failed, how much back then I would disappoint Elizabeth who believed in me but also our friends. I had no choice but to turn all those doubts and all that fear into my own motivation. You literally don't stop! You have to fight and be persistent, like a lion when hunting prey. You have to be that lion that runs and doesn't think about how hard it is, until the moment it catches its desired prey.

Step by step, things started coming in our favour. By the time we can say that we have become firmly stable, a good half a year has passed but it was worth it. It was well worth it.

The apartment, which was so difficult to get, was only 28 square metres in size. For a start, more than enough, although many would mind such a size. Given when we heard what kind of apartments some people live in and for how much money, we were grateful for the small kitchen, bathroom, and one room. When Elizabeth got the papers, we were lucky that she immediately got a job in a Japanese-Peruvian luxury restaurant whose income helped us a lot.

In late April, my older brother got married. The celebration was great with a lot of joy and laughter. What I will always remember, as I replied to my mother who was worried since we had gone to Germany a few months earlier, would we be able to have the opportunity to come to my brother's event?

*'If I even came back from North America and terminated my contract just to come and not miss the World Cup, then I will also come from Germany, which is a couple of hours away, for my brother's wedding'.*

As summer was slowly coming, we returned to Croatia in mid-August. I had to keep the promise I made to Elizabeth. She wanted to see the Krka National Park, which is adorned with natural beauties such as numerous lakes and beautiful waterfalls. Although I had visited this place twice before, I didn't mind going to see one of these masterpieces again. We stayed a couple of days in Šibenik as well, a very nice city.

Things were getting more and more in place, so it was the final time I got back to my favourite soccer. During the year while we were still burdened with many things, I went jogging and did some smaller workouts just enough to slowly get back in shape. Our apartment was near the famous Olympia Park which has great green areas and running trails as much as you like. It also houses a soccer stadium (which Bayern used before but has been moving to the amazing Allianz Arena since 2005), an Olympic hall designed for numerous concerts and a capacity of 15,500 people, and sports pools.

Munich has quite a lot of green space but the Englischer Garten and Olympia Park are the two largest. It means a lot when you live in the city and have a little nature by your side where you can run and clear your head. As I started getting back in shape more and more, it was time to find and join a club. I wasn't sure how and in what way to do it until the idea of Google maps came to me. Since it meant a lot to me not to spend time on longer trips to the club and the field where I can train on my own, I searched on the Internet for the closest one. Once I joined the club, I started getting opportunities and returned to the long-awaited soccer game after as many as six long years, from the very beginning when I started with ship life. It was a great feeling to be back on the field, wearing the jersey and soccer boots again, fighting in every duel, and sacrificing for the team.

In our first year in Munich, we had the opportunity to attend the most famous event for which, I believe, many even take a vacation. I think Germans consider Oktoberfest their most important 'holiday' how much interest there is! The event, which lasts more than two weeks (September/October), is filled by up to about 6 million people. Another name for this festival is 'Wiese'n'. About beer, it is particularly brewed by local first-rate breweries with a minimum Volume of 6% Alcohol. In 2018 people drank 7.5 million litres of beer. Also, another interesting fact is that even Albert Einstein assisted on a beer tent installing electricity in 1896.

During the summer, I changed my job in a different and better hotel. I worked there for almost two years. The first year I met a very good friend Isa, who grew up in Munich but of Bosnian roots. Since we both found ourselves in soccer topics from the beginning, he suggested to me if I wanted to go with him, to work a couple of times at the Allianz Arena, the soccer temple of Bayern Munich. They always looked for the staff there to work in buffets and similar services, in private spaces for special guests during matches. When I say special guests, I literally mean those who can afford something like that while we ordinary people with average salaries can't even get a normal ticket just like that. The point of this, of course, was not work or earnings, but to feel at least a little of the ambience in this beautiful stadium. I definitely accepted and went there three times.

I went for the first time when it was a Champions League match against Paris and the other two times when the Bundesliga was played against FC Köln and the DFB Cup against the great rival Borussia Dortmund. In all three games Bayern celebrated, which was a great experience to feel the voice of the fans at this huge stadium with a capacity of about 75,000 people, so you can only imagine the noise and atmosphere in those moments. Since I had to work there, of course, I didn't have the opportunity to watch the game too much, but again, those few minutes of seeing megastars in that field were something special. I got that great feeling again when you live your dream at least a little bit.

The last game was just five days before Christmas, for me the most beautiful day of the year. Since we had a small one-bedroom apartment, there was no room for a Christmas tree the size we were used to, so we were happy with a very small but cute tree as well.

We said goodbye to the old 2017 with thanks to God for helping us in all the struggles and obstacles from the beginning when we arrived in Germany and welcomed the new 2018, which will leave a big mark, especially for us Croats.

Waterfalls of Krka, Croatia ; At Olympiapark, Munich, Germany

Autumn in Olympiapark; At Alianz Arena, Munich, Germany

# 2.5 Travels, football (soccer) and Russian fairy tale

After Bayern Munich passed the group stage in the Champions League, in the next knockout phase, his opponent was Turkish Besiktas. At the end of February, when Besiktas was coming to Munich, I was excited because that club stayed in the hotel I worked for. That hotel hosted rival clubs that played in Munich. I remember that day when I finished work and left the hotel, the bus from the Turkish club arrived at that same moment. I immediately stood by the fence and waited impatiently with the prepared camera of the phone, for one of the players from the Croatian national team, Domagoj Vida.

*'Vida, majstore! (master), can I have a picture with you?'* I shouted as soon as he passed by me. After a few metres, he stops, turned, and approached me with a big smile. I was so excited that I was afraid just not to mess something up with the camera, and completely out of my mind with this happy moment so much, that I forgot to thank him for the picture at the end. My dear Domagoj, I hope you did not resent me that day, and I know such situations are already normal for you anyway so thank you very much for that picture! Vida had always a strong self-confidence and desire for firm soccer, which he has proven throughout his career so far, and a few months later when we needed him the most!

Since I was already there, it was an opportunity to take pictures with other famous players as well. After Vida, I wished for another one with Ricardo Quaresma. Although he was the 'executioner' of the Croatian national team at Euro 2016 and scored the goal that decided the winner, I considered him a great soccer player full of skills that I have followed since 2008, but unfortunately, I did not get any second with him because I was not the only fan there. Munich is also full of Turkish nationalities so I can think what it meant to them when the club from their country came to Germany. But I caught a moment with another Portuguese, whom the whole world knows, and I believe more because of the bad than the good. His often dirty way of playing has cost him his career many times. I'm sure you know who this is. Pepe, who 'gave me a face' as if he wanted to beat me up with some barely sour smile.

In late April, Bayern reached the semi-finals and hosted the great Real Madrid. How excited I was about that arrival, amazing! To see my life motivations as Luka Modrić and Cristiano Ronaldo. Of course, I also like other players such as Marcelo, Sergio Ramos, Isco, Kroos, Benzema, Bale, and our other national team member Mateo Kovačić. I was completely obsessed with it and waited impatiently and even bothered my supervisor countless times if he can try to find out when and where Real Madrid will come.

I went crazy with worry when I found out they weren't coming to the hotel where I worked. But thanks to my persistence, I found out that Real Madrid will be staying at the Hilton hotel located in the Englischer Garten and the day when they will arrive there. As soon as I got home from work, I ate something in a hurry and headed to the Hilton hotel! By the time I got there, there was already quite a crowd. Cristiano Ronaldo appeared in the next few seconds. He walked the other side in a suit and took pictures with fans over the fence. And yes, that wasn't the real Cristiano!

That was a man who only looked very much like him and who appeared more for fun. I have to admit to you dear readers, that as soon as I saw him, I was very excited but at the same moment as if something was very suspicious to me about him, so I was on the scales whether it was really him or not. Although I believed some 80% that it was him, I was waving to him to take a picture, and also I wished that he sign his jersey of Manchester United I bring with me. But as more I observe him, more was everything suspicious to me. All the fans there seemed to me way too calm. Then about that person, my eyes caught his height. Although it was some 20–30 m away, to me it was the first signal of suspicion. Then his movements, the way he walked… everything was 'blurry' to me. Kudos to that person who imitated Cristiano Ronaldo in a truly original way. Well, he blinded most of us there. But soon after those few minutes, it became increasingly clear that he was not the real Ronaldo.

After waiting a few more hours, the bus from the great Real Madrid finally arrived.

The bus door hadn't opened yet, my hand holding the camera was already shaking with incredible excitement!

Here they are! They started going out! I was standing right in front of the bus and the hotel entrance. One of the first to come out was a French legend, Zinedine Zidane! Then his assistant and behind him Cristiano Ronaldo! And yes, this time it was the real Cristiano Ronaldo! And fans, you could hear them a lot louder this time than a couple of hours ago. That moment, those few seconds I will never forget!

As they got off the bus, still in the dim light, I noticed Cristiano as soon as he got up from his seat. When the bus light came on, we all saw it even better!

In those seconds I didn't know where to watch what was eating away at me! Should I look at the camera and watch how I shoot so that it doesn't turn out to be a bad shot, or should I watch and not miss these special moments live! I guess situations like that are the worst! You came to see them live and at the same time you want to record that moment that you have as a lasting memory, to which you must also pay attention so that it does not turn out that you were filming someone in the back. Ah, terrible! I think my eyes in those seconds jumped every millisecond on the camera to check if I'm recording well.

After 15 years of following his games, I finally experienced seeing him live even for those few seconds that meant more to me than I don't know what! I just felt at that moment some special positive energy that kept me going even a few weeks later. Behind Cristiano, a couple of new, back then lesser-known players and two very well-known Brazilian players, Casemiro and crazy Marcelo, who I love to watch when they play, came out on the first door. Most of them went out the other door, which was less visible to me, but again enough to catch everyone for at least a few seconds, even from behind. Isco, Kovačić, Modrić, Bale, and others. Cristiano was the only one who waves to us, while everyone else just hurried into the hotel, which I can understand. The day before the game, everyone tries to stay maximally concentrated and not allow themselves the slightest distraction.

The next morning I went back to the same place hoping to see them again and maybe catch some opportunity for a picture. Unfortunately, none of that happened. I even tried to get into the hotel but it was simply impossible with too much security. Only guests staying at that hotel were allowed to enter. If Real Madrid stayed at my hotel where I worked, access would be much easier for me, and I am sure I would find some way for a few pictures even though after that I would get a warning for being fired. I don't know if you've ever felt that way when you want to see someone your favourite person, who in some way gives you meaning in life and you're so close and yet insufficient. But it is how it is, if dear God allows, maybe there will come another opportunity in life like this one.

Three days later, Kovač's Frankfurt arrived at the hotel where I worked. Niko Kovač and his right-hand man, brother Robert, did an excellent job with the soccer club from Frankfurt, which is why they later took over Bayern Munich. I caught Niko in the lobby to shake his hand and congratulate him on every success. Man is full of discipline and calm without limits. I'm sorry that it turned out that way in the end, for Niko and Bayern. No one deserved to be treated the way he was just because he had firm criteria and wanted to make the necessary changes. I hope he finds a club that will appreciate him and with which he will achieve even better results. Seeing the whole team of Frankfurt was an experience, especially our other national team member, Ante Rebić. I wanted to ask him so badly for a picture but I was not allowed because we who worked there need to follow the rules, ah those rules!

Also, a couple of other soccer legends came to the hotel where I worked. Martín Demichelis, Giovane Elber, Luca Toni, and Zé Roberto. One morning a person comes to breakfast, whom you can recognise from a mile away that he is a pro athlete type of person. He sat down and ordered green tea. As I go for his tea, I'm thinking who could it be, man, I know him from somewhere! The supervisor tells me—Zé Roberto. Wow! I read about him, and he seems like a great person to me. At that moment, I wished to go to him, sit down and talk. And again, unfortunately, I couldn't ask for a picture! Today, the man is more than 45 years old and still looks like a gladiator. I was surprised to find out that he was born on the same day and month as me.

*** 

A month after these soccer excitements, we booked a hotel in Mallorca, Spain, more precisely Calla d'Or. For this holiday we weren't sure until the last day where to go. As Elizabeth's parents arrived at the end of the month, a visit to Rome was in the foreground. I intended to take my parents with me because I know that Rome is my mother's life's wish, but due to various obligations, this plan, unfortunately, did not come about. We thought about where we could go without going too far.

Mallorca somehow seemed the most attractive to us back then. Since Elizabeth and I know Mallorca from before, more precisely the capital Palma de Mallorca where we came by cruise, this time we aimed at the other side of the island. Calla d'Or pleasantly surprised us with its natural coves which we joyfully explored. Although I admit, we had to walk a lot, it was worth seeing and feeling again a piece of that nature. Those were the days when the grand final of the Champions League was played between my Real Madrid and the likeable Liverpool.

Of course, I didn't want to miss a game like that, and we watched it in a bar with a lot of soccer fans. It was a very intense match with a lot of energy. My heroes Luka Modrić and Cristiano Ronaldo celebrated with the company while I admit on the other hand I was sorry for Dejan Lovren who cried for the missed opportunity that every soccer player has dreamed of since childhood. Who would have thought that as early as next year, his Liverpool would reach the grand final again and this time he would celebrate a big title! On 26 May 2018, Real Madrid thus registered their incredible 13th Champions League title.

Mallorca is a very pleasant place to rest but a small mistake we made is that we travelled there in late May which was still a little too early to feel that real summer. After a week in Mallorca, on our way back to Munich we were stuck halfway. We had a return flight from Mallorca to Munich via Hamburg where we had to spend the night because our flight was cancelled. We had to go to a hotel that was paid to us, and we had nothing to complain about when we saw this luxury. The Grand Elysée hotel was a nice experience. The return to Munich was in the afternoon so we had a nice time to explore a bit also Hamburg which was covered with hot sun most of the day.

When we returned to Munich, our brand new car was waiting for us, which we decided to buy about a month ago. It means a lot to you when you have a car, especially in the city. We opted for the Hyundai i30 Passion and a very pleasing to the eye blue colour. I can say that we are very pleased with this choice.

With Domagoj Vida, Pepe and Kovač brothers

Cala d'Or, Mallorca – Part 1

Cala d'Or, Mallorca – Part 2

Cala d'Or, Mallorca – Part 3

Thinking blue …

***

### *Russian fairy tale and tears of emotion*

The month of June is coming little by little. I believe that we all remember very well that special summer of 2018, especially we Croats who shot with pride!

It was the year of Croatian soccer, the creation of some new unimaginable history! It was also the year of one of our fiery, incredible combat leaders Luka Modrić! It was the year of all of us Croats and our magical community!

14 June—15 July was a period because of which if not the whole, at least most of the world cared. The biggest soccer spectacle has arrived this time in huge Russia.

Remember when I told you about the failed plans for Euro 2016, just two years earlier? This time I wanted with all my heart to travel to a couple of games and feel that fantastic euphoria that many crave. From the moment when everything was already known, which teams will attend and in which cities, I opened the map of Russia and started planning according to the schedule of matches where and when to travel. Jorge, the crazy Peruvian and adventurer was definitely for those trips especially now that his Peru has qualified for the World Cup after as long as 36 years. Unfortunately, here we now come to crucial decisions that have made me very sad.

The plan didn't work this time either, and I'll explain to you soon why. Russia is a huge size of the country. The schedule of matches and the distance between the cities—stadiums is extremely large, which was the biggest cause of our plans' failure. My plan was to attend at least the first game of the Croatian national team and since Elizabeth and Jorge are Peruvians and their country was eagerly waiting to participate in such a spectacle again, it is logical and understandable that they were eager to watch at least one game live. I had absolutely nothing against it, and I already wanted to see one of their games, and I must say that I had great respect and sympathy for the Peruvian national team.

It's an amazing fighting team that can stand up to any team without fear or doubt. I believe that many Croats would agree with me that the defeat by them in a friendly match before Russia was a huge cause and influence on our final results and such a miraculous success. The coach Zlatko Dalić himself admitted this, in his book published shortly after Russia, the man who brought us to the roof of the soccer world. For the third game, I wished it was at all possible to

378

finally see Ronaldo and his Portugal. I'm such a passionate fan of that soccer, and I haven't had a chance to live these real moments yet, to see at least my biggest idols and heroes. Ok, at least I have seen Luka Modrić before and it was a life experience that I appreciate a lot and keep in my heart.

Trying to connect the three games and be in each of them was impossible. Peru from Group C and Croatia from Group D played the same evening, the first at 6:00 p.m. while the second one at 9:00 p.m. and distance differences of more than 1,200 kilometres.

Another thing I didn't want to miss was the other matches of this championship. Regardless of either the World Cup or the European Championships, I never liked to miss a single game. Just travelling to Russia and from one city to another would spend a huge amount of precious time for which I was not at all suited, and I was becoming more and more aware that the whole plan was falling apart. Just spending that time on travel, while performing different national teams, I was not willing to take the risk, although maybe I should. Elizabeth and I agreed to go to my family in Croatia and enjoy that soccer differently and more modestly. It was also the first official time my parents met Elizabeth's parents.

And so we went from Munich on vacation to Croatia, to my Zagorje. You may have wondered what happened to Jorge then? Although I invited him to come to Croatia, he was and remains a crazy Peruvian and went to a couple of Peruvian games. He told me how he liked the girls from Russia, and he would like to come back one day and 'look around' this Russia in more detail hahaha.

We watched the first matches of Peru and Croatia in Munich, just like the other matches before them. It was tense for both, us and the Peruvians. Yet the first game opened up a lot. Peru lost 1-0 against Denmark, and I was very sorry for them because they deserved at least a draw. Our great Croatia beat Nigeria 2-0, which I was afraid of because every African national team is very uncomfortable and unpredictable, but this time Nigeria couldn't do anything to us! Croatia opened its doors great at this championship, and we left for my homeland after a few days.

If there is something I can't imagine following the World or European Championships without, then it's definitely the Croatian jersey, the ball that must always be present near me during matches, and a magazine with a list and details of all teams and the overall schedule of these competitions. I have been collecting magazines of these soccer types since the 2002 World Cup, and I keep each of them as if they were my millions.

Even today I can remember that excitement and nice feeling when I was driving back then a fresh, brand new car from the factory, on the highway to Croatia, with fan songs that created nothing more than that brutally positive euphoria both in me and in the whole nation. Having already mentioned these songs, I also want to point out how much my emotions explode when watching also all those Highlight videos, in which ones they put all the possible important details that influence and make this euphoria so special and great!

On 21 June, again the first game of Peru against France and again, unfortunately, lost 1: 0 and behind that, Croatia against Argentina. Dear God, what a game was that! How much we feared that Argentina, maybe not so much its national team, but only one man. You all know who I mean. The amazing Lionel Messi who held the status of one of the best for more than ten years! Wow! This match was just another proof of how much soccer means to be a collective game.

How important it is to be a team and not depend on individuals. The amazing Messi could do absolutely nothing to us! A big failure and a huge zero from his game. Our trio Brozović, Strinić, and Perišić closed it so well and with quality that it looked like a helpless bird in a cage. Mr Dalić has excellently prepared and compiled a list of names that have literally embarrassed Messi and Argentina. Do you remember the desperate Sampaoli—the coach of Argentina? Our Mr Dalić destroyed it in every way!

Rebić's beautiful volley, even better and more beautiful Modrić's rocket in the very corner of this one lost Caballero and for the sugar, in the end, Rakitić's confirmation of the total demolition of Argentina. 3: 0 and a huge step forward in just the second game!

Like the entire Croatian nation, we jumped for the happiness and joy that were given to us that day by our boys. Wow, already the tingling started when I remember how excited we were that day! In this match, it can be said that the real phenomenal strength of Croatia was truly felt! I'm not saying that they played badly against Nigeria but still, it was the first game that felt like they were somehow playing under the brake until this one!

Not even a week later, Croatia played the third and last game in the group stage, against Iceland, which came to this World Cup with high expectations. After their performance at Euro 2016, everyone started to respect them much more seriously. Our Mr Dalić decided to rest the main players because we were safe to pass anyway, but again he did not want to take this game easily because of that. Another great performance is full of struggle and intensity. The match ended with the victory of our team 2:1 and with that secured the maximum number of points in the group and moved towards the knockout phase of the competition.

Peru also won the last game against Australia 2-0 but unfortunately, that was not enough for their passage. If by some miracle they passed and were in the second position in the group, fate would reunite us in the knockout phase. It would be a duel, Croatia against Peru, me against Elizabeth, my family against hers hahaha… of course I don't mean any physical clashes, but only that soccer charge, passion, and love we share for homeland and the national team.

1 July Croatia against Denmark! Agh tough these Denmark! Tough and too tough! The match starts and in the first minute we get a goal, a goal we don't understand still today. The first game of the knockout phase, and we got an unfortunate goal in the first seconds! Horror! But before we all started looking for an Aspirin and similar pills, thank God we didn't even manage to find them because in the 4th minute our Mario Mandžukić already equalised!

Two fastest goals in the championship and both in a very funny way. It doesn't matter, it's good, let's move on, the game has just opened.

As much as ours struggled and exhaustion to score the winning goal and finally finish this drama, what we feared most was actually just coming. In the last minutes we had a perfect opportunity to bring everything to a happy end, but to our Luka Modrić this frightening Kasper Schmeichel, the son of the Danish legend Peter, stops and gives new hope to his homeland.

The winner will be decided by penalties. Oh my dear God, if people didn't take those Aspirins in the beginning, after this drama they certainly did! Our crazy goalkeeper Subašić defended the first penalty to Eriksen, but as that hope came quickly, so it went, Schmeichel does the same to our Badelj. After that, Kjær and Kramarić and Krohn—Dehli, and Modrić scored. Agh omg how close it was for Schmeichel not to stop for the second time our already back then frustrated Luka who was angry at himself for that first miss when they still played.

Then another great defence of our Daniel who read Schöne brilliantly and thus gave us a second hope for a better tomorrow but again, the drama instead of ending only grew into an even worse scenario! Schmeichel stops Pivarić, and you no longer know who can endure this psychic struggle and disorder of stress in the head.

Danijel Subašić, a guy from Zadar, this time is even safer and for the third time, he instils hope and self-confidence that stays on the edge of this Russian roulette! It is Jørgensen who this time becomes the new tragedian of Danish destiny. After all, this follows the most beautiful sound you could hear: *'Raaaaakiittiiiiiiiiiiiić!'*

Croatian national team beats Denmark 3: 2 on penalties! Finally, finally, we can breathe more! Without a doubt, this was for me (and I believe 99% of Croatians) the most dramatic match our team ever played!

These penalties are a tough and too hard game of nerves! Watching it was as if someone was loading large blocks of rock on your back or head, however, and after Rakitić's last blow, it was as if all those blocks had fallen and crumbled to pieces, and you flew high from this joy. That's why this soccer is so special because of moments like this. Until the very end, you can't say for sure who will win. In a few minutes, some scenarios change and turn around, from which you almost go crazy.

Although such moments can cost someone's health, it is still worth feeling that indescribable joy and happiness, in the end, that pride for our guys who give so much of themselves in this field. Croatia is qualifying for the quarterfinals of the World Cup for the first time after 20 long years of waiting! This was the main trigger and a big test of ourselves, are we really capable of great things. Something that was necessary to happen and thus 'destroys' the Croatian heads of self-confidence.

On 7 July, the day after my birthday, we are playing against the hosts, this huge Russia! Amazing what an ambience it was. Croatia not only played against the Russian national team but also against the entire stadium, but for that duel, there were our fans who, no matter how small they were, destroyed their throats by singing and cheering. Since I was starting to work soon, we had to go back to Munich. In Munich, it was organised for that match in front of a big screen where all Croats living in the city and its surroundings could come, which gave us a much better atmosphere, since we couldn't all go to the stadium. The atmosphere there was great but what should I write to you about this match? Another Russian roulette…

A tough, hard game started from the first minute and it didn't take us long to realise how difficult it will be with Russians. After half an hour of play,

Cheryshev scores, dear mother of God, what a goal! We need to admit, with great left foot in a bombastic style hits Subašić's right corner, which he could only helplessly follow by watching.

Here we go again, the opposing team took the lead, and we have to come back again. After only less than ten minutes, Kramarić scored with his head on Mandžukić's assist!

Dear Jesus, as the game goes, the Russians don't let go, we don't let go! And again we came to the end without a winner, we have to go into overtime, for the second time in a row. Who has the nerve and strength now for this? We still haven't recovered from that Danish drama before…

After ten minutes of overtime, Domagoj Vida scores! Slavonian 'jolly fellow' and his head give the people a new song and a reason to celebrate! Immediately, the picture with him near the hotel, flew by my mind! A smile I will never forget.

But Russia is still knocking on our door, I no longer know if they have become more aggressive or ours have already started to give in from fatigue. Fernandes scores in 115' and thus open a new page of drama at Sochi Stadium. Another penalty arrived. But OK, there was a little less drama than with Denmark but still, there was drama.

Our goalkeeper opens the penalty with an excellent defence, while after him Brozović scores and already tells us that it will be easier this time. Yeah right, you wish! After Dzagoev's goal, our Kovačić does not score. Akinfeev defends and salts our wounds. The Fernandes is coming again omg! As our commentator said, he scored from the game, he doesn't have to score from the penalty spot, when here is the next scene, he misses the whole goal! Aaaww, come on now, finish with this already!

Luka sets up the ball. When it burst it was as if some slow motion shot had happened. A shot in which we all experienced a small heart attack for a second. The ball bounced and danced near the goal line, omg hard to watch. But the ball was in!

There are four penalties left until the end. Ignashevich, Vida, and Kuzyayev tear the net to the goalkeepers and again everything remains on our dear Rakitić.

If he scores, he leads Croatia to the semi-finals of the World Cup! If he misses… thank God I don't know what it would feel like! Once again stronger: *'Raaaaaaaaaaakiittiiiiiiiiiiiiiiiiiiiiiiiiiiiiiiić! Ivan Rakitić taking us to the semi-finals of the World Cup! Russia also fell!'*

Happy birthday Goran, I thought.

11 July semi-finals Croatia—England

The day before the game, I had a training session with a club that I went to and played proudly in a Croatian jersey! Modrić's number ten on my back is an inspiration that cannot disappear. I played, and I felt much stronger and better! Every time I wear a Croatian jersey, I remember what it means to play with a brave and full heart, firmly and persistently but always humbly as our golden Mr Dalić teaches us!

Never stop, never give up and always carry the fighting spirit within you! Such we are Croats! Our guys taught us that best, especially after that game with England.

How much they just underestimated us on some news, I believe you (Croats) remember very well! Our guys also listened to these provocations but they took it into their hearts and not into their heads. With their hearts, they also responded, on the field.

One very important detail should also be taken into account, Croatia had two very difficult matches behind them, both with overtime. We had injured players more than half of the team but as soon as the day came, the fight for the World Cup finals, as I said, a strong will and desire, the heroic heart comes on the scene.

The match is about to open, all of Moscow is in Croatian jerseys, where we were joined even by the Russians, the hosts of this championship that we knocked out, just a game before.

The national anthems are accompanied by those special emotions, the teams are ready, the match begins. Already in the fifth minute, a shock for Croatia, to which we were honestly already used. Trippier hits relentlessly from a free-kick and leads the English into their world of imagination. I can't even imagine what it was like for our Luka who committed a foul from which he hits. Croatia gets the first goal for the third time in a row, which means that it has to come back for the third time. Regardless of that goal, nothing disturbed the Croatian game. Each of their matches in this championship was above all expectations. From game to game their desire and fighting spirit only grew and grew!

For me personally, this match with England is my most favourite so far, although it is a difficult choice among all the others.

Seeing 1:0 in the semi-finals in the fifth minute, at first glance, of course, does not give any optimism. But here we are talking about Croats! ☺

Our boys were attacking from all sides, like a meteor shower of fire, without mercy. They didn't give up at all! This was a real tense, solid, brave, and phenomenal Croatian game!

The English started to lose their rhythm of the game and created just a couple of chances in front of our goal which I admit, there was also a bit of luck for us. But they also become nervous every time we approached Pickford—the goalkeeper who made our Mandžukić bleed. But our Mario wouldn't be Mario if he didn't grit his teeth, get up and continue this tough game! Mario is a real warrior and will forever remain one of my favourite general soccer players. Let's be realistic, this whole generation!

We bite and bite, it feels like the English are hanging dangerously in the air when here we meet our 68th minute! Vrsaljko, an icon we only heard about until recently, sends a beautiful cross-shot where Ivan Perišić scores with his left foot! And how! It is almost impossible in which way Perišić sends the ball into the goal, and thus the English into despair!

Finally, the goal that we have been waiting for, for so long, Croatia is coming back with the result, it throws us all into a trance because we can! We believe from the deepest bottom of our heart, that we can and will win these Englishmen! After that goal, Subašić, Vrsaljko, Vida, Strinić, Lovren, Rakitić, Modrić, Brozović, Perišić, Mandžukić, and Rebić, so means all XI, all exploded with the desire to play! No one felt tired in those moments anymore, no one wanted to get out of the game, everyone was willing to play stronger, better, with more persistence, to take Croatia to that long-awaited final!

The Turkish referee announced the end of the match. Croatia is going into overtime for the third time. Omg, dear mother of God, let's hope we will not get a penalty drama again, we all thought!

109th minute a moment that changes everything! A moment that erupts the Croatian people with happiness and enthusiasm! Not a wave but a tsunami of emotions shaking all possible white red jerseys! Squares in Croatian cities send strong vibrations to each other, they have already started with fireworks, 'The fiery heart' (fan song) destroying every speaker, celebrations and madness are not lacking, and tears… it is not easy to keep them in such a situation!

Pivarić, who has been criticised by many after missing a penalty against Denmark, is finding the initiative. He tries to cross, Walker bounces the ball in the air, Perišić encounters, jumps high and bounces the ball with his head into a small empty space in front of Pickford, which is followed by Mandžukić who in an incredibly difficult situation finds a hole and drills the man who made him bled before!

The most important goal of the Croatian national team in history happened! Everyone ran like crazy, jumped on Mandžukić, and knocked down a photographer from Mexico. What scenes to remember! After that goal, the English still tried to hurry and to trick our boys to score a goal, which the referee did not fall for.

None of us could believe what happened, are we dreaming?

It was necessary to bring the game to an end and not give up in any way, but as much as the heart still wants to leave everything on the field, the body cannot. Slowly, our team is starting to slow down, to which Dalić starts making changes—substitute. The English acted after that goal, with no sign of strength that they could change anything else. 115th minute—Ćorluka, back then soon retired, enters, and one of our warriors, the great Mario fighter Mandžukić, comes out! Thank you, Mario, for making us so happy, there are no words to describe such emotions! Here is something from Luka Modrić's book about that moment.

'Dalić brings Mandžukić off in the 115$^{th}$ minute. I watch him, the tank, leave the pitch; he's so tired he can barely walk. If this man, who can run non-stop for two straight days, has been so battered, I can only imagine what it is like for the rest.. With these words, Luka said everything about Mario as he is.

On 27 April 2010, a charity match was played between Dinamo Zagreb and Mladost Klenovnik, a place not far from my village. That was the first time I saw Mandžukić live, and he looked too brutal. Yes, they played against total amateurs who did not pose any threat to him, but again, as soon as you see him on the field, you feel that a gladiator is walking on that grass! We adore this type of player precisely for these reasons—his dedication, fighting spirit, and selflessness. As we often say, where others do not dare even with a stick, he goes there with his head.

Four minutes later, another hero comes out of the game! A fighter who also left everything on the field. Our doctor of soccer, who was ridiculed and underestimated by the English media before the game, ran like never before. I don't think we've ever seen him in such an edition eager to prove himself. The English 'sharpened' him very well with their provocations. The man, who played three consecutive games of 120 minutes each, showed no signs of fatigue until the very end.

Our little Luka is a born leader, not because he is a soccer genius but because of the hard life, he had before as a child. Days before the grand final of the World Cup, a video of little Luka Modrić in his oversized jacket grazing goats and the song *My Croatia* in the background appeared. The tingles not only passed through me but almost exploded from me when I saw that scene! I admit I was really struck by this but in that extremely magical and positive direction.

120th minute + 4 minutes of extra time has finished, the referee announces the end!

*'Croatia is in the finals of the World Cup! How nice is to say that! How nice sounds that!'*—shouted a Croatian commentator full of emotions. Yes, it's over! Croatia is truly in the finals of this tournament, which still sounds unreal to us today. Dalić's first comment on our game was: *'They are not normal! How much they just ran and played!'*—he did not believe, so how can the rest of us? While one Brozović ran more than 16 km! Until the very end, regardless of fatigue and exhaustion, no one even wanted to get out of the game, how much that game meant to them. I think for most, this match with England was the match of a lifetime and not just the one coming up, the last of this tournament, the final of the 2018 World Cup in Russia.

After these crazy scenes, an even crazier night follows, celebrating and singing until the morning, both for our boys and for the entire Croatian people. Well, they deserve, a lot!

15 July 2018. Final of the World Cup France—Croatia

How to describe that day now? How to talk about something that both you (Croats) and I do not want to remember, that so painful day?

France, which knocked us out in the semi-finals in '98 and after twenty years, remained a thorn in our side. The result at the end of the game was 4: 2 in the advantage of France, which made them world champions, but when I looked at the game… it was something completely different.

That day the result and the game were two different concepts. The fact was that the French did not have as hard a tournament as we did, not even close to the fact that they had a day off more and practically a game less when we look at our three overtimes. A huge advantage for them if we took that into account, and they were still struggling with us.

The match started very well for us. We took the initiative, held possession of the ball, and combined perfectly. The French looked helpless on a couple of occasions and then out of nowhere, suddenly a lot happened! A controversial foul that mentally cut us off and from which our fighter Mandžukić unhappily scored an own goal. We losing 1:0. What a pain in the 18th minute and again as against Denmark, Russia, and England we have to chase the lead of the opponent.

This was really too much for all of us, but there is nothing to complain about, it was the last game, that big final that someone has been waiting for all their lives and many do not get that moment. But even then, we didn't stop believing, we knew deep in our hearts that our guys wouldn't stop now in the last game, we believed they would leave literally everything on the field without any doubts because there is nothing to lose. And it was like that! After only ten minutes, Perišić masterfully launched a torpedo into the net. It was wonderful to see the ball fly past the net. We're back! Hope has come to life and ours seems unreal again, there is no end to the enthusiasm… unfortunately there is this time…

38th-minute penalty for Griezmann, a decision made by VAR—This is not happening! Pitana himself isn't sure what to judge after confused looks at that screen box. It's really amazing from which situations we get goals and as Mr Dalić himself said, we played perhaps the best halftime in the whole tournament. Even in the second half, we started strong and full of confidence, but here comes the third goal by the French. We haven't even recovered yet, here's the fourth. As catastrophic as it seemed to lose so much, we didn't give up. Mandžukić once again confirms why he is so stubborn in his perseverance, makes Lloris panic and scores his third goal in the World Cup, to which he shares the same number of goals with Perišić.

Pitana, a referee we will not sympathise with after this match, marks the end but also the beginning of indescribable sadness for our heroes. Half the team after that whistle fell to their knees from exhaustion and fatigue, which clearly showed that they really did their best, to the last atom of strength. It's unimaginably hard to face the thought when you know we were stronger and better, in every way! We played the whole championship phenomenally! I said, and I will always stick to my opinion, if we played after that two, three more times with the French, they wouldn't get us! France did not delight in the games throughout the tournament. That is why it is so difficult to face the realisation that one such team that gave us goals from two fouls, an own goal, and a penalty, now raises the trophy and not us who have proven countless times what it's fight and perseverance! But this is soccer, unfortunately. It's neither the first nor the last time, that win a less valuable team.

There are no easy ways and words to describe this success of our guys! How much emotion and joy they have contributed to us, we will remember and talk about for generations!

That day, even the sky cried for our misfortune. I sit petrified in grief, and I still don't believe it, I'm looking at TV and see Modrić being called out to receive the award for the best player of the tournament. Poor Luka comes all broken physically and mentally, receives an individual award for the best and his face says it all. He takes that trophy without emotion, without happiness, on the edge of tears he tries to control himself, to not look towards that other trophy that he wanted so much, but he simply couldn't resist. When I saw that scene, I couldn't either. Tears began.

We watched the game in a bar full of our fans and when we went home, I walked like I was lost. Lost in thoughts... *what would be if this or that happened...* I was wondering.

I look at the streets, Croats celebrate, sing, honking with cars, and I think, well, we did, we really achieved great success, but I only became more aware of that a day later.

I can't even imagine what it was like for our boys in Russia! To the last! It took a couple of hours for all those emotions to subside and a new page to turn in the morning. From Croatia and around the world, moments of defeat turned into hours of celebration and that lifted them up! They return home after 35 wonderful days with silver medals, leave Russia with wonderful memories, and arrive in Zagreb where they are greeted by half a million people! If the square was bigger, there would be even more. From the airport itself, they were accompanied by both old and young. It took them more than five hours to reach the square, which is about 10, 15 km away. Event and scenes to remember!

The only thing we all resented about the Zagreb organisation was that the welcome of our boys in the square was too short. The team was indeed in Russia on the last day without normal sleep, and they were completely torn, even a few beers splashed them easily and quickly in the bus when they were coming from the airport, but they were still willing and eager to celebrate a few minutes longer. They seemed to be looking for ways to thank all of us for the support we provided them. The real truth is that we are grateful to them for uniting and making us so happy and of course for writing that silver history!

Even days after these beautiful pictures, there was no end. When they all went to their families in different parts of Croatia, they also had their own individual welcomes there because all this meant so much to people.

Mr Dalić also arrived in my hometown of Varaždin, where they gave him a wonderful welcome. I went crazy worrying that I couldn't at least attend those moments. My family was there, and they told me it was great, which is easy to conclude when you see those pictures from Varaždin.

We may not have become champions but we have conquered the world! The whole world bowed to us after our tournament, it just felt that day before the final that we got a lot more sympathy and fans than the French. People fell in love with our jerseys and our guys, how could they not after such a spectacle that they provided and left! No matter what, they are champions for us! They were and will remain.

### A letter to our players and a message to all fans Written 19 July 2018

*What to say, with which words to start and end this wonderful Croatian fairy tale?*

*I think it all started from the moment when our great and humble Mr Dalić took over the guys who were so eager and hungry for success.*

*These days I read all possible media, the impressions of our people but also in the world and when I see all this, something inside me forces me, my heart and mind come together to throw some pictures of emotions out of me on paper.*

*Indeed, a man can see thousands of images for the history of Croatia that will be remembered for centuries as long as we exist because this is something so huge and large that there is no size to measure, which in fact dear Croats are not even aware of, and we just think that we are.*

*Due to my circumstances, I did not have the opportunity to attend and greet our boys in Zagreb, but also in my hometown of Varaždin. I followed everything live online and what can I say other than that I shot with pride. Like me, so do the rest of the people in Munich where we live, but I believe the rest of the Croats all over the world. On the other hand, I was on the verge of tears because I wanted to live that moment there so much, I would be lying if I said that I did not wipe away tears when I heard my homeland sing in a loud voice for our boys and all Croatia. I wiped away tears even after the finals. I tried so hard to hold back tears because I felt so sorry for these guys, we all know they deserved that world trophy, but sometimes unfortunately sport has its downsides and it doesn't ask you if you will accept it or not.*

*Regardless, these guys left their hearts on the field, in every game, at every moment, and became our champions but they also won the hearts of many in the world. All that... and much, much more....*

*People who used to provoke, insult, and underestimate our players changed their minds after that dramatic final and bowed to our 'small' country. After all this, there are a lot of things to learn from our heroes and not small, but huge life lessons!*

### Mr Dalić

*It all starts with one man, who these days is known in every corner of our small homeland, but also in some parts of the world.*

*A gentleman, humble, simple, wise, collected, thoughtful, modest, small but again so big, dedicated to God but also to his country, a patriot who shows how much he loves Croatia in every way, in any situation...*

*Ladies and gentlemen, every Croatian mouth utters with indescribable pride a name that changed us, if not for a long time, at least for a short time, a name that woke us from the pits of negativity and pulled us to the very top! A name that has brought thousands of us together. A name that first associates us with a fighting spirit, humility, and love. The name that our Croatia needed and needed so badly. I present you our golden Zlatko the great Dalić.*

*A man who changed Croatia in just over a month. A man who does not know about greed, arrogance, stinginess, who even responds to provocations in a non-arrogant and realistic mood. A man who should be a role model to many. A man who teaches with humility and discipline.*

*On behalf of all Croatia, we thank you with indescribable pride for returning our faith, for filling our hearts, for helping us to see, that it is possible, that it is possible to make dreams come true, and most importantly, that you reminded us how our homeland is truly loved. We love you always and forever and Thank you for everything! We truly hope that you will remain the selector of the Croatian national team and that you will continue to allow us to dream new dreams.*

### Danijel Subašić

*Dear our crazy 'octopus' from Zadar! You showed more than you should in the most difficult moments. You pulled out the team when it was most required of you. Thank you legend, we all know you wouldn't have succeeded so much without your 'favourite' T-shirt. Don't worry, your dear friend was also there, every time with you, and he shared that silver with you. Enjoy these moments Danijel because one day you will tell your grandchildren about Russia, how you defeated Messi, stopped the tough Danes and Russians, and Englishmen...*

### Dejan Lovren, Domagoj Vida, Šime Vrsaljko, Ivan Strinić

*Fellas, Croatia has not had such conductors in defence for a long time! You have instilled indescribable security in everyone. Such caution and movement in defence have not yet been seen. I saw every opponent's attack in advance as unsuccessful because I believed so much that we have rocks in defence, which turned out to be the case. Amazing how strong our defence is!*

### Luka Modrić, Ivan Rakitić, Mateo Kovačić, Marcelo Brozović

*What to say to names like this?*

*Pure fantasy! We have the strongest midfield in the world! For the world to put together the strongest midfielders in today's soccer, no one can compete with us, you can't against ours in any way, and that has been confirmed.*

*Luka is my hero and teacher. I try to learn so much from him both in soccer and as a person. I watched Luka live for the first time against Italy in 2012 in Poland and from 90 min. of the match, I watched Luka closely for at least 75 minutes. Amazing what a beast, what a doctor! He moved from Tottenham to Real Madrid that year and never, but I really never doubted his quality like most people that year. My lifelong desire is to meet or at least get a picture with two players. One of them is our master Luka! I burst into tears of pride with joy when Luka took the award for the best player in the World Cup. Just remember, dear Croatian people, how much we were all afraid would Luka be able to play the whole game with the Danes, Russians, and English due to exhaustion, but when the 'little' Luka was inexhaustible sprinting and running, fighting in all directions in 120 minutes—a detail that I will remember and which will always remind me how to fight to the very end!*

*Luka the master, for me you are the best midfielder in the entire history of soccer, and I don't care who says what because you have proven your qualities and more than enough! Dear Luka, if you ever read this, if I had a moment with you, it would mean a lot to me, which means, everything in soccer.*

**Mario Mandžukić, Ivan Perišić, Ante Rebić, Andrej Kramarić**

*'It's hard to beat someone who never gives up, almost impossible'. (Babe Ruth)*

*This is how I would describe your performances in the shortest possible way. Thank you for leaving your heart on the field. Thank you for all the goals, thank you for running for every opportunity, for every pressure on the opponent, even for those balls that you knew you would not reach but you still tried. Thank you Heart of Fire!*

**Lovre Kalinić, Dominik Livaković, Duje Ćaleta—Car, Vedran Ćorluka, Tin Jedvaj, Josip Pivarić, Milan Badelj, Filip Bradarić, Marko Pjaca**

*'You can't hang out with negative people and expect a positive life'. (Joel Osteen)*

*This was the key to a good atmosphere in the team. Although you did not play too much, I believe that you contributed a very important part to the success and that is the support and motivation of our first XI. Thank you from the bottom of my heart for the fact that you were the ones who could influence our boys even more.*

**Coaching staff (Assistant coaches, Goalkeeping and Fitness Coaches, Physiotherapists, Doctors, Team manager and everyone else)**

*Thank you very much to you who were with us in the same way, 'patching' them and doing your best to cure them for every difficult game because it was also very, very important.*

**For all Croatian fans but also foreigners**

*Once again, a big THANK YOU guys, for every second of joy and happiness that you have contributed to us and that you have united us so much as one 'small' nation!*

*THANK YOU also to our fans, there is no point in writing the same words anymore because there really is no dictionary and description that would describe what you have achieved, for us and our homeland! How nice it is to watch today the videos of our fans celebrating everywhere…*

*When someone asks me about Croatia, I just send them scenes and pictures of our fans.*

*What I recommend to many, to do the same as me. Print a big picture of our team and hang it in the place where you pass every day, to remind yourself how combative and persistent you have to be to achieve your goals. Our fiery guys showed us the best way. From the first to the last!*

### 3 pictures that will remain in my memory forever from Russia

1. *One hundred times more, fighting spirit in absolutely every situation. The attitude 'never give up' and 'believe in your dreams' will always cross my mind when I think of this 'Russian fairy tale'.*
2. *Before the grand finale, when suddenly, unexpectedly, a video of little Luka Modrić, only five years old, appeared on the Velebit mountain, in his oversized jacket grazing goats, and in the background the song 'My Croatia'. I was so shaken by the tingling when I saw it, with the fact that everything our Luka went through and broke through, came to the very roof of soccer.*
3. *Tears of Joško Jeličić—Croatian pundit and retired soccer player. After the final, when our Joško Jeličić commented in tears on the entire championship and the games of our team, when he said it with so much emotion and how much that furious pride in our boys could be seen in his eyes.*
*'I feel proud because no one did how they united Croatia. This is therefore especially difficult to watch, them crying and it will take time to recover. What they did, they died on the field, they did their best, they united us and not only did they unite us, but we also became better people because of them. And they did it with their sacrifice, their suffering, and everything they have done for all of us in the last month'.*

*Joško Jeličić*

*Without the slightest doubt, this soccer generation can be used as an inspiration to every team but also to an individual. Truly this is a story that can motivate any person who hunts for their dreams, no matter what life career they choose.*

<3 ONE HEART ONE SOUL ONE CROATIA <3
Your fan, Goran Žganec

### *About Luka Modrić...*

Although he scored only four goals (three from the penalty spot and one from the game) in the entire tournament, Luka won the hearts of many with his games and qualities. The leader and captain of this already now, a silver generation who achieved the dreams of many and thus enrolled, as we like to say, in the immortality of soccer.

After the match with England:

*'After the final whistle I stay on the pitch, taking my time to enjoy the view of the stands. It's taken 12 years of playing in Croatia's shirt to see this. It's the moment I've hoped for since I was 13 years old and watched the generation that came third in the world. This is where my career and my story as a footballer reaches its conclusion. I've won everything with Real. I'm playing with Croatia in the FIFA World Cup Final. No matter how it ends, I feel I have accomplished what I hoped for.*

Luka, who went through scenes unimaginable to us, such situations made him stronger and capable of great things. He broke through from nothing to his biggest dreams and for that very reason, he is just another proof that nothing is impossible in this life! Without resentment to everyone in the national team and others in general soccer, there are a lot of great and fantastic players who play in the midfield, and they will always have my respect and let no one be angry with me for what might sound like an exaggeration to many, but Luka Modrić is for me the best midfielder in soccer history! And I'm not saying that because we are both Croats.

My dream would come true if I could exchange at least a few words with him.

After the World Cup in addition to this great success, Luka won and conquered the world on a couple of occasions. As he says, the pleasant consequences of great success are coming to each other, which was shown during that special 2018. So let's take turns.

Before the World Cup, he won Europe with his Real Madrid four times (for the third time in a row) in his career.

At the World Cup, he was named the best player in Russia, where he was also selected as the best team in the championship, and won and brought home silver.

UEFA declared him the best midfielder, but also the best in the 2017/18 season, where he got 90 points, even more than second-placed Cristiano Ronaldo.

The best player in the world The Best by FIFA in the 2017/18 season. I was touched when I saw Zvonimir Boban, a legend from the bronze generation shed tears at Luka's speech. Zvone was Luke's idol and an example to follow. What a feeling could that be, when you made cry someone you admired and followed, someone who motivated you all your life.

After all these awards when a man thinks it's over, here's just the real highlight of his career. Luka did not lift the World Cup trophy, but he did lift the highest possible individual award that exists in soccer, that beautiful Ballon d'Or! And even ahead of which players! Luka is the first player to break such a long dominance (as much as 11 years) and the eternal rival between Cristiano Ronaldo and Lionel Messi! These two geniuses who have greatly changed soccer history are certainly not easy to surpass. Who will be more proud of our Luka, than we Croats after such recognition! And right behind us, a crowded Santiago Bernabéu stadium, which gave him as well a standing ovation for such recognition.

In addition to these most important ones, Luka also won a good number of other awards, such as being proclaimed an honorary citizen of the city Zadar, and even being named the best Croatian soccer player for the sixth time. He closed the year with another club trophy, the title of world club champion.

Without a doubt, this was Luka's year, the crown of his career! A couple of years later, he received another great recognition. They ranked him among the 100 best athletes in the world in the twenty-first century.

Luka is a player and a person I admire and learn from as much as I can, but also an example I can pass on to my children one day. A year later after all these events, he released his autobiography which I read at lightning speed. Twice. Luka is a true example to follow—humble, brave, intelligent, combative, persistent, simple, wise, and charismatic.

*Every one of us has their own path. Every story is as different as we are as players and people. But the foundation of every success is the belief in yourself, even when someone tells you, 'There's no point.' There's always a point, trust me. I have already been told that, after reaching my zenith at 33 years of age and after becoming the best player in the world, playing for the best club and for the national team that came second in the world, I would not be able to play at the same level. This has only given me the motivation to show this up as a prejudice – one of the many that have followed me in my life and my career. But my biggest motive, the one that led me from the first training session until today, is my unconditional love for football. This love is the reason I'm going to play for as long as my feet can carry me and the ball will listen to me. And I'll continue to give it everything I've got.*

*I know it won't be simple. I know my career has always taken the more difficult road, but, in the end, I reached the top. Staying on it is difficult, but I know from experience – the best things in life never come easy.*

*Luka Modrić*

By all these texts you can clearly recognise all my passion for our national team. The best test of my love for soccer and our team I 'passed' back in 2012. when the European Championships were held in Poland and Ukraine. A prize game was published on the Internet in which a 'fan verse' was to be designed to support our team, and as a reward for the best verses, tickets for the matches of the Croatian national team were distributed. There I saw and felt an ideal golden opportunity, and threw myself into work the same minute.

With my verses, I won two tickets for the match against Italy! When the answer came to me that I had won the tickets, I didn't believe it and somehow everything seemed like a scam to me. I didn't answer anything when in the next message they sent me the address where I could come and pick up the tickets. Wow, this is seriously I thought! Well, I really won something here! Since I had a friend in Zagreb, I asked him to pick up those tickets. When he sent me a picture of those tickets, then I just realised and became aware that I have the opportunity to attend one of our team's games against Italy.

*'Wooow this is not true'*—it was banging my head! I got the opportunity to watch live Modrić, Mandžukić, Perišić, back then Pletikosa, Kranjčar, Da Silva, Srna, and others against one Italy, back then led by the incredible Pirlo and one of my favourite goalkeepers Gianluigi Buffon! This was a touch of a dream!

Until then I didn't have a passport and believe it or not, that match was the reason I ran to make a passport, which I really needed later! To have as a souvenir, I put those verses on my jersey, and with that same friend, we travelled to faraway Poland, for an unforgettable feeling! Cheering in the city, euphoria in the air, songs, and Croatian jerseys—that's the feeling that exploded on every corner, especially in the silver 2018!

Here are these verses, which I should have written a little differently in English, as they differ from the Croatian—the original version:

*What beats in our chests hard and clear,*
*attracts even the youngest Croat without any doubt and fear.*

*Prayer and fight is their way,*
*tears and sweat are the pride of the mother's bay.*

*To the European Cup, red and white carry us,*
*joy and optimism always bring as a full bus.*

*The stands are ours every fan believes,*
*when the team goes after our dreams.*

*Goran Žganec*

Euro 2012, Poznań, Poland – Italy vs Croatia

In Croatia at my parent's house

During my time in Croatia, I tried to include in my match schedule some free time for Elizabeth's parents. It would not be fair and nice of me if after I brought them to Croatia and introduced them to my parents, I just left them to watch the World Cup matches with us, even though they had absolutely nothing against it because they love soccer too.

I took them to many places in Zagorje. To the city of Varaždin a couple of times, although we all like to spend time in a natural environment, such as vineyards, peaceful Castle and Lake of Trakošćan, the shrine of Marija Bistrica, and a little bit to Krapina and the famous museum Kraneamus—Neanderthal Museum, which I admit, is very creatively made.

Since we were already in Croatia, I wanted to feel a little of our sea, so I took my Peruvians, together with my father, to feel what it's like to spend the summer on the Adriatic. We didn't travel anywhere too far because again there was no time to waste. About three hours to Selce, a place I always happily remember from my childhood.

When my father, as a professional bus driver, drove regular lines from Varaždin to the Croatian coast, I had the opportunity to go with him as a little boy. Who would have thought, literally from a young age I loved travelling. I enjoyed sitting behind him, right in the front seats of the bus, and watching everything I could see, through all the places we passed. As hard as it was back then for a boy of my age to get up around 4:00 in the morning, I didn't even think to miss such adventures.

We usually left early in the morning and reached our last destination in the afternoon where we stayed for a good part of the day, and only in the evening, we set off again to Varaždin. My father has always loved swimming in the sea because he is aware of how much it helps the human body in many ways. Sea salt makes miracles on human skin. That day we reached the place I mentioned above, Selce. I didn't know how to swim until that day, but what you read next will change my life in some useful way.

As it was his habit after a long drive to rest and cool off in the sea, we were on a beach whose entrance to the sea was already about 2 metres deep at the beginning. And now it was in Goran's head, either you go or you don't. I could only jealously watch my father enjoy swimming in the sea or decide, now that's enough, I'm going to learn to swim!

It's not I didn't care about staying on that hot sun, while my father was cooling off in one of the Adriatic beauties. It had to come once, I think. After my father explained the swimming technique to me, I jumped into the sea and swung my arms and legs as if it were my last.

When I think back to that moment in my childhood, I also realised that as a child I was already beginning to create the habit and trait of a persistent character. As much as I was afraid of that deep water at first, I promised myself that day, that I would not go home without learning to swim. The first few minutes were torture but no matter how fast I was wasting energy, I didn't leave the sea until I learned. That day, not only I did learn to swim, but I naturally adapted to the depths. Today it is not a problem for me to jump even into the ocean no matter how deep. Of course, the other story is whether I would really do it, regardless of whether everything is hidden in that water. But no worries mom, when I say so, it doesn't have to mean we literally jumped off the ship. Although we once planned to do a bungee jump but calm the stress, we didn't do that either. ☺

Here, now you know the story of how I learned or more precisely was 'forced' to swim.

After all these little adventures, the moment came that we had to go back to Munich, and those were the days before the Croatian national team's match with Russia.

This summer really passed unexpectedly for everyone! I mentioned before that for me personally the best year was 2016 and that was because of the different days filled in each month throughout the year. When we talk about soccer, it's definitely that silver 2018! When our team passed that hard Danish team, something told me: *'Okay, if they really reach the top this must serve not only as of the infinite joy of the whole nation, but I must know it and personally use it as the main inspiration that will carry me closer to my goals'.*

I didn't believe that our little Croatia would really reach the grand final! When Modrić missed a penalty in the final minutes against Denmark, it hit me in the head like a UFC fighter's slap and yelled in my head that this was going to cost us the whole game.

The second time I felt a shockingly emotional high kick was when Schmeichel stopped our Pivarić from the penalty. I was drenched in sweat at first when he stopped Badelj, but since they had just started, it was as if I hadn't become aware of it yet, so I didn't take too much to heart. Yeah, right, to whom am I lying! I was on the verge of a stroke.

After Pivarić's penalty of 99, 99% I was sure that we would not return! It's over, here's a scenario and endless sadness like we experienced that Turkey in

2008 and Portugal from 2016 together, I thought! We are not destined, not for this so ingenious generation, I could already imagine how the newspapers comfort us like heroes, I was convincing myself... until the last series of penalties, the Danes miss, our calm master Rakitić sends Croatia into a new trance of madness!

When I think of that game, both the first the incredible physical fight and later the mental ones, and then I combine that with what I felt, I have to take them as an example of inspiration... there is no better example than the one they made! That is why I have suggested to you, dear readers, to hang a big picture of our team in your home, to always remember with great pleasure those heavenly days, but also the message they left at the end.

*'Follow your dreams and ambitions. And never give up! '*

*Zlatko Dalić*

\*\*\*

After this positive madness, when everything calmed down, it was our second wedding anniversary. Elizabeth and I decided to celebrate this with a three-day trip to Prague.

Since the year before, for the first anniversary, we were still catching the stable rhythm of the first year spent in Munich, this time we deserved to treat ourselves with such a gift. Prague is about four hours away by car, which did not cause us any problems, but we embarked on another small adventure with our, back then new Hyundai.

Europe has beautiful places, believe me when you are told by a person who has visited the good north of it, and quite a number of places in the Mediterranean. Of so many interesting ports, I regret that Prague cannot be one of them! Personally, Prague surprised me very, very extremely! For me, Prague is the most beautiful European city I have seen so far, and I have seen many of them. Amazing architecture of buildings that follow each other not only from older history but also from more recent times. I prepared for this trip a week in advance. I studied various interesting locations in the city, wrote down where best to change money, which restaurants to visit and of course the tradition that does not change during my travels, where to taste the best beer that is so famous when Prague is mentioned. Even though we got there in late autumn we still captured extremely beautiful natural scenes. From the first day we arrived and sat down to eat something, I ordered the famous Prague speciality Svíčková which won my appetite from the first! In those three days every meal we had I ordered just that one, I just couldn't resist how good it was. Especially in combination with Czech beer.

The history that this city has is very attractive. I was surprised by the size of the famous Charles Bridge which I believe looks creepy at night as from horror movies. Along with it are a couple of locations in Prague. One of them is Vyšehrad. If they weren't so far, great horror movies and thrillers of mysterious themes could be made. The ambience itself evokes a feeling of tense fear. Fortress, basilica, chapel, cemetery... all in one package.

On the main square is the third-oldest astronomical clock in the world, which was set back in 1410. The watch still works perfectly. The centre of Prague contains around 60 churches, while the outer part of the city has a little more. There's quite a lot to see when I talk about churches. The Cathedral of St. Vitus gives an impressive picture. One of the squares that also impressed me is the one that leads to the National Museum. Quite a wide avenue my eyes had never seen before. The National Theatre also has stunning architecture. It doesn't make sense to me to explain to you all the buildings in Prague because you have to see them for yourself to know the right words that give you the best personal description. I can only tell you that it is worth the time and money to see this amazing Prague!

Due to work in Munich, we were not able to get more free time which is also the reason why I wanted to prepare well for the Czech exploration. In those three days, we found ourselves like camels carrying a load through the desert but it was worth it. We went from north to south as much as possible and not in a very relaxing rhythm. The only real tourist relaxation was the moments when we sat down to eat and drink something.

Prague doesn't really look like such a big and complicated city, at least judging by the subway which is far simpler than this one in Munich. After our wedding anniversary celebration in a magical city full of different styles of architecture, on the way home, we remembered that we forgot to bring the most important souvenir from Prague—at least a few Czech beers that I admit have proven themselves so well known. Believe it or not, we stopped at the last gas station before the German border, only to take a couple of Czech beers to Munich.

Our second Christmas in Bavaria has arrived. Like last year, still a small Christmas tree but therefore a great Christmas spirit. Advent time in Munich is very filled with Christmas lights and all kinds of decorations and on every corner, houses where you can drink traditional mulled wine. We travelled to Croatia for a few days after the holidays. My first long hour ride through the white ambience outlines new versions of natural beauty. The snow followed us all the way, so you can imagine those beautiful Austrian green landscapes you see in the commercials, this time covered with a white blanket.

The year 2018 closes its last pages but also inscribes one of the best for our Croatian people, which neither I nor my parents remember that we have ever been so filled with joy and happiness. My father told my brother and me 98' about the back then matches of the Croatian national team (when they finished third at the World Cup):

*'My children, watch and remember well this success of the Croatian national team because the question is whether it will ever happen again in your life, whether you will ever experience it again'.*

After this 'fresh' success of our team from Russia, my brother, and I gladly remind our father of the words he addressed to us in those ancient days. I am very glad that our father experienced the even better success of our team than the one from '98. Although I was indescribably sorry that we didn't share those bombastic emotions together when Mario scored against England, for the passage to the final. I knew in my heart that my father was overjoyed at that moment! I knew that my father and mother were as proud of Modrić as the society as well!

Castle Neuschwanstein, near Munich, Germany

Prague, Czech Republic – Part 1

Prague, Czech Republic – Part 2

Prague, Czech Republic – Part 3

# 2.6 Second — the church wedding

Here we are in 2019, which started great for us by changing the apartment. With Isa, a friend I met at the hotel in my previous job, and because of whom I had the opportunity to feel the atmosphere at the Allianz Arena, I stayed in touch, and we often hang out and usually talk about soccer topics. After two years spent in a one-bedroom apartment, I knew we needed to be more persistent in looking for a better and bigger apartment. I was no longer sure where better to look, in which neighbourhoods of Munich, so one day I sat down with Isa and asked him for advice.

Isa grew up in Munich and knows very well both the people and parts of Munich, and I knew I could confide in him about such things. Unterföhring—he says, after a few minutes of thinking. He convinced me that I would have to look for an apartment in that part of Munich because it is somehow the most suitable for living. A quiet neighbourhood, without any excessive noise, has everything you need and the best part is that the place seems more like a village and not part of the city, and yet it is quite close, by car to the downtown around 15–20 minutes. Perfect! I threw myself into looking for apartments and this time I hit even harder!

I sent about 20 applications a day and after a couple of weeks, I got an answer and the opportunity to visit and see the apartment in Unterföhring. Elizabeth couldn't because of work, so I went to check the apartment by myself. The apartment didn't look the most attractive to me, since it was in the attic of the house. The two-bedroom layout too. It wasn't very affordable either, but when you look at the neighbourhood that the apartment is in, I believe that the price is more because of that than because of the apartment itself.

When I got home and told Elizabeth what kind of apartment it was, it was logical that she wasn't thrilled either. We thought for days, whether to take the apartment or not. We had a 100% chance to take over that apartment, but because of the price it was too expensive for us, so we gave up in the end. Shortly afterwards, I received an email from another application, also regarding the apartment. Since we had a lot of rejections by then and every expected opportunity fell into the water, we somehow lost more hope in being able to find a better apartment.

Although I didn't plan too much to go and see that apartment, Elizabeth still wanted to try our luck. The first thing I noticed, when we got there, was that the apartment was literally across the street from the one we had given up before. This apartment was great compared to the other one. Only 14 steps to it, also two rooms but much more convenient. Balcony on the other side, large garage, basement, and laundry room. Everything we didn't have in the first apartment, we had here. Although we fell in love with that apartment right away and filled out the application the same day, again I didn't dare to hope after seeing quite many interested people who also applied for that apartment.

After about a week, I sent an email about that apartment because we knew absolutely nothing whether we had a chance or not. When the lady who was supposed to forward our papers reported that she forgot to do so. OMG, so now it is certain that we will not get an apartment I thought. After all, those who applied surely someone got it because as I already mentioned, here the apartment goes like € 100 on the sidewalk. There is no theoretical chance that we have any more chances, this one forgot to forward the papers and those are the precious minutes we lost. Next week again email, from that same lady. Elizabeth was the first to read the email while I was working the morning shift, and she texted me, *'We got the apartment!'*

It took me a few minutes to figure out which apartment it was. Simply, shock! How I wonder! What a joke! After a few days when we took over the apartment and sorted out all the paperwork, I had to ask, *'Ma'am, please now explain to me how it happened that you chose us?'*

The lady kindly replied, *'You see, we had two candidates in front of you. The first was an older lady who didn't like the view from the balcony, so she gave up. The others were a young couple who had a dog, and we don't approve any pets in the apartment, so you came in third to take over the apartment'.*

Hallelujah with them then, I thought with happiness. We are moving to Unterföhring!

Here, this story of how we got an apartment is another proof of how patient and persistent you need to be in life. It means a lot to you when you change better, more convenient, and nicer living conditions, and remember that I almost gave up looking at this apartment at the beginning. You may not be able to best understand how difficult it is to get an apartment in Munich but that is why those who live there know best.

*'Never give up because maybe exactly that last attempt will lead you to the so much desired goal'. – Unknown*

This year we have chosen to finally get married in the church. Since we got married for the first time in Croatia, due to fairness and respect for our parents, we planned to have a second wedding in Peru, to satisfy both parties.

Things did not go exactly as expected (as usual) and the plan for the Peruvian wedding became quite complicated, which led us to the conclusion that it is best to repeat the wedding in Croatia. It was not easy to plan all the preparations in Croatia from Munich. I couldn't expect much from Elizabeth as she still doesn't speak Croatian well, although she understands it quite well. But step by step, we managed to sort it out.

We chose one of the churches in Varaždin, the same one I mentioned earlier in this book. It was the *Church of the Good Shepherd*, next to which I welcomed 2015 by myself. I came that evening lost and worried and left full of hope, courage, and God's blessing.

While we were still together in Croatia three years ago, we met a priest who served the Masses in that church. We liked him so much that we only wanted him to marry us and exact in that same church where we met him. The date of the church wedding was 3 August, with just over 30 people. What I have to mention to you is how I felt that day, first of all.

We arrived a week before the wedding from Munich and those were intense days for me. What I had arranged by phone from Germany, now I had to personally check and make sure everything went well. The rhythm of running to different places totally exhausted me. If you haven't gotten married yet and prepared everything for the day, you don't know what awaits you, what kind of stress. For those of you who have been through this, you know well and too well what I am talking about. ☺

A couple of hours before the wedding, when we had prepared everything to the last, I went to the living room and simply had to lie down on the couch. I also told you many times about the ship, how much exhausted me at times but to this day, until the wedding, I was totally emotionless. Not because I wasn't aware of my own wedding but because all those preparations had exhausted me that I couldn't think anymore. I love Elizabeth, but in that condition, you think, I don't care, just give me to rest a bit. I tried to sleep for at least half an hour but I couldn't do that either. When it was time to jump into my suit and head for the church, somewhere inside rang in my head, *'Hello! You're getting married today! I know you're on the edge of strength, but now is the real-time where you need to muster even more energy! Then God, please give me a little strength just to push through this day!'*

As the moment approached, my batteries became more and more charged. From entering the church until coming home from the celebration, I was totally fine.

From Elizabeth's side, only parents and a couple of colleagues from work were present, while from mine, close family and friends. I noticed how much everyone present at the church wedding gave compliments and admired our priest, who found a phenomenal way to maintain the wedding. Because of Elizabeth, the ceremony had to be held in English but this did not disrupt the priest's desire to perform our wedding in two languages, Croatian and English. He performed it very creatively and so emotionally at times that I noticed in some even tears, including the two of us. That day, I think he touched even God himself with his words.

After the Mass and ceremony, he gave us a cross made of Brač stone (stone from the island of Brač) which we keep in the apartment, and we often remember to touch that cross in passing, with the thoughts of God and his blessing. We are infinitely grateful to him for making our special day even more special. Without any doubt, our good friend and priest left us some of the most beautiful memories.

*Thank you very much for that, we wish you from the bottom of our hearts that dear God bless all the ways that await you.*

A celebration followed. A party that is not forgotten! Place, food, band, service, cake, company… everything was great! The mood did not drop at any moment! Singing, dancing, no one showed any signs of fatigue or boredom, everyone had a great time, which was the most important thing for us!

It is a mystery how all those preparations before the wedding take an incredibly long time during which I was on the edge of my strength, and one evening that you finally welcome flies by with lightning speed and without any fatigue. It was celebrated until dawn. I have to thank once again the whole company who provided a fantastic atmosphere throughout the evening and night until the morning sun rays. As soon as we pulled out the two national flags from the start, we were attractive to others as well. We were surprised when we even saw the staff at the restaurant taking photos of our crazy and fun scenes, of course, we were totally fine with that.

An interesting fact is that a very good friend with whom I attended high school, during all those years from my high school days, both he and I travelled and had different lives, far from our homeland. After all these years, it turned out that he also lived in Germany, only an hour away from Munich by car. Fate brought us closer again after hitherto crazy life adventures. That friend is my wedding best man today, and I am very proud and grateful that he accepted such an important role. Friends like him are rare today. Always in a good mood and strong will ready to help anything when needed.

Another interesting fact that we noticed later and that happened totally by accident is that our date of 3 August was the same date three years before when I asked for Elizabeth's parents 'blessing, and just a few days later proposed to her at the magical Machu Picchu.

To end this chapter regarding this particular day, we still fondly remember and comment on that night filled with fun and laughter. I hope that others do the same because, in our opinion, everything was perfect. Long live the newlyweds! ☺

*** 

After an unforgettable 3 August, we stayed in Croatia for another week and spent time with my family. Although I wanted to stay longer, of course at home is always the most beautiful, we had to go back to Munich because on 11 August we had a new but very special trip—our honeymoon, this time in the original version. You will be surprised when you find out where we decided to celebrate this very important trip of ours!

A couple of days before that, we spent a relaxing time in the vineyard, with my father's barbecue, my mother's salad, and a lot of laughter that just continued us through a series of great days.

The Second Wedding

Let's party!

# 2.7 Back to the Aries

Here it is, you found out! We return to the ship that connected us! The ship that changed my life from the moment I stepped on it, the ship that awakens all those best and craziest adventures, emotions, and memories, the ship on which we met so many great people, the ship that sailed into our lives and in some way never sailed out! But this time, we will also feel what it is like to finally be a guest on a cruise! I mentioned and promised myself, when I left the ship, that I would return one day but as a guest, I fulfilled that. Now you have the opportunity to hear my experience of how that feels too. As for the destinations, the ship was visiting, we didn't care as much about it, although we saw them many times. The most important thing for us was to mark our honeymoon by travelling to the place we met—the ship Aries!

*Ship's Itinerary (11–18 August)—Mediterranean*
*Sunday—Embarkation day—Venice, Italy*
*Monday—Kotor, Montenegro*
*Tuesday—Corfu, Greece*
*Wednesday—Santorini, Greece*
*Thursday—Mykonos, Greece*
*Friday—Argostoli, Greece*
*Saturday—Dubrovnik, Croatia*
*Sunday—Disembarkation day—Venice, Italy*

We decided to travel by bus from Munich to Venice, we arrived at around 8:00 a.m. From a fairly great distance, we spotted cruisers from the bus, as many as three of them. Elizabeth couldn't recognise which one was ours, as we saw them like that from the semi-fog, while I recognised our Aries by her shape immediately and surely exclaimed, *'That's the one, that's our Aries!'*

When we arrived and got off the bus, our cruiser was in front of us, in the most beautiful picture, all from the profile, so we had to shoot the first pictures with the camera to start our honeymoon even better. There was that feeling *'where I left you, that's where I found you'* because the truth is, Venice was the place of our last disembarkation three years ago, when we decided to drop anchor. We didn't have to rush to the board, we had plenty of time and headed to town for morning coffee and breakfast. Once we did that, it was time to board.

416

We had quite a bit of way back to the boat, our legs almost fell off in that heat. Elizabeth told me nicely, let's each take smaller luggage, it will be easier. But no, I had to make one big one that was 'easier' for me to drive and carry all over Venice. It would still be OK if we didn't get lost on those streets when we were looking for a shortcut. I almost dropped my soul carrying our luggage up those stairs that are every 20 metres uphill and downhill over hundreds of small bridges. But no worries, we were not late for boarding.

It took about an hour and a half from entering the terminal to boarding the ship. I literally started to feel like a guest when we got the key card with which you open your room, use to pay for everything else you want that isn't included in the package, and without which you can't go out on the ports. So here we are, after six long years, since the last we were here, we stepped on the ship Aries again! And only three years since the last official sign-off and closing of the maritime career. What excitement! Our gazes flew as far as they reached, all over the ship, at every moment. Memories began to return. We thought about whether we would run into our former colleagues, but that was a little too much to expect, many years have passed, and people can change their lives every day when they work in such a place.

Throughout the cruise, however, we came across a couple of them. We got a pretty good room, on the twelfth floor, the same one where the buffet is, the gym, the spa, and an outdoor pool with four Jacuzzis. The room didn't have a balcony, not even a window but that was completely irrelevant to us. You don't spend all day in a room when you're on a cruise like that anyway, literally almost like in the good old days. We left our things, got a little comfortable, and hurried to lunch. All the other guests had lunch at a buffet that was full of people, but we knew where to go and have lunch in peace.

Few new guests know that during lunch, in addition to the buffet, also only one restaurant is open—*Royal Blue*, so here, now you know. We got a table by the window in an almost empty restaurant. As soon as I saw our waiter, I noticed the Bosnian flag on the NameTag. He was very friendly, starting with that introductory monologue with which he was obliged to begin with the guests so that they could feel as comfortable as possible at the very beginning of their vacation. I told him briefly that it was not necessary and explained our story in which he could not believe what fates we had gone through. During the cruise, we were a couple more times at the restaurant where he worked and asked exclusively for him to serve us.

After this lunch, we went to ask something at the front desk where we ran into my ex-roommate. If you can remember, it was in that first contract that I was in a room with a Balkan team and a guy from Grenada. I couldn't believe we ran into him. He progressed quite a bit but not as fast as he should have. Unbelievable that we came across him just when he decided to do his last contract. I was very glad to see him, it is always a nice feeling to meet friends after a long time.

After one cold refreshing shower, we escorted Venice from the open twelfth deck. A real pleasure to watch the city from the cruiser as it sails. It immediately reminded me of the Liberty Wave when I worked at an outdoor buffet, by the pool, and along the way, cast glances at the *Queen of the Adriatic*, as some call it. When we set sail from Venice, there was still a lot to see but we decided to take a walk through the *Aries* and open the chest of good old memories. We returned to the *Royal Blue* restaurant for dinner.

We wanted food from that restaurant because we remember it very well. Most of the specialities have remained and there are only a few minor changes. For an appetiser, I couldn't resist a French onion soup. It may not sound tempting to you, but trust me, it tastes great. So good that I took two servings (laughs). The food onboard is one of the things we don't see so much quality and delicious as on the land when I talk about restaurants. Trust me when I tell you because we know well the difference in the restaurants behind the kitchen on board and on land. There are no jokes about the food on cruise ships. Also with a delicious dinner, we could hardly wait to re-enjoy a bottle of white wine, *White Zinfandel* from California.

The next morning my eyes saw the sight they had been waiting for so long! View of the blue Mediterranean without any clouds and any land on the horizon. With that special breeze that passes over your face and body that makes you tingle, how much you enjoy that moment. Something amazing! In a couple of hours, we arrived in a very hot Kotor. It was extremely hot, but I guess it was because of the rocks above the city. A large mountain that stretches behind the entire city. We were thinking about whether to go to the top of the famous fortress, but when we saw what the walking path was like, it would take us a long time and despite this hellish heat we preferred to stay in the city and cool off in the sea on one of the city beaches. The place is nothing special but again cute.

On the way back to the *Aries*, refreshing cold towels and something to drink were waiting for us in the cruise terminal, as it is with CL2 company, but also with every other one. And again during dinner, we enjoyed a bottle of the same wine we had taken the day before. Later we took a walk on the open seventh deck and enjoyed the night ambience of this cruise.

New port—Corfu. Elizabeth has friends who are from that place, but also live and work in Munich, more precisely her work colleagues. They arrived there a couple of days earlier, also on vacation, and contacted us and offered themselves as our main guides, which of course we didn't mind. I have already mentioned, that Corfu has a beautiful clear sea, and I believe a good part of all Greece. It is no wonder that in addition to its rich history, Greece is visited annually by more than 25 million tourists.

The country is beautiful no doubt about it. After our friends took us a bit through the city centre and introduced us to a couple of traditional things like the type of food and liqueurs, they took us for a finish, to one of the beaches if I remember correctly called Barbati beach. Great atmosphere, fantastic water temperature, beautiful beach with an even nicer view of the hills we came. Unfortunately, we didn't have a chance to taste that real Greek food, and yet besides such friends who are professional chefs, we had to go back.

Later that evening a few more scenes that I particularly missed—sunsets escorted from the cruiser. Who does not know how wonderful this experience is, let him not try to imagine but achieve that moment! I wrote about how much I enjoyed such ambiences, especially in my first contract when I worked the night shift.

This time the dinner was at *Japanese Nigiri*, an Asian restaurant where everything was also great but plentiful. Me, who can usually eat quite a lot, could not 'clean' everything this time. Overall, I was just surprised that during the whole cruise I didn't have as much appetite as at home, and I thought as soon as I got on the ship, that I would come back with a few pounds more, especially with so much variety of delicious food. To be honest, you don't even expend too much energy when cruising. That's why there is a gym and an outdoor jogging track on the 13th floor.

During the cruise, I visited the gym a couple of times and the other days ran down that open jogging track. Finally, this time I didn't have to be afraid of being caught by some supervisor with thoughts of whether I'm allowed to do 'this or that' like it was before when I was a crew member. Yes, we were on vacation and it's best to sleep without worrying about having to get up early, as I used to get up for work around half past four in the morning, but again, when you are offered the opportunity to run on the open deck at dawn at sunrise, that's stronger than me! I could not, nor did I allow myself to miss such magical moments. Plus with that, after a good run, even breakfast suits better! In those few days that I also visited the gym, I met an older lady whose life hides an amazing story.

It was another one of those life stories of how nothing is impossible. It was about her health. She was very active and constantly in training, but she was hit by an illness that prevented her from returning to the same training sessions as before. She ran a lot but after that illness unfortunately her running was taken away. After that, she could choose two options in life, or she would let it all go and have every excuse for the disease and turn her back on training forever or continue training only different types with a smiling face. The lady was about 60 years old and her body 20 years younger. I remember noticing her developed shoulders.

When you meet someone to such stories then exactly this kind of thing shakes you, in that positive way. When you think it's hard for you because of something and then you meet someone with an even better story, then you actually just realise how much more you have to harden. That's why I think that you need to meet new people as much as possible because just one person is enough to change your thinking guidelines. Here is a saying that goes:

*'Become friends with people who aren't your age. Hang out with people whose first language isn't the same as yours. Get to know someone who doesn't come from your social class. This is how you see the world. This is how you grow'.* (Roumaissa)


This lady, whom I met by chance, is just one of the thousands of examples of how there is no easy way in life, there is always a harder way and a struggle and fight all over again so that in the end your life gets meaning, satisfaction and happiness that many crave, but only if is your desire strong enough to go through that same struggle, without the excuse that it is too difficult.

The next morning another beautiful sunrise which I greeted around half-past five. That day our port was Santorini. The third time we go out into this Greek pearl but here at last this time I can say, we have time! We have a lot of free time! We explored a good part of the city and captured beautiful pictures from different angles towards our *Aries*. We walked a lot and this time from one end of the city to the other on the west side of the island. Santorini is an island that makes it one of the most desirable destinations for tourists in all of Greece but also in the world.

It is visited annually by about two million tourists and has been becoming a tourist destination since the 1970s. If you are a romantic type of person, forget about expensive Paris or already a bit tiring Venice, Santorini is a place where you want to spend great moments with your better half. It is no wonder that over a thousand weddings a year are held at this place, the number of which continues to grow. A spectacular sunset with the most important day in life really cuts deep into a wonderful memory.

Again, I personally wouldn't recommend staying in Santorini for too long unless you really plan every day for something. There are many things to try on this island. From food (not the one I mentioned in the last contract), various famous Greek wines, visits to the prehistoric city of Akrotiri, various beaches (for which we didn't have time to visit), hiking trails (for those who like to explore the island that way) or even a tour around the island by boat, visits to the volcano by helicopter, an open-air cinema in Kamara, a large number of entertainment bars and even attractive diving or relaxing fishing if you like. Yet under number 1 the priority and reason for visiting this place I would put the sunset.

If you think I'm wrong, just google a bit to see for yourself. This specific sunset is, I think, somehow the biggest reason for the arrival of a large number of cruisers that do not set sail even a minute before that sunset. After a good exploring, Elizabeth and I sat down with a cocktail (it is not easy to find a place in those hours because a large number of people want such a relaxing experience) and send the sun 'to sleep'. But don't think that only the sun's rays adorn this island because what follows, this place during the night also gives a special ambience because of its lights that stretch along the whole island.

On the way 'down' we took the cable car and spent another beautiful Mediterranean night on the *Aries*. We had dinner at the *Royal Blue* restaurant again, as if it was the only restaurant on such a huge cruise ship hahaha. But I was surprised to see an old friend who was my supervisor in 2014 at ship Aquarius. He has always been fair to me by which I retaliated with the same measure, this time had the role of restaurant manager which is a very high position. I was glad to run into him and talk a bit.

Mykonos, another place known for Greek mythology but also for the charming city with tight streets as in Santorini. This white and blue combination is something beautiful. When you see this, you wish to paint your house in this Greek style. And this time we had to take a tender, to the island because the parking spaces for cruisers on the island were occupied. When we took a closer look at the cruiser anchored on the island from a distance, we realised that it was another member of the CL2 company and that, we couldn't believe it, our good old friend, the ship Liberty Wave! Wow, memories flew through my head once again, as soon as we saw the ship from which we disembarked in 2016 in Venice.

Since I'm mentioning Venice so many times, there is also one on this island, believe it or not. It is called Little Venice and makes up only a small side of the island which once you see it is clear to you why it is so-called. In addition to Little Venice, there are also attractive icons of Greek islands—windmills, as many as 16 of them on the entire island.

These streets of Mykonos are too cute. Clean, without any rubbish, full of colourful flowers and greenery, and as I already mentioned, a wonderful and pleasant combination of white and blue colours. Since this place is known to us from before, with of course more freedom this time, we decided to visit one of the beaches and try the water temperature of Mykonos. It was refreshing but a little too cold. After only an hour, we decided to go back to the city and enjoy it a bit more. We had to take a couple of souvenirs from this place because they are just too good and there are a bunch of them to choose from. Upon returning to the ship, we enjoyed Greek beers by this clear and beautiful sea.

When we arrived at 'our hotel', quite hungry but also in a good mood (offered by beer), we sat down at *Laguna* restaurant for lunch. When here suddenly a former roommate appeared to take the order. Along with the meal, he 'accidentally' brought one beer too much. Oh, how could he just make such a terrible mistake hahaha! He made us quite a good laugh when start telling us about well-known situations with the guests.

That day, a *'One Colour Party'* was organised on the open deck—twelfth floor, next to the pool, so we danced a bit. I remember from the crew entertainment staff at that party, there was one guy from Africa, I don't remember which country or name but I think his nickname was Simba. Wow, when we saw that person dancing and making guests laugh, you really rarely see something like that. Amazing, what a talent for such things this guy has. Even then, I think he had a good position, and I am sure that all the promotions that follow in his career onboard will come soon if he continues like that. Truly when you see someone doing something with so much passion, it's not hard to recognise that that person is born just for it. I really wish we could meet him again one day.

Argostoli, a port we have not known before, just like the first one, Kotor. We knew almost nothing about this Greek port. We took a short walk and a taxi to one of the beaches, which is, I have no words, great! We used to realise that Greece is a very beautiful holiday country, but only now can we say that we honestly felt that climate and atmosphere. We didn't plan to return to the city as quickly this time as we did in Mykonos so we stayed there until the last minutes.

When we got back to the ship, I looked at this crew and thought, how we felt before in that situation, waiting for guests to return on this hot sun. How many times back then did I just think, how I would like so badly to jump into this beautiful water! But no chance back then.

This time as a guest, I come back still wet from the beach, with a relaxing rhythm, a bit tired, and with thoughts of taking a nap and the only concern in my head was where and what to eat. That's why I felt sorry for them—the crew because I know very well what it feels like.

We opted for lunch at the buffet on the twelfth floor this time. When we filled the plates, we tried to look for an empty table because at that time the buffet was full. After a few minutes of searching, Elizabeth headed to one side and saw empty seats next to a young married couple like us. From that moment on, we made new friends. That young couple from Colombia who lives in New York kept us company until the end of the cruise.

We talked about the port we visited that day, and they showed us pictures they caught from some hill on the beautiful Greek sea full of different shades of blue. When we realised how much fun we had with each other, we regret not having met earlier but again, who would say, our first cruise (as a guest) and their first cruise somehow brought us together. We stayed in touch today and try to plan a vacation to finally go somewhere together from the first day and enjoy the pleasant company. Later that evening we drank cocktails at the back of the ship and spent another night with a good amount of laughter.

The last port was Dubrovnik. The pearl of our Adriatic that we have visited before but never personally went to the city. This time with the company, we came out in an even better mood to make the most of every minute. When we reached the old town and walked within those walls, we could not miss the detail of how expensive Dubrovnik is. It is clear to me that such an opportunity is used because of such a tourist destination, especially since the famous series *Game of*

*Thrones* was filmed in Dubrovnik, but again, OMG, it is a great shame how rudely expensive everything is. I can say that one Santorini is expensive, but Dubrovnik… without shame.

When we walked around the city and realised that there was nothing more special to see, Mauricio suggested we do a tour of the walls. Of course, this tour is charged, I will not mention the price because it is excessive in itself, and it is not to me because of the money, but again, I think that a little more respect should be shown to tourists. So that we don't lose our good mood, I said let's go, let's see Dubrovnik from all angles, and I don't plan to come here anymore. I can't say, the views from those walls are beautiful. After some two hours of walking in the relentless sun, we decided it was time for some refreshment! We played tactically, we sat in the nearest bar next to the bus station so that by no chance we would be late for the bus if we stayed longer.

Our friends wanted to try Croatian beer, so I felt like a host, as they asked me which one was the best (the best is the one they didn't have). After each half a litre of draft beer, to this day I do not remember how the topic of rakija (Croatian spirit) began. Well, who knows what I'm talking about, it's a tough topic. When all of a sudden they start asking for it, *we want to give it a try! Let's try rakija!* I said good, I take the menu and start looking for what kind of rakija to offer the best. I think I chose one made from different herbs, I don't remember for sure but anyway, there's not too much of a difference in all of them because each one 'slaps' you quite well. We ordered one each, after a few minutes I realised the good mood was growing. Everyone took another. It didn't take long for the comedies to start.

The man should relax and laugh, after all, that is the main reason for going on vacation. Those hours flew by, and we already had to get on the bus. When we got up and just got out of the bar, there was already a column of people which was leading to the bus. One lady from CL2 company started explaining something to us while suddenly Mauricio hugged her, and we all burst out laughing. We were in a great mood and our friends, I think they remembered the rakija very well.

I remember we tried to even order another round, and we practically didn't even stand in the bar area. From that day, our motto was—*rakija connecting people* hahaha. When we arrived at *Aries* everyone went to their rooms for a little nap and later a little more socialising by the pool. We had our last dinner at *Aries* in the already known *Royal Blue* restaurant.

Here we are at the very end of the cruise. How time flies fast when a man has a good time. Why does it always have to be that way, we wondered, but I believe all the other guests as well. We are leaving the ship *Aries* once more, not after nine months this time but for a small one week. Wow, what a difference! I was feeling a bit bad because I didn't ask my ex-boss, an old friend to allow us a little tour through the crew area. Then even stronger memories would ring in my head.

I know it wouldn't be a problem for him, but honestly, we realised that the cruise wasn't as relaxed as we thought. It just seemed like we didn't have time for anything. The ship arrived at the ports at dawn and left after a few hours (except in Santorini, it was an exception). When you get back on the ship, you eat something, and you get tired because you have the thought in your head that you are not in a hurry anywhere, everything is relaxed. You get some nap, dinner comes, here—there, watch some show that Cruise Line offers, have a drink at the bar, maybe dance, the night flies by, you go to sleep, and you have to wake up in a couple of hours to get out as soon as possible at the next port make the most of your time there.

I'm telling you, we started to feel that old rhythm of a couple of hours of sleep, as it was when we were crew. But I don't mean anything bad about the cruise, it's a great pleasure but personally, if I could really enjoy and spend the holiday very relaxing, without running, it would take us at least 14 days. Who knows, maybe one day. I definitely plan to get back on the cruise again but not so fast and not for that short.

The only downside I share with Elizabeth regarding this cruise is the ship's air conditioning. The hallways and larger rooms are pretty cold because of it. On one hand, I think logically that it must be so because it is still a place full of people and the air must circulate while on the other hand, my advice to you is, if you are planning a cruise, bring long sleeves. When we felt that cold air, it was only then that we became aware of how much we were used to it before and how it was normal for us to spend time in the guest zones at that time.

Once more, I turn my head to our *Aries* with that old, accustomed look. I may be getting out of it again now, but no matter how many times I do it, *Aries* will never get out of me. As I once wrote before, you can remove a man from a ship but you cannot remove a ship from a man. Thank you once again, you beautiful remarkable thing for still filling our lives with special memories, you have always done that, and you will remain that forever, the strongest image of our lives!

Not goodbye, but until next time. ☺

After we disembarked, our friends intended to stay in Venice for a few more days, so we left our luggage in their room, and spent the rest of the day in their company around the city. In the evening, we took the bus to Munich again, and closed with it our honeymoon, which left a lot of beautiful new adventures, made new friendships, and marked a new beginning of our life together.

Back to Aries

Venice Mood'

This is the view that I missed

In Kotor, Montenegro

Chilling out in Corfu, Greece'

Elizabeth and Me.

Free in Santorini, Greece

Santorini adventure

Mykonos, Greece

Wandering around Mykonos, Greece

Amazing colors in Argostoli, but also the beaches!

This is vacation!

Dubrovnik, Croatia

On this occasion, I decided to suggest useful tips if you ever find yourself on a cruise. Follow these ten rules and no doubt, you will have an unforgettable vacation, so let's go in order:

1. For starters be sure to choose your dream cruise! Investigate well what places you want to visit and what you will do there, what type of cruiser you want to choose (although most of them are the same) but I personally recommend that you avoid ships with more than 3,000 guest capacities! Also, don't forget to pay attention to what types of activities that ship provides. Regarding your luggage, it is not necessary to overcrowd it, but I definitely recommend that you bring a couple of long-sleeved clothes, keep in mind that there is a high possibility that you will want to buy a couple of clothes in a few places (for example a T-shirt as a souvenir). When talking about clothes, check what rules individual restaurants you plan to enter have. Companies have their own dress code in such places (for example casual or formal).

2. Arrive at the boarding terminal as soon as possible, the sooner you board, the better so that you can start using as much free time as possible on the same day on the ship and thus become more familiar with the place where you will spend the next minimum a week.

3. You have come on vacation but that does not mean that you will only spend your days lounging, sleeping, and eating when you are hungry. Get out of the room the same day you boarded and enjoy the magical views while sailing outdoors, with the proviso that I don't think that should only mean on embarkation day! Sailing out of most ports looks amazing! Some of the best I've seen are those from Scandinavia and cruising the Baltic. By such an occasion, the man could admire many things all day long.

4. Both by day and by night. Whether you're somewhere in the middle of the ocean or not, catch a moment with the stars that will amaze you! Don't even plan to come on a cruise unless you think of catching both sunrise and sunset a couple of times because then you are committing a sin! It is something unthinkable and a cruise cannot be imagined without such an ambience. I guarantee you, your day will be great if you welcome it at dawn with a cup of coffee, and see off in the evening with a cocktail or a glass of wine.

5. *'Become friends with people who aren't your age. Hang out with people whose first language isn't the same as yours. Get to know someone who*

*doesn't come from your social class. This is how you see the world. This is how you grow'.* (Roumaissa)—remember that well. Once you start applying these words in your life and especially in such a place that is perfect for such occasions, you will feel and understand the core of this concept. Not only will you thrive and mature as a person but you will also have a good time.

6. Food on cruises is something you don't see every day or have a chance to taste. This is a great opportunity to try something new. You do not have to dine every day in various special restaurants, which need to be paid extra to feel the new cuisine. Each cruise has an already offered complimentary package that also contains more than enough options. But also, keep in mind that this is a unique opportunity that you could eat the whole vacation uncontrollably, whatever you like—very unhealthy, or choose the safer and healthier option that is also available in large numbers. Of course, I'm not saying you need to feel guilty if you take dessert before bed or a glass of alcohol too much, that's why you're on vacation, to relax and enjoy but trust me, you don't want to be intemperate in eating and drinking every day.

7. Learn and try something new! Don't allow yourself to get bored after a few days even though it's impossible. I mentioned that it would take me 14 days for a real vacation on a cruise. What do I mean by that? Well, just that the ship contains so much that it's very hard to see and try everything in just a week. Take a walk around the entire ship, bring your favourite book you can read on a deck chair, or listen to a list of your favourite songs at sunset. Have you ever tried meditation? Not? Learn and enjoy the ocean breeze. Spend some time in the spa, enjoy the various shows on offer each night, have fun with the many activities on offer, meet new people, talk to the crew (just no stupid questions please), or take a dip in the pool.

8. No Internet, elevators, casinos, and shopping while cruising!
   Don't allow yourself to waste this phenomenal time or more money, which you've already spent quite a bit. The Internet on board is expensive and very slow. Don't be a slave to your cell phone like you are at home (admit it, we all are sometimes) by reading meaningless and useless information on web portals and Facebook. Understandably, you're bursting with the urge to post pictures of the place you've visited as soon as possible and want to brag to your friends at home, but still wait a moment for that until the next port, where you'll sit down for a drink. I am sure you will also find faster and better Internet on ports.

If you do not have health problems with walking, avoid elevators onboard unless really necessary. Use stairs because it is a faster and healthier option. Just ask yourself how many times you waited for the elevator and when it finally arrived, you muttered to yourself that during this waiting time you could have already reached the stairs to the desired room.

Casino, and shopping?

If you are a gambler and addicted to shopping, I do not interfere in your private life, you are the one who wants to spend time and money that way and that is absolutely your right! However, I think it is much smarter to save that money and use it for much better purposes on ports, such as numerous excursions, places where you will catch a break and eat or drink something, or even those real original souvenirs such as postcards, magnets, T-shirts, cups or other similar souvenirs. Our fridge is full of different magnets that we took in every new place we visited and guess what?—there is still enough space on the fridge for new magnets and the fridge is pretty big.

Don't come home from a cruise and become aware and regret the moments you missed because you 'didn't have time' which will lead you to frustration and get the wrong picture about everything. This type of vacation you may not be able to afford every year, use every day in a natural and best possible rhythm!

9. On behalf of the entire crew please have patience and common sense with every kind of service on board. Every crew member does their job the best they can, and you have to believe it! A job on a ship is not like some jobs on land where you can slack off. The eyes of a supervisor are everywhere whose if they see something that is not in the job description, it can lead that person to more serious problems. That is enough motivation for the workers on the ship to make sure that they complete each task successfully and without the slightest problem. Working on a cruise is hard, you know now, pretty well, if you've read my experiences so please don't lose your temper if you need to wait a few minutes longer to be served. Everyone is doing their best to meet your requirements and expectations!

10. Don't do anything that has nothing to do with common sense! Avoid any physical conflicts, quarrels, thefts or, God forbid, any illegal things because the company has a very right to throw you out in the middle of a cruise (of course I don't mean literally from a ship to the sea), provided that you can respond to the consequences the country where you created the problem.

When I write to you like that, I also mean the typical human nonsense type of doing something abstract just because you think you're going to become very popular because of it. Here are a couple of crazy examples to get a picture of what I'm talking about, which really happened whether you believe it or not: jumping from a ship into the sea, jumping into a pool or Jacuzzi from unsafe and inappropriate heights, using a slide in a very unsafe way, throwing sports equipment into the ocean because of your frustration (golf clubs, balls, cones, etc.) or any other objects and breaking and damaging other people's property.

Common sense, please!


The cruise is something wonderful and special! Once you try, you will fall in love with cruisers and their travels. But that's not the only point.

Let me ask you, why do people like to travel? What makes travel so special? Is it because of the beautiful places? Natural wonders or popular cities? Is it because of making new friendships? Enjoying with average friends? Is it because of getting to know new world cultures and customs? To see how different the world is from your country. Is it because of the desire to learn a new language? Do people travel because they love food and want to try new flavours? Do you think people like to travel to have something to write about, like me for example? Do they simply desire new challenges, to test their own limits? To find themselves, how they say?—For such things, it is best to travel alone! Do people travel because they are running away from something or someone? Is it due to climatic conditions, stress, worries, or failed relationships? Or quite the opposite, to find a soul mate? Have you wondered and imagined in these lines?

Travelling is not just about seeing a new place because as you can see for yourself, by all these questions, travel is all that and much more! Life was not created to be lived in only one place, I have already mentioned that! Travel as much as you can! As far as you can! As long as you can! (Lifehack.org).

When I first left the ship, part of me stayed there and seemed to be waiting for me to come back! And so every time! It doesn't have to mean that it's the same for you because the whole same principle is created once you start travelling no matter how, by what, when, where, and why. It always pulls you back! You are drawn to that adventure! A new adventure calls you every time! Don't miss such bright moments in life! Without excuses, find a way, and make your long-dreamed dreams come true because those same ridiculous excuses always sound best to the people who invent them. The only reason why you don't have something is the story you keep telling yourself why you don't have it. (Jordan Belfort)

***

After returning from Croatia and having an unforgettable wedding and celebration, we left Elizabeth's parents in the apartment and made sure they had everything they needed for the week we cruised. They stayed until our traditional 'harvest in Zagorje', which I never want to miss. We wanted them to see what the grape harvest looks like in our Zagorje. We last arrived in Croatia in mid-September that year for just a few days.

After we arrived and had a relaxed day with my family, what greeted us the very next morning was the worst news in this whole book. The worst possible news came from Peru. Elizabeth's three-year-old niece, unfortunately, and with great misfortune, that day, left us all. Disaster! Terribly! We were all in shock and for Elizabeth and her parents, I don't even have to try to describe how it was just for them. I don't want to write too much about it because no one wants to remember moments like that. We all believe she is in a much better place now.

No matter how terribly and indescribably difficult it was for us, we had to do the harvest for which we came. On the other hand, I thought, maybe it's better to have that harvest now in such a terrible situation because we needed something to divert our thoughts, some distraction from this huge shock. Me and Elizabeth and her parents especially!

After we returned to Munich, in a few days Elizabeth's parents had a return flight home. Elizabeth also wanted to go and spend time with her whole family, especially back then in those very difficult times, which I fully understood. A new problem arose at the job where she worked. They did not want to give her more than two weeks of free time to visit the family watching the whole unfortunate situation. Of course, she didn't care about anything except about her family, so I told her:

*'Take the ticket, go to your family in Peru, stay as long as necessary because I understand your situation. You don't travel to Peru a couple of times a year because it's not a few hours away like Croatia. Stay if you want for up to a month.*

*And don't worry about work, this is Munich, and you can find a job here whenever you want! '*

And it was like that. She took a ticket for a month and flew with her parents to Peru.

# 2.8 Prayer and training – the last chapter

After Elizabeth travelled to Peru for about a month, I dedicated myself to myself and training. I will first describe to you a few more things about my job, then the topic I kept for the very end.

Let's go back for a moment to the beginning of 2019 when I was still working at the hotel, the morning shift for breakfast. I mentioned that the year before was great for me because of the big soccer names I had a chance to meet. When I started thinking about what 2019 might look like during one working morning, the answer came to me even earlier than expected. Another big soccer name arrived at our hotel but this time one of my true soccer role models that I started following from a young age. Although he has been retired for a good couple of years and was an assistant of the Croatian national soccer team, a person of an incredibly persistent character, whom many have compared to our Mario Mandžukić.

Without a doubt, if these two people have anything in common in terms of playing style it is certainly impeccable and stubborn persistence! If you have not guessed who it is, it is our Slavonian legend Ivica Olić. How much we loved watching his dedication and tireless character on the field, which amazed us all. Our 'Ola' as we all called him, was never a particularly talented player in technique and other skills with the ball, but he ran on the wing, like an express train, and always sniffed the place where the ball should be thrown into the goal. At the European Championships in 2008, he was the fastest player to reach a speed of as much as 31.76 km/h against Germany, a game in which he scored a goal, as I mentioned, from 'insidious' situations.

When I saw that person taking food from the buffet, I began to doubt in my eyes whether it seemed to me or I was really looking at one of my soccer idols. Due to the rules at the hotel regarding taking photos with celebrities, I tried to find out when he would leave the hotel to catch him at that moment, outside the hotel, 'in a safe' but unfortunately, such an opportunity never came. I spoke briefly with him and let him know how much I had always admired him for his courage and perseverance, and wished him much success in his further roles. He promised me a picture because he came to the hotel a couple of times later but because of his commitments and a busy schedule, I understand and can't expect him to just wait for me because after all, I'm just one of his many fans who are nonetheless grateful for the opportunity to meet him in person and exchange a few words.

After Ivica Olić, Mario Mandžukić has been playing in our national team for some time, and you know the story and the unforgettable goal against England. After that Russian fairy tale, he also decided to retire from his national team career, which we Croats must not blame him for because he made us so happy, even though he could have stayed at least for the next Euro. Such two gladiators that Croatia had, really deserve great respect!

But who is the third, who could now inherit by such hard and steely perseverance, these two names? Let people talk, but for me, it is without a doubt Ante Rebić. A player whom I also had the honour to see in person but also him, unfortunately, I did not have the opportunity to bother for a picture, to have as a souvenir. Although as a player he still seems a bit insecure technically, I am sure that he will develop if he continues with this 'character of aggression' because that is what we adore, and I believe others, to see in him. When he goes as furious as some beast full of anger where it can be clearly seen in his eyes how eager he is to win, not just a game but every duel with an opponent.

As for situations with famous soccer players, I was always trying to find some suitable way to get a picture or at least a short conversation.

But not only because of the hotel rules about it, but also for a couple of other reasons, I was getting very bored doing such a job. It was not difficult but monotonous. Every day the same thing I started going crazy about. Life on a ship has left a big mark on me in many ways and especially in terms of work. Looking from that side, I can now say that life on land is a bit boring. When you work on a ship for nine months, you are accustomed to such an unusual routine where you do not have a single day without some scenes, events, or experiences.

In nine months every day is different! Here, on the hard ground... 80% of work is monotonous, all the same, uninteresting and pointless which prompted me to understand even more the difference between work on a ship and on land. Unless you are looking for a serious hobby in your free time and turn your life only on the basis of home and work, your life is not reduced to anything. Working on a ship is a different story. There you always have twice as much motivation just because of that journey that makes you more mature every day. Something realistic that pushes you forward while on land is quite the opposite, unless you force yourself to something new. In my case it's a sport, otherwise, I will get crazy.

Don't get me wrong, but since my first working day on land after the ship, I haven't taken anything too seriously. I've always done my job the best I can, correctly, and I still do, which is a result of great training and school off the ship, but when I consider and compare the professionalism of the ship and the mainland it's like day and night. You don't believe me? Ask others who have had experiences like me or better yet, google a bit why it's good to hire a former seafarer.

In the first hotel where I worked, darkness immediately fell on my eyes when I realised how many people do not pay attention to detail when we talk about only one of the most common, but also the most important example in gastronomy and that is hygiene. If I were always trying to explain proper cleaning procedures, people would misunderstand it in such a way that conflicts would start to arise, and I don't need that. Kudos to the exceptions who are realistic and aware of such an important detail. In another hotel where I worked, it's a little better and most of them follow a few rules but again it's the individuals who make a huge difference and distort the whole picture.

Unfortunately, that's how we are, we can't expect everyone to do the same from the first to the last, while onboard is another story. I don't know why things like that upset me and sometimes completely frustrate me. I guess that's why you don't have a serious inspection on the mainland every week like the USPH, which came to us more often than the wind in the open and 'beat' us with all those procedures and regulations that eventually became part of us, which I consider the best thing we were taught about work. On land, inspections come once a year (if they come) so people are more relaxed and don't take that part of the job seriously.

During the summer, I decided to change the working place and kind of job. I switched to the bar. I turned to learn about cocktails and the job of a bartender that I wanted to learn while still working on the ship. After only a few months, I felt a big difference. Although unfortunately not as popular soccer players come here, the job is more interesting for that reason because I somehow deal more with guests like it was on board.

One of the biggest reasons why I love this job is because in 80% of cases I use English which I really missed in communicating with other people. I missed talking to people, meeting them, sharing stories and experiences, joking, etc. because this kind of work requires talking to guests as well. At that job, I also met a person who has been working there for an incredible 20 years. Here's a great example, when I asked that person, what keeps him in one bar for so long, he described a very similar experience as I had on board.

Constant communication with different people from which all those important things in life come—experience and fun. And not only that but my colleague today has also travelled to a lot of destinations in the world, which gives us a common experience and different views of the world, unlike the percentage of people who do not go beyond their cities or countries. He has an amazingly fun character and a great friendly spirit! Since he's from Portugal, you wouldn't believe the island of Madeira to be exact, the next vacation Elizabeth and I plan to take, along with our friends from the cruise, is exactly that one. To the beautiful island of Madeira, which although we have seen before, we really want to expand our horizons on this, another natural wonder and with another host and private guide—my great colleague who, without a doubt, wants to present his island in the best possible version.

When he showed me only a part of that paradise through some pictures, the place where he has a house, I immediately wanted to jump into the picture. Another very important thing if not the most important you can learn from my colleague is how much he does not regret for a second all the trips he has chosen. He has travelled to some locations more than once and all those trips have cost him a lot of money but that's the point. He often said that money was not important to him at all, except to use it for such purposes. Life is too short and the most important thing is to create as many memories as possible. The money will come and go, while with life it is not so simple, so once again, create memories that cannot fade and live a life of calm but fulfilled conscience.

Speaking about colleagues, in January 2020, also another colleague invited me to join him in the 'B2Soccer' tournament by the German organisation for soccer (indoor) tournaments. Since I couldn't get a day off for that tournament, I still left intending to play at least a couple of games, so I get back in time to work. That day I was supposed to start working at 6:00 p.m. while the tournament started just after 3:00 p.m. Half of our team were guys from Croatia and Bosnia. Around 5:30 p.m., I called my fellow Portuguese, who was already at work. I explained to him that we were playing a tournament and asked him if I could come to work around 7:00 p.m., which he allowed me, plus the team wanted me to stay as long as possible.

When the time came for work, unfortunately, I had to leave the team. Later after a couple of hours, the team calls me and sends pictures. They won the tournament! Oh, come on! I wanted to eat myself alive! I was both sad and angry at the same time! In the first five games we played, I scored four goals and had one assist which was a great start for me. Who knows, if I had the opportunity to stay and continue with that rhythm, I would undoubtedly compete for the best player of the tournament, i.e., the player with the most goals scored, and that was another reason for my frustration later. That but also the moment you lift the trophy of the first place! I couldn't believe how I missed such an opportunity! Since our team represented in that tournament the hotel where we are working, I still had the opportunity to feel the weight of the trophy in my hands before we left it in one of the offices. I was so close but OK, this came to me as another motivation to fight for the next opportunity!

***

I turn to the last topic of this book—Dreams.

If a person does not have dreams in life, some desired future, some ambitions, to achieve something unexpected… then I do not know what he can have, without still having the desire to live. Here I am thinking exclusively of personal goals in life and as one of the examples, I will put myself.

Before my biggest change, in 2013, I had only one wish, one dream. Succeed as a professional soccer player. Although I was completely alone in it, with no interest in anyone advising me and showing guidance, my commitment to training and desire for progress was never questioned. Over the next three years, I went through the hardest, most beautiful, but also the most valuable moments in my life. I travelled to parts of the world I never thought or dreamed of, met nationalities and languages I didn't even know existed, traversed and steeled my own boundaries that I had never felt in my body before, strengthened and matured as a person in ways I would never manage to do that if I hadn't left my 'comfort' zone. Here I want to advise you i.e. shake you up and wake you up about the first lesson.

*If you do what is easy in life, your life will be difficult. If you do what is difficult in life, your life will be easy.*

Les Brown

When I first read this saying, someone would think that it refers more to material things. That if people work hard and learn, they can afford whatever they want. I'm not claiming that's not true but these days that saying has actually shown me a different side of the answer. The one that has been negligible so far. Often times life tests us more on the inside than on the outside and this is actually where these quotes are found.

It is very important to become aware of your daily impact on your own life. If you do things that are normal to you, without any changes, ask yourself if these habits and actions lead to the achievement of your goals. Does your personal mentality progress for the better and is your wisdom broader and greater than the day before. Do not comfort and convince yourself by saying to yourself that you have time, that you do not yet feel that the time for change has come, that you are waiting for the perfect moment, etc. There will never be a perfect moment if you plan to welcome it because after that, during your waiting, your life will fly by and suddenly you will be in the years when you no longer have as many possibilities to create new opportunities as before. Never allow yourself to be lazy (it's not without reason one of the seven deadly sins), being manipulated by others, and leaving things you can do today, for tomorrow because who can ultimately promise you that you will get tomorrow. (from Benjamin Franklin quote)


*One day your life will flash before your eyes. Make sure it's worth watching.*
Gerard Way

Always, but you always have to find ways to believe in something you want to achieve and when you succeed, hold that faith firmly! Do not let it out of your hands and thoughts, fill it every day with even stronger self-confidence and good healthy habits. Become the greatest optimist there can be.

*The pessimist sees difficulties at every opportunity. The optimist sees an opportunity in every difficulty.*
Winston Churchill


The real truth is that if you look at most things negatively, you miss those very important and crucial moments because those very moments can force you to look for better solutions that are out there somewhere, it's just up to you if you want to open your eyes and see them. Try to understand how necessary and inevitable this is for your progress, ability, and power to change any situation you are in. Always believe that something good is in your way. Be open and honest for every moment that comes to you, do not ignore it because I believe that this is the only way to live a true life. Maybe I confused you a little now with these words, so here is an example to give you a clearer picture.

When I travelled to Kansas in 2015 for professional open soccer try-outs, every day until those try-outs, I filled myself with confidence and high concentration. During the day, I strengthened my body with physical training while before and after sleep my inner spirit. My mentality, my focus on all those individual things that eventually merge into the main source of energy and strength. I didn't allow even a second to be stunned by some negative thoughts or people's voices, I always listened loudly to what my heart was telling me.

*Your faith will not work if contains even the slightest piece of doubt.*
(from the Bible Matthew 21:21)

When I arrived at these try-outs, I felt incredibly mentally ready (that's how I thought and created such a mentality) but the real truth is that I may not have been so ready, but because of that power and faith in myself, I 'fed' only the positive energy, which led me to the second round of these soccer try-outs. If I had big doubts from day one and started directing my thoughts to that dark side, then it would be called failure.

*Whether you think you can or you can't, you're right.*

Henry Ford

True, I failed in the second and final rounds of those try-outs due to a couple of important factors. There was not enough energy for physical or mental struggles but that is not the point of this story. What I want you to pay attention to and take the idea out of it, is how strong I was in my head, and only because of that, I managed to pass the first round. This is the kind of strength and firm faith that I want with all my heart for you to practice too!

When I got home, it took me a while to understand and see the whole picture of this opportunity I was hunting for. I stopped looking at it all as a big failure and just because of that, I changed some of my life habits and became even better than I was in those days. I analysed each course of events in my head and took these examples so that I could look at them again but this time from a different angle, attitude, and character. The only thing that makes my conscience not completely clear is the knowledge that I could have learned and applied such golden lessons and changes much earlier and faster. So don't procrastinate for that long. Take from this my own example, an example that can serve in your life.

Time flies, years go by, the clock is ticking and it's something you can't change or stop. When you face your own obstacles and dedicate yourself to finding better solutions and necessary changes, it will take some time until you learn everything important and prepare yourself for the next step because a new obstacle is already waiting for you around the corner, which will also take time to crush and move on. Once you start making such important shifts, only then you will realise how much you are actually lagging behind and how much you have to learn, to reprogram yourself into a stronger and more intelligent version. That's why I insist on how important it is to work on yourself every day.

No day off! When you are not training your body physically, train it mentally. Your mind is the strongest weapon and no force can change it. Always strive to be better today than you were yesterday and better tomorrow than you were today (Lorenzo Snow)! It is not said in vain that nothing is achieved overnight. These are the steps that lead you to the top very slowly but surely.

The only time you don't get more opportunities is when you stop taking those same opportunities. As long as you create an opportunity for yourself, you have the opportunity to win.

*Life opens up opportunities to you, and you either take them or you stay afraid of taking them.*

Jim Carrey

I learned from that example of mine and became a better version than I was back then in those days. But that absolutely doesn't mean I can stop here, with the conceited thought that I'm ready for anything because I'm not. I still have to create new opportunities, run into new obstacles from which I can learn even more, and thus prepare myself and climb as far as I can. It's my passion, my obsession, my path.

There is only one way, the hard way.

\*\*\*

Something has always told me that I would get a very important and life opportunity at 23 years old. Given my passion for soccer, I expected it to be an opportunity in those directions, and I couldn't even predict it would be anything else entirely. I followed my dream in all possible options, even to the point of being so insane that I believed I could get to the right soccer opportunity by meeting someone important while working on a cruise ship. I don't know, dear readers, what's crazier here? That I truly found such an opportunity or that I fell even more in love with such an experience of travelling and learning new undiscovered things that eventually touched my heart so much that I realised my second dream, which I did not think I would have. Yes, you read that right. Because I was following my first dream, on the way to it, I came across another dream, which also grew in my heart.

*'Shoot for the moon! Even if you miss it, you will land among the stars!'*

Les Brown

After Elizabeth and I anchored once, I had days where I doubted if I had done the right thing. Not about her, but about the ship's career. Questions began to come to my mind as to whether I had withdrawn from the ship too quickly. Could I have stayed a few more good years, to reach the desired position and then turn to the mainland? There were days when I started to think more seriously and even about the return option. These were actually the first days when I started writing this book.

When I remembered everything and realised how much I miss it all. And I admit, I miss a lot of it! From travelling to airports, important friendships and socialising whether in a crew bar or cabin with always a lot of laughter, those views of the wide ocean and ports no matter what time of the day, different experiences with guests, going through that I—95 corridor, even the time spent in that crew mess all the way, to the parts of going out at different ports. When I just remember how much I adored, not only with the team but for myself, going out to that hot Mexico, just to enjoy my own company, both there and everywhere else!

All these details mean something but unfortunately, I can't describe how much, to those who haven't experienced them. It all calls me back, while another voice says, *'You have passed the ship and now enjoy this way of life! But who knows, if God wants and thinks I have a better place there, He will find a way because let His Will be done!'*

Writing this book, on the other hand, connects me in some way to the ship and calms me down at the same time. Sometimes, I feel like I'm stuck between two dreams. Between that return to the ship that would allow me to continue life's adventures and that first one, the soccer dream I still crave because that 'candle' is still burning!

\*\*\*

At the end of September 2018, I was hit by an injury that took me away from soccer fields and training for as much as half a year. I would have recovered earlier, but at the beginning of that injury I 'forced recovery' and because of my overwhelmed desire to return as soon as possible, I made a counter effect. It was another shock from which I began to fall slightly depressed and doubted whether my leg would be the same once I recovered. The injury was a stretched adductor in my leg that hurt so much that I could barely walk.

Thank God, nothing was broken and more serious. After a couple of months, I was already quite frustrated with this injury to the point that I was seriously looking for any other occupation just to divert my thoughts from the sore leg. Here we come to the main factor and mover of this book. In February 2019, I remembered that I once wanted to write about my experiences on the ship. This came as an ideal opportunity to write a book, which took me too long to figure out. I knew and believed that one day I would start writing and this was the main trigger when I will actually start.

During the first contract, I mentioned how much I watched all those soccer videos on my mobile phone in the middle of small breaks, which gave me incredible strength and motivation to continue believing in my soccer dream. That no matter how hopeless everything seemed about soccer in those moments, I still somehow remained connected in some way with this wonderful sport. My body was physically exhausted from such a rhythm of work on the ship but my inner spirit and mind were because of my faith, unbreakable! Because of that mentality, it was not a problem for me to sleep an hour less and train in the gym.

Because of that spirit, it was not difficult for me to go out to the port with the team to the soccer fields and run for the ball in that unbearable summer sun, while the others either stayed to sleep on the ship or went out into the city. My love for soccer is true, complete, and moral. Countless times certain situations and people have tried to distance me from this passion and thus extinguish the spark that is still full of undiscovered energy.

A few moments ago, I mentioned that sometimes I feel like I'm immersed between two dreams. That there are only two sides from which I can choose only one. Either left—soccer or right—ship life. I chose the left side. I just couldn't give up and ignore something that fills me so much and calls me constantly all these years!

From a young age when I had almost no skill at all with the ball, but anyway I still ran after it. When I was often rejected by popular society on several occasions, I was still coming to the field kicking the ball, no matter how bad my self-confidence was, so bad that I didn't even have it. Later in my teens, I felt I could. I felt a stronger presence of faith and hope that I could do something that many thought I couldn't, and wasn't capable of. But even back then, I still hadn't jumped out and been as effective as I had hoped.

Something unseen and unexpected was needed for a real jump and maturity. Let's call it astronomical change. Something that will truly test me, not only my desire for soccer but also my character, my overall potential in all aspects of this life.

If I had stayed on the ship for many years, I'm not saying I would have been unhappy but still, first love is the first one with a reason. After this different type of life, a much sharper mind and wiser spirit, my heart pointed again to the mainland and sent me a clear message that it was time for a new beginning, a new chapter, and new emotions that remained undiscovered and unfinished.

Suddenly, I was no longer a lost teenager with a broken self-confidence and a small handful of hope. I have become a person who is aware of my abilities. I have built a self-confidence that no one can poison me with, a self-confidence on which I am still developing my roots with the help of very wise people. Life is simply too short and that's why I decided on this comeback.

*You can accomplish anything but you can't accomplish everything.*
David Allen

I would like to point out one of the essential details that affect your personal progress, no matter in which aspect. No man is born to be able to understand and know everything. A lot of people don't realise this because if they did, they wouldn't continue to insult and consider those weaker than themselves as if they were the last scrap. If you see someone that needs help, that they want, and that is willing to make a better and healthier change if you feel that you are the one who could help, do not hesitate! Do it! It's so boring to listen when people compare their type to who's better. Only the wrong ego can make you do something like that.

Watch how you understand these words! I don't think it's wrong if you want to create a habit of thinking in yourself, that you're the best (because of stronger motivation) but publicly, don't compare yourself to anyone. Be humble! The only person you can and must compare yourself to is the person you were yesterday, who you are today! Are you better than that person? Domination and not a competition! For example, when I play soccer either in training or a game, I always want to be better than my last performance before this one. I don't want to fill my head by watching an opponent how much weaker or stronger he is than me.

If I beat my old version, I will beat him too, end of discussion! If I find myself in the inevitable situation where provocations are directed at me and where I am underestimated, great! I feel less pressure, and I don't have to think about some necessary proof, with the opponent relaxing and not considering me a more serious threat. I play the best I can and surprise everyone who doubted me. It happened many times before, and it will happen again.

One of the most useful tools for sharpening your skills is available everywhere to almost everyone today. Internet. I think this is the best and cheapest help you can get in this world. There's almost nothing you can't find there, you just need to look for answers. But again, it is very important that you become aware of who you are asking for help from. As much as the Internet can be useful so much it can be harmful, so watch how you spend time on it, were those hours spent useful? Did you get the solutions you were looking for? Or you started so you ended up with some pointless nonsense and threw away once again this so precious time that was given to you.

I mentioned before, when preparing for Kansas, how I ran into Dylan via a YouTube channel and learned carefully from his videos. That person greatly influenced my soccer views. I threw my conceited ego in the trash and became open-minded, willing to listen to a complete stranger who infused me with ideas and knowledge in all aspects as far as soccer is concerned and sometimes even more so. He is the reason I went through the first round of try-outs.

After a year or two when I came back from the ship and started hunting for stability in Germany, I couldn't even think of going back to training without his help. He has developed even better and more advanced programs that in my opinion are worth their weight in gold and 'food' for every soccer player. He still helps everyone who wants to succeed in soccer in some way and as far as I can see, he has become a highly regarded person, which does not surprise me at all. A person like him is a huge rarity. What I want to point out here is how I found a huge advantage on the Internet and used it for my personal progress. You have to do the same! Wherever you get stuck, seek help, write down a couple of ideas, change your plan, try again, and never give up on your dream.

*'If your plan doesn't work, change the plan but never your goal!'*

positlive.com

Something that you love with all your heart and that lives in you can never die. How much longer I will be able to train and fight to become the strongest and best version of myself, I do not know. As much as dear God allows me, as long as I can, I will not stop and one day when my legs give way and my heart cries because of the impossibility of playing, it does not mean that I will leave everything. There are always ways to stay in what you love so much, but until then, age is just an ordinary number. I follow Ibrahimović, the man who passed his 40s, which is amazing for soccer. I admit he is also one of my favourite players and also the motivation. He is not the only one who is living proof that age means nothing. If you live healthy habits, there is rarely anything that can stop you.

This will sound fictional but believe it or not, I often dream at night, how I am preparing for some big game but most strangely, I never play it. I always wake up when I go out on the field. It often happens that I dream of my favourite players from whom I always ask and get a jersey, but again, I wake up every time disappointed and often very confused because sometimes these dreams seem very real.

My comfort zone

***

After all, now that I look and think where all my life has led me and in what crazy but wise ways I was educated, how many times in it, a hundred times alternated some situations from which unexpected guidelines emerged and led me to the next ones…

From the very moments when I didn't find a job, finish courses, and even fail part-time college, all of which actually led to that real true opportunity…

From the day I stepped on the ship for the first time (a day I will always remember fondly) and when everything back then started in a new light, some new boundaries that only you, and I have to move in order to see how many of us our lives it can indeed lead us far, to do all those things that we once feared and that limited us to live fully!

So many things happen unexpectedly in life. Both the bad ones and the good ones. But don't allow those bad things to damage you from the inside. Don't regret a single day in your life. Good days give us happiness, bad days give us experience, the worst days give us lessons and the best days give us memories! Struggle to create new memories that one day you can leave this world with a clear conscience, a calm soul, and a full heart. To say to yourself:

*'Yes, I did a great job! I took advantage of the opportunities this wonderful life offered me!'*

But don't think only of yourself! I believe that the purpose of life is made up of three parts:

1. Achieving your own dreams—work hard and believe in the things you want to achieve! The only real enemy that can stop you is yourself (Friedrich Nietzsche). Be aware that there is a good and a bad version in you. If you feed a good version with positive thoughts and strong self-confidence, the bad one will evaporate and only from time to time knock in your subconscious. Remember, always strive to be a better person tomorrow than you were yesterday and today! And don't stop every time you get a little tired, stop when you're done (David Gogins). When you go to the store to buy something, you don't stop halfway to take a break or vacation right?

2. Be exemplary to others—Whatever you do, do it in a clean and honest way! Do not harm others in any way! Good deeds never come from bad intentions!

3. Think of the next generations that are the future—when you reach adulthood, do not keep all the wisdom that life has taught you just to the grave. If the gift of wisdom is given to you by nature or God, return the favour! Share every healthy piece of advice to newer and younger generations because if you don't, they will take advice from the wrong people.

Imagine you have two of the same seeds. If you nurture and water one, something wonderful will sprout from the seed, a new life that looks so clean and correct. And as it grows, you can use something to adjust it to grow upright. If you damage this other seed in some way before you plant it, hardly anything will sprout from it or there is a greater chance that nothing will sprout. It's similar to humans. Don't let, those who are responsible for the future of this world, be damaged by the wrong people before they start caring about that same world because no matter if in a good or bad direction, the roots will continue to grow.

Remember, the opportunities that life offers appear on every corner and in many different forms so open your eyes widely. I am truly grateful from the bottom of my heart to dear God for all the gifts He has sent and given me. And I still thank him for those gifts he still sends me. The year 2013 changed me as a person, that is, my ways of thinking, while the year 2015 totally turned into a new chapter and a stronger level of wisdom in terms of my personal ambitions. The years continue to flow, which means the possibility of constant progress. Use it every year wisely and get the best you can out of it and so constantly for as long as you can!

I wrote my book, which I hope you like at least a bit. Now it's your turn to write your own if you decide on such an amazing life adventure. Of course, it doesn't necessarily mean it's just a ship. This version is just one of the hundreds that still exist, undiscovered. It's up to you to step out of your comfort zone and push those already so boring and common boundaries in which you have been living for too long anyway. Because that's the only way you can experience something new.

I really think and believe that everyone should have one day in their lives which changes everything. My 'day' like this one was the ship. If you don't have yours yet, it's only a sign that you need to create for yourself.

I wish you with all my heart and deepest part of soul crazy happiness, eternal health, wisdom without borders, unforgettable new friendships, and many magnificent, magical, fantastic, hilarious, phenomenal, and indescribable wonderful adventures! So compass (wisdom) and map (dream) in your hands and embark on a life that has been waiting for you already for a while! ☺

Climb your mountain, no matter what it takes!

And finally, I want to share with you the sources from which I draw wisdom and motivation.

Dylan Toobie, Les Brown, David Goggins, Luka Modrić, Cristiano Ronaldo, Zlatan Ibrahimovic, Ben Lionel Scott, Above Inspiration, Nick Vujicic, Eric Thomas, Elliott Hulse, Tony Robbins, and many others.

Quotes that help achieve goals and that are so strong that they clear your every path filled with obstacles and doubts. The energy that cannot be extinguished or weakened. The wisdom that feeds you with the strongest natural vitamins. Read one every day and think about it when you need it the most. When you are fighting for your place, for your name.

*The future belongs to those who believe in the beauty of their dreams.*

Eleanor Roosevelt

*Who/What should we become? Someone/something no one ever thought.*

David Goggins

*Your mind is an incredibly powerful thing. Once you fill it with positive thoughts, your life will start to change.*

positivitysparkles.com

*Think positive, train daily, eat healthy, work hard, stay strong, worry less, dance more, love often, be happy.*

goodreads.com

*The days you don't want and avoid are the days you need most.*

progressivesoccertraining.com

*I don't stop when I'm tired, I stop when I'm done.*

David Goggins

*A man is never too weak or too wounded to fight if the goal is greater than his life. Go with all your might.*

Oenomaus

*Great things never come from a comfort zone.*

*Invest in yourself first. Expect nothing from no one and be willing to work for everything.*

Tony Gaskins

*It is very important that you only do what you love to do. You may be poor, you may go hungry, you may lose your car, you may have to move into a shabby place to live, but you will totally live. And at the end of your days, you will bless your life because you have done what you came here to do. Otherwise, you will live your life as a prostitute, you will do things only for a reason, to please other people, and you will never have lived. And you will not have a pleasant death.*

Elisabeth Kübler-Ross

*Keep your thoughts positive because your thoughts become your words. Keep your words positive because your words become your behaviour. Keep your behaviour positive because your behaviour becomes your habits. Keep your habits positive because your habits become your values. Keep your values positive because your values become your destiny.*

Mahatma Gandhi

*Pain doesn't tell you when you ought to stop. Pain is the little voice in your head that tries to hold you back because it knows if you continue you will change. Don't let it stop you from being who you can be. Exhaustion tells you when you ought to stop. You only reach your limit when you can go no further.*

Kobe Bryant

*Impossible is just a big word thrown around by small men who find it easier to live in the world they've been given than to explore the power they have to change it. Impossible is not a fact. It's an opinion. Impossible is not a declaration. It's a dare. Impossible is potential. Impossible is temporary. Impossible is nothing.*

Muhammad Ali

*Give God your weaknesses and He will give you His strength.*

daleblack.org

*You only lose when you surrender.*

Anonymous

*I asked for strength and*
*God gave me difficulties to make me strong.*
*I asked for wisdom and*
*God gave me problems to solve.*
*I asked for prosperity and*
*God gave me body and brain to work.*
*I asked for courage and*
*God gave me obstacles to overcome.*
*I asked for patience and*
*God placed me in situations where I was forced to wait.*
*I asked for love and*
*God gave me troubled people to help.*
*I asked for favours and*
*God gave me opportunities.*
*I didn't get anything I asked for…*
*But I got everything I needed!*

poemsonly.com

*This is your life. Do what you want and do it often. If you don't like something, change it.*

*If you don't like your job, quit. If you don't have enough time, stop watching TV. If you are looking for the love of your life, stop; they will be waiting for you when you start doing things you love. Stop over-analysing, life is simple. All emotions are beautiful. When you eat, appreciate every last bite. Life is simple. Open your heart, mind, and arms to new things and people, we are united in our differences. Ask the next person you see what their passion is and share your inspiring dream with them. Travel often; getting lost will help you find yourself. Some opportunities only come once, seize them. Life is about the people you meet and the things you create with them, so go out and start creating. Life is short, live your dream, and wear your passion.*

*Many of life's failures are people who did not realize how close they were to success when they gave up.*

Thomas A. Edison

*Life is 10% what happens to you and 90% how you react to it.*

Charles R. Swindoll

*Do It Because They Said You Can't!*

*Take a chance, you never know what might happen.*

*Remember, years are just a number.*

Joan Collins

*Don't forget that life is full of ups and downs. Without downs, ups would mean absolutely nothing.*

*The day I changed was the day I quit trying to fit into a world that never really fit me.*

JM Storm

*To be successful you must accept all challenges that come your way. You can't just accept the ones you like.*

Mike Gafka

*It Feels Good To Be Lost in the Right Direction.*

*Excuses will always be there for you, opportunity won't. Use every moment you get.*

*If you want to succeed, stop telling yourself you can't. You can and you will only if you really and truly want to. Up to that point, you just choose not to.*

progressivesoccertraining.com

*How hard do you work when no one is watching?*

Ray Lewis

*Today, they will laugh at you for trying. Tomorrow they will ask you for advice.*

progressivesoccertraining.com

*To be successful, the first necessary thing is to fall in love with your work.*

Sister Mary Lauretta

*Eight main steps on the way to the top: 1. I won't do it. 2. I can't do it. 3. I want to do it. 4. How do I do it? 5. I'll try to do it. 6. I can do it. 7. I will do it. 8. Yes, I did it!*

quote.byethost10.com

*Life doesn't get easier, you just get stronger.*

Steve Maraboli

*You are only one decision away from a totally different life.*

Mark Batterson

*In moments when you plan to give up, think about why you managed to stay in it for so long.*

progressivesoccertraining.com

*If the plan doesn't work, change the plan but never the goal.*

positlive.com

*Life has two rules: 1. Never give up. 2. Never forget the first rule.*

Duke Ellington

*Stop hating yourself for everything you are not and start loving yourself for everything you already are.*

Tiny Buddha

*Don't let small minds convince you that your dreams are too big.*

Bruce Van Horn

*Not caring what other people think is the best choice you will ever make.*

treasurequotes.com

*I need to believe that something extraordinary is possible!*

Alicia Nash, from the movie A Beautiful Mind

*Imagine with all your mind. Believe with all your heart. Achieve with all your might.*

goodreads.com

*In order to succeed, your desire for success should be greater than your fear of failure.*

Bill Cosby

*The difference between talented and successful is a lot of hard work.*

Stephen King

*The only time you run out of chances is when you stop taking them.*

Alexander Pope

*Stress makes you believe that everything has to happen right now. Faith reassures you that everything will happen in God's timing!*

weheartit.com

*Discipline is just choosing between what you want now and what you want the most.*

Abraham Lincoln

*Never regret a day in your life. Good days give happiness, bad days give experience, the worst days give lessons, and the best days give memories.*

quotespedia.org

*Never stop doing your best just because someone doesn't give you credit.*

lifehack.org

*People will never truly understand something until it happens to them.*

wisdomquotes4u.com

*I don't know where I'm going but I'm on my way.*

Carl Sagan

*People are often unreasonable, illogical, and self-centred;*
*Forgive them anyway.*
*If you are kind, people may accuse you of selfish, ulterior motives;*
*Be kind anyway.*
*If you are successful, you will win some false friends and some true enemies;*
*Succeed anyway.*
*If you are honest and frank, people may cheat you;*
*Be honest and frank anyway.*
*What you spend years building, someone could destroy overnight;*
*Build anyway.*
*If you find serenity and happiness, they may be jealous;*
*Be happy anyway.*
*The good you do today, people will often forget tomorrow;*
*Do good anyway.*
*Give the world the best you have and it may just never be enough;*
*Give the world the best you have anyway.*
*You see, in the final analysis, it's all between you and God;*
*It was never between you and them anyway.*

Mother Teresa

*It's hard to beat a person who never gives up.*

Babe Ruth

*If you keep doing what you're doing, you will keep getting what you're getting.*

Stephen Covey

*If you can't fly then run; if you can't run then walk; if you can't walk then crawl, but whatever you do, you have to keep moving forward.*

Martin Luther King Jr.

*No, we don't always get what we want. But consider this: some people will never have what you have, right now.*

me.me

*You seriously have no idea what people are dealing with in their personal life so just be nice, it's that simple.*

greatestquotes.net

*When you lose hope, it's an opportunity to reconstruct it. Remember the caterpillar, yesterday it was weak and ugly, today it looks stronger and beautiful with its wings. Don't lose hope because you never know what tomorrow will bring.*

Anonymous

*If they say 'it's impossible', remember that it's impossible for them, not for you.*

Leonardo DiCaprio

*Don't worry about where you are, focus on where you want to be.*

progressivesoccertraining.com

*Your mind will always believe everything you tell it. Feed it hope. Feed it the truth. Feed it with love.*

quotlr.com

*You play the way you practice.*

progressivesoccertraining.com

*Work hard in silence. Let your success make the noise.*

progressivesoccertraining.com

*The only person you are destined to become is the person you decide to be.*

quotefancy.com

*The greatest weapon against stress is our ability to choose one thought over another.*

William James

*Practice like you must win. Play like you can't lose.*

progressivesoccertraining.com

*Never underestimate your opponents or your own talents.*

progressivesoccertraining.com

*Every morning you have two choices, continue to sleep with your dreams or wake up and chase them.*

Carmelo Anthony

*The greatest pleasure in life is doing what people say you cannot do.*

Walter Bagehot

*Don't tell God how big your problems are. Tell your problems how big your God is.*

ownquotes.com

*Motivation is what gets you started. Habit is what keeps you going.*

Jim Ryun

*Don't lose faith! Humanity is like an ocean—it will not be polluted by a few drops.*

Mahatma Gandhi

*There is nothing so easy to learn as experience and nothing so hard to apply.*

Josh Billings

*The greatest reward for effort is not what we get for it but what we become with it.*

John Ruskin

*The essence of life is in constant trying, without giving up.*

Anonymous

*Everything we are is the result of thought. The mind is everything. What we think, we become.*

Buddha

*Every experience enriches you and you never know when you will need it.*

brainyquote.com

*Perseverance is failing 19 times and succeeding the 20th time.*

Julie Andrews

*The hardest thing is to listen to a man who does not have enough soul to speak well, nor smart enough to be silent.*

slideserve.com

*Your talent is God's gift to you. What you do with it is your gift back to God.*

Leo Buscaglia

*The greatest possible adventure is to live the life you dream of.*

Oprah Winfrey

*God, I am not asking You to free me from the sufferings of life, but I am asking You never to leave me in those sufferings.*

Anonymous

*Look forward to the little words. Maybe one day you turn around and realize they were actually big ones.*

Anonymous

*Be thankful for what you have; you'll end up having more. If you concentrate on what you don't have, you will never, ever have enough.*

Oprah Winfrey

*Life is not a problem to be solved, but a reality to be experienced.*

Soren Kierkegaard

*Do I get up with the decision, that I will use the day and get the most out of 24 hours!?*

Anonymous

*Destiny is no matter of chance. It is a matter of choice. It is not a thing to be waited for, it is a thing to be achieved.*

William Jennings Bryan

*For real dreams, it's never too late.*

quoteslyfe.com

*You see things, and you say 'Why?' But I dream things that never were, and I say 'Why not?'*

George Bernard Shaw

*All the knowledge you have is worth nothing if you don't put it into practice.*

Anton Chekhov

*Be not afraid of going slowly, be afraid only of standing still.*

Chinese Proverb

*It is very important not to give up. Only then, you can actually do something.*

Anonymous

*I have not failed, I have just found 10 000 ways that won't work.*

Thomas Edison

*Miracles only happen to people who believe in them.*

Bernard Berenson

*Good, better, best. Never let it rest. 'Til your good is better and your better is best.*

Tim Duncan

*One who wants to listen to the sincere voice of conscience must first learn to create silence within himself.*

Anonymous

*Learning without thinking is useless. Thinking without learning is dangerous.*

Confucius

*The will to win is not nearly as important as the will to prepare to win. Everyone wants to win but not everyone wants to prepare to win.*

Bobby Knight

*Only a man who is good because he wants to and not because he has to can be moral.*

Anonymous

*Success means going from failure to success without losing the will and passion.*

Winston Churchill

*It is not the strongest of the species that survives, nor the most intelligent; it is the one most adaptable to change.*

Charles Darwin

*You can't change the direction of the wind, but you can adjust the sails to reach your destination.*

Jimmy Dean

*The human soul insults itself if it allows pleasure or pain to overcome it.*

Anonymous

*It's easy to be grumpy but making people laugh is a real art.*

Anonymous

*People often do not see their own happiness but they never miss the happiness of others.*

Anonymous

*If you aim at nothing, you will hit it every time.*

Zig Ziglar

*By giving 110% of yourself you become the best. When you can't anymore and then push just a little more, that makes a difference!*

Anonymous

*The past cannot be changed and the future is contained in the present.*

Anonymous

*With a goal in front of their eyes, even the slowest progress faster than the fastest without a goal.*

Anonymous

*Sometimes, you have to get knocked down lower than you have ever been to stand back up taller than you ever were.*

quotespedia.org

*Before you speak—listen, before you write—think, before you spend—earn, before you pray—forgive, before you hurt—feel, before you hate—love, before you quit—try, before you die—live.*

William Arthur Ward

*Every achievement begins with the decision to try.*

John F. Kennedy

*You won't always be motivated, you must learn to be disciplined.*

fearlessmotivation.com

*Don't practice until you get it right. Practice until you can't get it wrong.*
flickr.com

*You don't have to see the whole staircase, just take the first step.*

Martin Luther King, Jr.

*Be happy but never satisfied.*

Bruce Lee

*When it seems difficult, it means you are doing the right thing.*

Anonymous

*I'm not in this world to live up to your expectations and you're not in this world to live up to mine.*

Bruce Lee

*If you stay ready, you don't have to prepare to be ready.*

Will Smith

*One small positive thought in the morning can change an entire day.*

Dalai Lama XIV

*Always choose the paths you fear because those are the paths that will help you grow.*

Anonymous

*Monday is the perfect day to correct last week's mistakes.*

ponwell.com

*If you can't feed a hundred people, feed only one man.*
*Those who condemn people do not have time to love them.*
*Some people come into your life as a blessing and some as a lesson.*
*We are not all created to do great things. But that's why we can do little things with a lot of love.*
*Loneliness and the feeling of not being loved is the greatest poverty.*
*It doesn't matter how much you work, it matters how much love you put into what you do.*
*To restore peace, we do not need weapons and bombs. We need love and compassion.*

*Peace begins with a smile.*

*Greet each other with a smile because a smile is the beginning of love.*

*I found a paradox. If you love someone to the point of pain, it means that there will be no more pain, but just a lot of love.*

*Find time to play. It is the secret of eternal youth.*

*Everyone who approaches you should leave you better and happier.*

*There is more hunger in the world for love and respect than for bread.*

Mother Teresa

*You can't hang out with negative people and expect a positive life.*

Joel Osteen

*Everyone wants happiness and no one wants pain. You can't get a rainbow without a little rain.*

Anonymous

*Shoot for the moon. Even if you miss, you'll land among the stars.*

Les Brown

*It's not about how to achieve your dreams. It's about how to lead your life. If you lead your life the right way, karma will take care of itself. The dreams will come to you.*

Randy Pausch

*You don't have to be great to start something, but you have to start to become great.*

Zig Ziglar

*Never let fear decide your future.*

Shalane Flanagan

*It's not a sin to get knocked down, it's a sin to stay down and not get up.*

Carl Brashear

*Strength does not come from winning. Your struggles develop your strengths. When you go through hardships and decide not to surrender, that is strength.*

Arnold Schwarzenegger

*Your excuses lead you 0% to your goals. Remember this the next time you decide to avoid a busy day.*

Anonymous

*No one becomes the best without anyone's help. Learn to appreciate teamwork and you will see how far you can go.*

Goran Žganec

*The pain you feel today is the strength you will feel tomorrow.*

Stephen Richards

*Never give up on a dream just because of the time it will take to accomplish it. The time will pass anyway.*

Earl Nightingale

*It is not the size of a man but the size of his heart that matters.*

Evander Holyfield

*The best things are the hardest. Happiness is not mostly pleasure, it is victory.*

Harry Emerson Fosdick

*Stop being afraid of what could go wrong, and start being excited about what could go right.*

Tony Robbins

*When we put God first, all other things fall into their proper place or drop out of our lives.*

Ezra Taft Benson

*Your best teacher is your last mistake.*

Ralph Nader

*If you think the same as most, then obviously you are not thinking.*

Anonymous

*The surest way to forgive our enemy is to forget and dedicate ourselves to something that is extremely greater than ourselves. Then nothing will be able to offend and provoke us because we will be 'dead' for everything but not for what is most important and what we are fighting for.*

Anonymous

*Invest your heart, mind, and soul in the smallest deed you do. That's the secret of success.*

Swami Sivananda

*Keep striving, for God gives His hardest battles to His strongest soldiers.*

Habeeb Akande

*Sometimes the people around you won't understand your journey. They don't need to, it's not for them.*

Joubert Botha

*Being negative only makes a difficult journey more difficult.*

Joyce Meyer

*A comfort zone is a beautiful place, but nothing ever grows there.*

John Assaraf

*I'm going to succeed because I'm crazy enough to think I can.*

Friedrich Nietzsche

*Sometimes you must fail to fuel your desire to succeed.*

Anonymous

*One day your chance will come! Prepare like it's tomorrow.*

progressivesoccertraining.com

*I hated every minute of training, but I said, 'Don't quit. Suffer now and live the rest of your life as a champion'.*

Muhammad Ali

*What you do speaks so loudly that I cannot hear what you say.*

Ralph Waldo Emerson

*The only bad training session is the one that didn't happen.*

Anonymous

*Move out of your comfort zone. You can only grow if you are willing to feel awkward and uncomfortable when you try something new.*

Brian Tracy

*Nothing is more stronger than a broken man rebuilding himself.*

reddit.com

*What you do not find in yourself, do not look for in others...*
*And don't strive to have what is someone else's...*
*Let your only goal be for you to really be you, not someone else...*
*And when you reach it, then you will have everything you need,*
*all your own and all unique.*

Anonymous

*Your competition isn't other people. Your competition is your procrastination. Your ego. The unhealthy food you're consuming. The knowledge you neglect. The negative behaviour you're nurturing and your lack of creativity. Compete against that!*

movemequotes.com

*A healer is not someone you go to for healing. A healer is someone who helps you to find the key within you, for your own ability to heal.*

handserenity.com

*Everything will be okay in the end. If it's not okay, it means it's not the end.*

John Lennon

*Never give up and you will see others giving up!*

Anonymous

*It's not what you are that holds you back, it's what you think you are not.*

Denis Waitley

*Twenty years from now you will be more disappointed by the things that you didn't do than by the ones you did do. So throw off the bowlines. Sail away from the safe harbour. Catch the trade winds in your sails. Explore. Dream. Discover.*

Mark Twain

*If you can't you must, and if you must you can.*

Anthony Robbins

*A bad attitude is like a flat tire. If you don't change it, you won't go anywhere.*

Joyce Meyer

*If we want more, we must become more. If we want to become more, we must do more.*

Jim Rohn

*If you want to confront your greatest enemy, look in the mirror. When you can stand up to him, anyone else will be easy to beat.*

Anonymous

*Never argue too much with stupid people, because they simply live in their own world and will never understand the real truth, which you want to prove.*

Anonymous

*When people hurt you over and over, think of them like sandpaper. They may scratch and hurt you a bit, but in the end, you end up polished and they end up useless.*

Andy Biersack

*If you talk about it, it's a dream, if you envision it, it's possible, but if you schedule it, it's real.*

Tony Robbins

*To get something we never had, we have to do something we never did. When God takes something from us that we cannot comprehend, He does not punish us but opens our hands to receive something even better. God's will, will never take us somewhere where God's grace will not protect us.*

Anonymous

*If you don't go after what you want, you'll never have it. If you don't ask, the answer is always no. If you don't step forward, you're always in the same place.*

Nora Roberts

*Your biggest fear carries your greatest growth.*

youareyourreality.com

*The idea is to die young as late as possible.*

Ashley Montagu

*Life is the most difficult exam. Many people fail because they try to copy others. Not realizing that everyone has a different question paper.*

dailyinspirationalquotes.in

*If you get tired learn to rest, not to quit.*

Banksy

*Everything you've ever wanted is on the other side of fear.*

George Addair

*A ship in harbour is safe, but that is not what ships are built for.*

John A. Shedd

*Our best friends and worst enemies are our thoughts that we have about ourselves.*

Yomi Joshua

*Push yourself because no one else will be there to do it for you.*

Rhyanna Watson

*Don't live the same year 75 times and call it a life.*

Robin Sharma

*The only difference between a good day and a bad day is your attitude.*

Dennis Brown

*People have the right to their opinion and you have the right to ignore it.*

Joel Osteen

*Don't be upset by the result you didn't get with the work you didn't do.*

yourquote.in

*In life, you don't get what you wish for. You get what you work for.*

Daniel Milstein

*Don't be afraid of failure. The only thing you have to fear is to remain the same person for the rest of your life because of fear of failure.*

Anonymous

*Your life does not get better by chance, it gets better by change.*

Jim Rohn

*Take good care of your body because you have been given only one, in this life.*

Jim Rohn

*Most people fail in life not because they aim too high and miss, but because they aim too low and hit.*

Les Brown

*All change is hard at first, messy in the middle, and so gorgeous at the end.*

Robin Sharma

*Strength doesn't come from what you can do. It comes from overcoming the things you once thought you couldn't.*

Rikki Rogers

*If you don't sacrifice for what you want, what you want becomes the sacrifice.*

quotefancy.com

*You can't get much done in life if you only work on the days when you feel good.*

Jerry West

*Admitting your mistakes is not a sign of weakness but a sign of maturity.*

94quotesz.blogspot.com

*We make a living by what we get, but we make a life by what we give.*

Winston Churchill

*Leaders become great, not because of their power, but because of their ability to empower others.*

John C. Maxwell

*Most people don't listen with the intent to understand; they listen with the intent to reply.*

Stephen R. Covey

*Wise men speak because they have something to say, fools speak because they have to say something.*

Plato

*Sometimes later, becomes never... so do it now!*

Tiny Buddha

*Little things, make big days.*

Isabel Marant

*Sometimes we're tested not to show our weaknesses, but to discover our strengths.*

Anonymous

*This world has become very dangerous not so much because of the bad things that happen, but because of the bad people who brainwash others with the greatest possible poison, so make sure to brainwash yourself too but only with those good things that will keep you away from all these bad people.*

Goran Žganec

*If they stand behind you, give them protection. If they stand beside you, give them respect. If they stand against you, show no mercy!*

yourquote.in

*Through action, a man becomes a Hero.*
*Through death, the Hero becomes a Legend.*
*Through time, the Legend becomes a Myth.*
*And by learning from the myth, a man takes action.*

yourquote.in

*Your life does not end when you die. It ends when you lose your faith.*

Itachi Uchiha

*I didn't come this far to only come this far.*

fearlessmotivation.com

*Insanity is doing the same thing over and over and expecting different results.*

Albert Einstein

*You can never make the same mistake twice because the second time you make it, it's not a mistake, it's a choice.*

Lauren Conrad

*Everyone shapes their destiny with the decisions they make.*

Tony Robbins

*If you do not believe that you are the best, then you will never achieve all that you are capable of.*

Cristiano Ronaldo

*Always give a hand to the loser, because if it weren't for him, you wouldn't be the winner.*

Anonymous

*DREAM is not what you see in sleep, DREAM is something which doesn't let you sleep.*

Dr A.P.J Abdul Kalam

*Stars can't shine without darkness.*

D.H. Sidebottom

*You will never have this day again, so make it count.*

dreamstime.com

*Pain is temporary. It may last for a minute, or an hour, or a day, or even a year, but eventually it will subside and something else will take its place. If I quit, however, it will last forever!*

Lance Armstrong

\*\*\*

*A Little bit more of soccer…*
*My ideal XI in soccer and substitutes*

| | |
|---|---|
| (GK) Gianluigi Buffon | K. Navas, Kasper Schmeichel, David de Gea |
| (DF) Marcelo | Virgil van Dijk, Philipp Lahm |
| (DF) Sergio Ramos | Joshua Kimmich, Dani Alves |
| (DF) Domagoj Vida | |
| (DF) Šime Vrsaljko | |
| (MF) Eden Hazard | Xavi, Ivan Perišić, Philippe Coutinho |
| (MF) Ronaldinho | Iniesta, Isco, Son Heung—min |
| (MF) Luka Modrić (c) | Coman Kingsley, Willian, Douglas Costa |
| (MF) Cristiano Ronaldo | Dani Olmo |
| (CF) Zlatan Ibrahimović | Erling Haaland, Ante Rebić |
| (CF) Mario Mandžukić | Carlos Tevez, Francesco Totti |

\*\*\*

**What I did, I did for everything I believe in.**
**Goran Žganec**

**Turn on the sound, let the rhythm flow because music is the initiator of great vibes…**

*All Saints—Pure Shores; Chicane—What Am I doing here; Coldplay—A Sky Full of Stars; CMA—You're Free; James Blake—Voyeur; CMA—Caught in Our thoughts; Todor Kobakov—Lost in All; Avici—Heaven; The XX—Angels (Kygo edit); Dario G—Sunchyme; The Naked And Famous—Young Blood; Jai Wolf—Indian Summer; Wiz Khalifa—Young Wild and Free (Konglomerate Remix)*

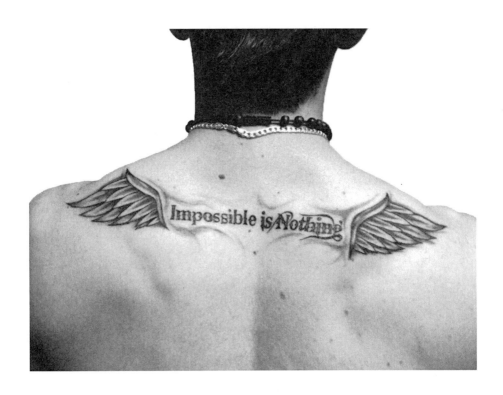

Live like a coward or die as a warrior

# 1. Life on a ship

1.1 Short version – All you need to know about the preparation and work on a ship
1.2 My side of the story about ship life – introduction
1.3 Cruise Line – Aries
1.4 Two and a half months of rest (10 weeks)
1.5 Cruise Line – The Aquarius (4 months)
1.6 Kansas and Sporting KC
1.6.1 The American experience
1.6.2 Back to my own – preparation
1.6.3 Wake up
1.6.4 The two most important days
1.6.5 Conclusion – a look into the future
1.7 Back to the sea – Cruise Line Liberty Wave – the ship that offered me the best opportunities
1.8 Conclusion and end of ship life


# 2. Life on land

2.1 After the ship
2.2 Peru
2.2.1 Cusco and the history of the Incas
2.2.2 Machu Picchu
2.2.3 Return to Lima
2.2.4 Madrid
2.3 The first wedding
2.4 Beginning in Germany
2.5 Trips, football (soccer), and Russian fairy tale
2.6 Second – the church wedding
2.7 Back to the ship Aries
2.8 Prayer and training – the last chapter